Tan's book offers remarkable insights about domestic work, gender, and exploitation. Drawing on richly textured narratives that center the perspectives of female domestic workers, her analysis reveals how gender dynamics are amplified when employment takes place in private homes, profoundly impacting the very meaning of safety and security. Highly recommended!

Nancy A. Wonders, *Professor, Department of Criminology and Criminal Justice, Northern Arizona University*

The book *Gendered Labour, Everyday Security and Migration: An Examination of Domestic Work and Domestic Workers' Experiences in Singapore and Hong Kong* brings to light some of the most hidden and vulnerable voices in the contemporary globalised economy. After completing this book, the reader will be familiar not only with the precariousness of women migrant workers. The book paints a complex picture of women's everyday life that includes challenges, exploitation, surveillance, abuse, as well as women's struggles, agency, belonging, resistance, and fight for safe and sustainable living and working conditions. Regardless of your knowledge and expertise on the topic, each of the stories presented in the book and the richness of data and analysis will make you think. Ideally placed to study these issues, Dr Shih Joo Tan's first book is a call for action for the policymakers, the international community, and all of us.

Associate Professor Sanja Milivojevic, *Bristol Digital Futures Institute/School for Policy Studies, University of Bristol*

Shih Joo Tan's evocative research with live-in domestic migrant workers in Hong Kong and Singapore generates a powerful argument for thinking beyond conceptions of exploitation defined in purely legal terms. By showing how domestic workers negotiate the contours of a peculiarly intimate workplace that is steeped in affective relations between migrant women and the families that house and employ them, Tan demonstrates how binary paradigms of exploitation/lack of exploitation may miss the most important features shaping domestic workers' everyday experiences. *Gendered Labour, Everyday Security and Migration* sets out an alternative vision of workplace safety, informed by inter-personal relationships, that places close attention to the concerns and aspirations of domestic migrant workers themselves. In so doing it not only enriches the labour exploitation scholarship but also expands the field of intervention for those seeking to safeguard the wellbeing of women involved in this work.

Professor Leanne Weber, *Professor of Criminology, Australian National University, Canberra Law School*

A unique, comparative insight into the lives of female domestic workers based in Singapore and Hong Kong, this book gives voice the everyday living and working conditions of these workers. Clearly and sensitively written it offers an alternative view on what a safe working environment might comprise for these women. Essential reading for anyone working in the field of labour relations, feminism and abuse more generally.

Professor Sandra Walklate, *Eleanor Rathbone Chair of Sociology, Liverpool conjoint Chair of Criminology, Monash*

Gendered Labour, Everyday Security and Migration

Drawing on original empirical research from Singapore and Hong Kong, *Gendered Labour, Everyday Security and Migration* interrogates women migrant domestic workers' experiences of work and workplace exploitation. It examines the ways in which these women negotiate everyday security and safe work against the backdrop of affective employment relations and institutional structures of labour and migration law. It challenges the current emphasis on the language of exploitation and legal approaches to identifying, understanding and rectifying poor employment conditions for women migrant domestic workers.

This book addresses the limited research literature that examines the extent to which regulatory or criminal justice responses are relevant to, and utilised by, women migrant domestic workers in their everyday negotiation of safe work and offers a unique contribution to the field.

An accessible and compelling read, it will be of interest to researchers from across the fields of criminology, sociology, labour migration studies and women's studies.

Shih Joo Tan is a Postdoctoral Researcher with Monash University's Gender and Family Violence Prevention Centre, Australia. Her research is interdisciplinary and focuses on gender violence, women's migration and temporary labour exploitation, and the intersections of temporary migration and family violence.

Routledge Studies in Criminal Justice, Borders and Citizenship

Edited by

Mary Bosworth
University of Oxford

Katja Franko
University of Oslo

Sharon Pickering
Monash University

Globalising forces have had a profound impact on the nature of contemporary criminal justice and law more generally. This is evident in the increasing salience of borders and mobility in the production of illegality and social exclusion. *Routledge Studies in Criminal Justice, Borders and Citizenship* showcases contemporary studies that connect criminological scholarship to migration studies and explore the intellectual resonances between the two. It provides an opportunity to reflect on the theoretical and methodological challenges posed by mass mobility and its control. By doing that, it charts an intellectual space and establishes a theoretical tradition within criminology to house scholars of immigration control, race, and citizenship including those who traditionally publish *either* in general criminological *or* in anthropological, sociological, refugee studies, human rights and other publications.

Re-thinking the Political Economy of Immigration Control
A Comparative Analysis
Lea Sitkin

Border Frictions
Gender, Generation and Technology on the Frontline
Karine Côté-Boucher

Policing Mobility Regimes
Frontex and the Production of the European Borderscape
Giuseppe Campesi

Gendered Labour, Everyday Security and Migration
An Examination of Domestic Work and Domestic Workers' Experiences in Singapore and Hong Kong
Shih Joo Tan

For more information about this series, please visit: https://www.routledge.com/criminology/series/CJBC

Gendered Labour, Everyday Security and Migration

An Examination of Domestic Work and Domestic Workers' Experiences in Singapore and Hong Kong

Shih Joo Tan

Routledge
Taylor & Francis Group
LONDON AND NEW YORK

First published 2023
by Routledge
4 Park Square, Milton Park, Abingdon, Oxon OX14 4RN

and by Routledge
605 Third Avenue, New York, NY 10158

Routledge is an imprint of the Taylor & Francis Group, an informa business

British Library Cataloguing-in-Publication Data
A catalogue record for this book is available from the British Library

Library of Congress Cataloging-in-Publication Data
Names: Tan, Shih Joo, author.
Title: Gendered labour, everyday security and migration : an examination of domestic work and domestic workers' experiences in Singapore and Hong Kong / Shih Joo Tan.
Identifiers: LCCN 2022022727 | ISBN 9781032168012 (hardback) | ISBN 9781032168067 (paperback) | ISBN 9781003250364 (ebook)
Subjects: LCSH: Women household employees--Singapore. | Women household employees--China--Hong Kong. | Women foreign workers--Singapore. | Women foreign workers--China--Hong Kong.
Classification: LCC HD6072.2.S55 T36 2023 | DDC 331.4/8164095957--dc23/eng/202205
LC record available at https://lccn.loc.gov/2022022727

ISBN: 978-1-032-16801-2 (hbk)
ISBN: 978-1-032-16806-7 (pbk)
ISBN: 978-1-003-25036-4 (ebk)

DOI: 10.4324/9781003250364

Typeset in Bembo
by MPS Limited, Dehradun

For Mum, Dad and Ah Ma

Contents

Figures

Tables

Series Editor Introduction

In this engaging study, Shih Joo Tan draws on rich, qualitative interviews with a small group of female domestic workers in Singapore and Hong Kong to argue for a broader understanding of labour exploitation that moves scholarship and practice beyond narrow legalistic responses which, she argues, inadequately protect domestic migrant workers. By centring women's everyday lives and experiences, she points to the gendered nature both of their abuse and of the solutions to it. In large part, these arguments chime with familiar feminist ones, in which the 'home', which is designed to be a site of comfort and safety, is, all too often, quite the opposite for women.

The problem, Tan shows is not just that the home as a site of work is often out of sight of the law but also that work that occurs within the home is devalued, and, by extension so are those who perform domestic labour. Thus, despite their centrality to the lives of so many middle and upper class families, women domestic workers, find themselves with few advocates or means of redress when needed.

The location of their labour in the home further complicates their relationship with their employer, since the domestic setting makes it both difficult to clarify the professional relationship and to draw boundaries around it. Being both within and yet not quite part of a family grouping is, even in the best of circumstances, emotional work; yet labour markets have no language or policy to manage that.

This book contributes original material to our understanding of migrant labour and the impact of migration. We particularly welcome the focus on Singapore and Hong Kong and are pleased to include it in our edited series.

Mary Bosworth, University of Oxford, April 2022

Acknowledgements

First of all, to all the participants who had very generously shared with me your stories and patiently walked me through your experiences and views, thank you very much. Without your contributions, this project would not have been possible. To all the domestic workers, it was a privilege to hear your stories, and I hope that I have done justice to the experiences and knowledge that you have very kindly shared.

This book began as a doctoral research project at the School of Social Sciences, Monash University, and I remain deeply grateful and indebted to the best supervisors there are, Marie Segrave and JaneMaree Maher. Your unwavering support, guidance and encouragement have been invaluable for this project, and I feel very blessed to have the both of you on this project with me. Thank you for the challenging but very fun journey. I am also grateful to the editorial team at Routledge Studies in Criminal Justice, Borders and Citizenship. My thanks also to Julia Farrell for the invaluable assistance as editor. Any errors are of course my own. A big thank you also to colleagues at Monash University for their friendship and support, including Nicola Helps, Nicole Ruslim and Ariel Yap.

To my family and friends in Melbourne, Singapore and Hong Kong – Isa, Beixi, Abel, Jas, Charlotte, Lis and Jo, thank you for being with me during this entire journey. This book would not have been possible without your constant encouragement and reminders to breathe, have fun (and memes).

Abbreviations

CEDAW	Convention on the Elimination of all Forms of Discrimination against Women
EA	Employment Act
EFMA	Employment of Foreign Manpower Act
FDH	Foreign Domestic Helper
FDW	Foreign Domestic Worker
GDP	Gross Domestic Product
HKD	Hong Kong Dollar
ILO	International Labour Organization
MECAB	Minor Employment Claims Adjudication Board
MOM	Ministry of Manpower
NGO	Non-Governmental Organisation
SEC	Standard Employment Contract
SGD	Singapore Dollar

Chapter 1

Introduction: Women Migrant Domestic Workers in Singapore and Hong Kong

The research presented in this book is based primarily on the everyday employment experiences of women migrant domestic workers in Singapore and Hong Kong. The women I interviewed for the research informing this book have emigrated from various countries in South and Southeast Asia (the Philippines, Indonesia, Thailand, Nepal and Myanmar), to work as live-in domestic workers in Singapore and Hong Kong. They are part of an increasing population of women migrants from less wealthy countries who are finding work abroad in the care and service sectors, particularly as domestic workers (Parreñas 2000; Sassen 2000; Lutz 2010; Islam & Cojocaru 2015). The most recent estimates by the International Labour Organization (ILO) indicate that there are approximately 8.5 million documented women migrant domestic workers globally, with 1 in 22 women working as a domestic worker across the world (or 4.5% of total female employment), making it an important source of employment for women (ILO 2021). While the outsourcing of care and domestic labour to migrant women is not a new occurrence, particularly in Singapore and Hong Kong (Constable 1996; Yeoh, Huang & Devasahayam 2004), in the context of globalisation and neoliberalism it is peaking as a gendered, global phenomenon. However, many of these women migrants continue to be excluded from full the protection of national labour laws and/or work without clear terms of employment, as well as being subjected to highly restrictive migration laws – the implications of which are precarious employment conditions and limited access to legal protections (Segrave 2009; Chuang 2010; Mantouvalou 2012; Mullally 2015). In recognition of and response to these issues, academics and labour rights advocates have identified the need to change immigration and labour laws, and thereby to enhance legislative protections, and to acknowledge migrant domestic workers as workers (Anderson 2010; Varia 2011; Blackett 2012; Sharapov 2015). In Singapore and Hong Kong, the policy emphasis in relation to the protection of women migrant domestic workers is on responding to criminal or employment law violations and punishing individual violators (that is, aberrant employers). Yet critical criminological research has documented the ways in which the persistent failure of state responses to address systemic connecting issues such as migration, gender, labour regulations and

DOI: 10.4324/9781003250364-1

controls as well as discriminatory border policing practices reflects a prioritisation of state security, which in turn works counter to protections and maintains conditions of exploitation and insecurity for women migrant domestic workers. In particular, restrictive labour migration regimes create an inherent tension between the protections offered by legal frameworks and migrant workers' lived experience of protection (see Lee & Petersen 2006; Constable 2014; Huckerby 2015; Palumbo & Sciurba 2015). Applying a gendered lens to the everyday security framework, this book documents and analyses the working and living conditions experienced by women migrant domestic workers and brings to the fore the specific aspects that shape safe and sustainable employment for women migrants. This book strengthens existing criminological understanding of the implications of legislation and policy in the domestic workplace by placing women migrant domestic workers' experiences and voices at the centre of enquiry and generating empirical data on their experiences and negotiation of safe work and everyday security.

There is a considerable gap in the existing criminological scholarship in the use of an everyday gendered (in)securities frame to capture the lived realities of women migrant domestic workers (and women more broadly) and the impact of systems purportedly designed to protect them. While the impacts of criminal justice and legal responses that drive countertrafficking frameworks and global responses to migrant labour exploitation are well documented in criminological scholarship, the focus of such analysis remains on exploitation. There is limited engagement with the complex and intersecting relations of power and violence in both the public and private spheres of women's lives, which structure and sustain exploitation. In this project, I began with a similar interest in understanding how women migrant domestic workers negotiate experiences of exploitative employment. However, during the research process, it became evident that, for the women I spoke to, their struggle not only involves navigating exploitation but is also about enabling safe and sustainable working and living conditions in their everyday work. In this context, legal protection from and/or resistance to exploitation is alone inadequate for explaining and determining what constitutes safety and security for women migrant domestic workers. Consequently, in this book I venture beyond concerns about justice and enforcement to undertake a broader interrogation of intimate labour, employer–worker relationships and workers' negotiation of everyday security against the backdrop of labour and migration laws. Additionally, as is highlighted in the chapters that follow, even though the model of labour and criminal justice protections is predicated upon an underlying assumption that the power and 'domination' of the employer is unilaterally enacted against the 'passive', powerless migrant worker (Tan 2010; Chan 2014), multiple actors, including employment agencies and state technologies (that is, border and immigration law), are deeply implicated in these power relations. In the governance of labour and migration, the worker and her employer are differentially impacted by laws and regulations, which subsequently inform their sense of insecurity *and* practices of security.

My research objective was to investigate how the women migrant domestic workers I interviewed in Singapore and Hong Kong understood and negotiated their labour, both in their everyday work and in the context of their long-term security. These two city-states[1] have vastly different regulatory environments for domestic work but share a similar socio-cultural, political and historical reliance on migrant domestic labour. This research is not intended to be strictly comparative; rather, it brings together the findings from 90 interviews conducted across both research sites, to better understand the ways in which their experiences of shared exclusion from labour migration regulations, the gendered norms underpinning employment practices and workplace relations shape workers' understandings and negotiations of employment conditions. This research is guided by three research questions. First, how do women migrant domestic workers experience their everyday workplaces, and how are these workers and their employers drawn into negotiations over everyday working conditions by regulatory and legal frameworks? Second, how do women migrant domestic workers in Singapore and Hong Kong negotiate their working conditions, and how are these negotiations enabled or challenged by regulatory and legal frameworks? And third, how do women migrant domestic workers in Singapore and Hong Kong define, experience and seek safety and security in the domestic labour context?

The literature on domestic labour, gendered migration, human trafficking and modern slavery informs these questions. Chapters 2 and 3 provide a contextual and conceptual foundation for this book. In Chapter 2, I provide an overview of the structural continuities between unpaid domestic and care labour and waged domestic care labour, which are characterised by the feminisation and devaluation of domestic labour across both the public and private spheres. This contextualisation of waged domestic labour as gendered, familial labour sets the scene for understanding the gendered work expectations placed on women migrant domestic workers, which contrasts with the ungendered definition of work and labour standards within legal and regulatory frameworks. The second part of Chapter 2 maps the labour migration regulatory context within which women migrant domestic workers' experiences of employment (and exploitation) are defined, understood and responded to. Against this background, Chapter 3 outlines the conceptual positioning of this work within a feminist, everyday human security framework. The first part of this chapter draws on critical criminological and feminist literature to consider the limitations of law and legal protection frameworks more broadly in terms of protecting women migrant domestic workers. The synthesis of this empirical scholarship highlights the need to (1) look beyond law and acknowledge that labour migration regulations produce structural precarity, and (2) foreground the lived experiences of women migrant workers to understand their needs, their assessment of risk and safety, and their responses to exploitation and harm. Building on these insights, in the second part of Chapter 3 I argue that the everyday human security framework helps us to contest the static conceptualisations of protection and exploitation dominating current policy and practice. This chapter offers an innovative interpretation of everyday human security by extending Crawford and Hutchinson's (2016) theoretical discussion on everyday security to encompass the context of female migrant labour in an intimate and relational setting.

Chapters 4, 5 and 6 answer the three research questions and, respectively, present the findings relating to (1) the socio-political and contextual factors that inform the everyday living and working conditions of women migrant domestic workers; (2) workers' negotiation of their employment circumstances; and (3) workers' perceptions of their employment conditions and the factors that influence their evaluations. Chapter 4 focuses on two participant groups (women migrant domestic workers and employers) and examines the everyday context in which waged domestic labour is performed by women migrants. This chapter addresses the first research question and examines the intersection of workers' and employers' needs, priorities, motivations and (in) securities and how they are informed by both the nature of live-in domestic labour *and* overarching state structures. Broadly, Chapter 4 draws out some of the socio-political and contextual features that inform the everyday living and working conditions of women migrant domestic workers. The findings reveal that the labour migration regulations of Singapore and Hong Kong differentially impact employers and workers, rendering both insecure. However, when employers are impacted by labour and migration laws and feel insecure, they are likely to adopt measures to control the mobility and freedom of their workers. By examining employers' and workers' experiences and negotiations of everyday security, in Chapter 4 I argue that the labour migration regime in Singapore and Hong Kong has created an employment situation where women migrant domestic workers negotiate their workplace security through their interactions and interpersonal relationships with their employers, rather than being protected by law. The final section of this chapter highlights the emotional and relational nature of the domestic workplace, wherein the interpersonal relationships between employers, workers and other household members have a significant influence on how workers perceive and evaluate their employment situations.

Chapter 5 answers the second research question by investigating how women migrant domestic workers negotiate their employment circumstances and which individuals or organisations they identify as a primary source of support when things go wrong. In this chapter, I argue that labour migration regimes in Singapore and Hong Kong have significantly constrained workers' access to various formal and informal mechanisms of support. Women migrant domestic workers' negotiation of their employment experiences – in particular, their resistance to subordination and exploitation – is a key focus of global efforts around domestic workers' rights, as evidenced by the burgeoning activist work and research in relation to individual strategies and collective actions (e.g., Chin 1998; Parreñas 2000; Lan 2006; Ford & Piper 2007; Lyons 2007; Constable 2009;

Anderson 2010; Pande 2012; Barua, Haukanes & Waldrop 2016). The findings presented in Chapter 5 offer a unique contribution to this scholarship by examining the type of assistance that the workers in this study sought and the factors that shaped their decisions around help-seeking. By mapping workers' perceptions of and access to various formal and informal mechanisms of support, this chapter reveals that while workers do employ various help-seeking strategies to enable safe work and better employment conditions, very few will do so via legal and regulatory interventions, due to the potential negative implications for their livelihood security. Through this analysis, I argue that there is a critical lack of commitment to recognising the work-related problems that women migrant domestic workers encounter and what is necessary to ensure a safe working environment for them.

Chapter 6 answers the third research question by detailing workers' perceptions of their employment circumstances, in particular what they consider to be labour exploitation or practices that are unacceptable, and the factors that influence their evaluations. This chapter offers an important contribution to the emerging critical criminological scholarship that problematises contemporary definitions of labour exploitation, which have tended to erase the complexities of workers' experiences by emphasising the most extreme and physically visible forms of harm (see, for example, O'Connell Davidson & Anderson 2006; Wijers 2015). By examining how women migrant domestic workers define and interpret their employment conditions – specifically, what they consider to be a problem – I suggest that current labour regulatory frameworks, which define exploitation, cannot fully capture and respond to women workers' experiences of domestic labour. The findings reveal that, alongside employer compliance with formal labour standards, workers' evaluations of their employers and work situations are also shaped by subjective elements such as individual expectations of domestic labour and the dynamics of the employer–employee relationship. In particular, affective relations of respect, trust and empathy were identified by the workers I interviewed as significant to their everyday employment experience. Based on the understanding that safe work for women migrant domestic workers is not simply the absence of exploitation, this chapter argues that the current predominant frame of labour exploitation is inadequate for understanding what is necessary for employment to be safe and sustainable for women migrant domestic workers.

Chapter 7 concludes the book by reviewing its key contributions to the critical criminological literature on gendered labour, migration and exploitation. It brings to the fore the need to rethink the current emphasis on a legal or criminal justice approach to identifying, understanding and rectifying poor or substandard employment conditions for women migrant domestic workers. The chapter also considers how the simultaneous devaluation of and reliance on gendered and emotional labour as performed by women in the private home impacts on the formal and informal employment standards governing waged domestic labour, and the continuing challenge this creates for establishing practices or ensuring access to protections that will enable these women to work safely.

The final section of this chapter provides a contextual discussion of female migrant domestic labour in Singapore and Hong Kong. Before doing so, however, the next section elaborates on the design and recruitment process of this study and explores the key ethical considerations relevant to feminist research with women migrant domestic workers.

Research Process: Designing the Study

To better understand the prosaic and diverse experiences of women migrant domestic workers, I chose to use qualitative, semi-structured interviews. The bounded flexibility of semi-structured interviews supports a systematic coverage of topics and offers the space to explore unexpected issues that may arise during the course of an interview, including shifting the discussion to cover the participants' priorities and concerns (Noaks & Wincup 2004; Reininger et al. 2005; Longhurst 2010; Allen 2011). I conducted interviews with a total of 52 women migrant domestic workers. Although the research foregrounds and privileges the voices and experiences of women migrant domestic workers, the objectives of this study also made it necessary to include the perspectives and experiences of employers and other stakeholders. In this regard, critical scholarship on labour exploitation has consistently underscored how frontline respondents, from state authorities to NGOs, have the capacity to define exploitation and in turn play a significant role in determining workers' access to protections (Ham, Segrave & Pickering 2013; Pickering 2014; Segrave & Powell 2015). To understand how these frontline groups define, understand and respond to exploitation in migrant domestic work as well as the expectations they hold in relation to support, protection and security, I interviewed a total of 10 employers and 28 legal practitioners and service providers. The interviews focused on three key areas: (1) 'exploitation' and its relevance to participants; (2) the relational aspects of domestic work and how they shape the everyday home workplace, and (3) workers' access to protection and security when employment problems arise.

Access and Recruitment

Recruitment of participants was conducted through a combination of snowball sampling and what Scott and Geddes (2016) colloquially term as a 'friend-of-a-friend' approach, which used the social ties of women migrant domestic workers to connect with more extensive 'weak-tie' networks (Scott & Geddes 2016). While access and recruitment via networks mean that there may be risks around privacy (such as the transmission of sensitive information), the extant literature on research recruitment demonstrates that access through 'insider' contacts is one of the most effective techniques for establishing trust with participants from 'hidden' populations (Jacobsen & Landau 2003; Sulaiman-Hill & Thompson 2011; Scott & Geddes 2016). I found this to be the case in my own recruitment process, as recruiting through these informal social networks was effective in helping to establish rapport, legitimacy and trust with women migrant domestic workers.

I started my recruitment phase in Singapore by reaching out to a former migrant domestic worker with whom I had become acquainted when she was working for my neighbour. Although she had returned to Indonesia a few years earlier, she put me in contact with her peers in Singapore. Prospective participants were given my contact details with which to contact me if they were interested in undertaking an interview. Following the initial contact, I provided further information about my project and confirmed their participation. This arrangement placed the respondents in an active role as they had the power to determine their degree of involvement in the research. After this initial round of recruitment and interviews, I then asked these workers whether they could help me with recruiting more participants, by circulating information about the research to their peers, in both Singapore and Hong Kong. Through this process, I was able to establish contact with three Hong Kong–based workers who agreed to participate in an interview and supported me further by offering to introduce me to their friends and persuade them to participate in the interviews. In addition, I applied a secondary sampling approach, where I sought the assistance of domestic worker support organisations that provided emergency shelter services to workers, and which participated in the interviews (as one of the four target groups). Following my interviews with staff members from these organisations, I asked whether they could help me by disseminating information about my research and contact details to their clients. In Hong Kong, the recruitment process was further supplemented by emailing labour unions that were managed and staffed by migrant domestic workers to inform them of the research. Leaders from three of the five migrant-led labour unions that I approached were receptive to my invitation to participate and agreed to be interviewed. They also offered to help me recruit participants from within their respective unions. This was a deliberate effort on my part to ensure a diverse representation of experiences and backgrounds among the research participants.

Access to employers of migrant domestic workers was also obtained through the dissemination of project information via key employer networks in Singapore and Hong Kong. Previous research on waged domestic labour has documented the difficulties of recruiting employers of domestic workers, as they are generally reluctant to be interviewed and grant access to their homes (see Chin 1998; Hess 2005; Killias 2018). In anticipation of these methodological difficulties, for my research I decided to conduct recruitment through local contacts and word-of-mouth, specifically by asking whether they could introduce employers of women migrant domestic workers to me. This proved to be an effective approach and while I am not personally acquainted with the employer-participants, an associated limitation was that these employers were not representative of the wider population as they all came from relatively similar socioeconomic backgrounds. Access to NGO staff members and state authorities was obtained through a different approach from that used for the migrant domestic worker and employer groups, for which I had primarily depended upon personal contacts and snowball sampling. For the former two groups, I reached out to a number of relevant NGOs, industry partners and government departments in both city-states, identified through desk-based research. As the migrant domestic labour industry is relatively mature in both city-states, I was able to identify a total of eight Singapore-based organisations and ten Hong Kong–based organisations. Initial contact with these organisations was made through cold emailing via which I provided information about my project and asked whether they would consider participating. Through this initial round of contact, six organisations from Singapore and five organisations from Hong Kong responded, leading to a total of 15 interviews. After completing the interviews with NGO staff members and state authorities, I also asked for suggestions of and introductions to any other individuals or organisations that they thought would be helpful for the research, such as other organisations working with female migrant domestic workers, or community leaders. This yielded quite a positive outcome for the recruitment phase in Hong Kong as I was made aware of a number of participants whom I had missed out on in the initial round of recruitment.

Negotiating Researcher Reflexivity and Power Dynamics

As an Australian-based female Singaporean Chinese researcher, conducting this research and interviewing both women migrant domestic workers and employers (among other participant groups) in Singapore and Hong Kong involved a complex navigation of the insider–outsider continuum during the entire research process. Recognising all of my identities is important as feminist research methodology locates research as a political process and emphasises the need for researcher reflexivity, in particular, by critically analysing how one's role, experience and social position affect one's research practice and the power dynamics that operate between the researcher and her participants (Marshall 1992; Gottfried 1996; Mason & Stubbs 2012). Campbell (2004, p. 163) describes reflexivity as requiring that questions be asked about 'who is representing whom', while at the same time acknowledging that the researcher is 'caught in representation'. In foregrounding researcher reflexivity, this approach assesses the impact of the researcher's involvement on the research, and in particular acknowledges the values, biases and prejudices that are embedded in the researcher's experience of knowledge formation and epistemological values (Kobayashi 2003; Ackerly & True 2008; Hamdan 2009).

Within this approach to reflexivity, acknowledging the continuum of insider–outsider researcher positionality is imperative as the researcher's social location (defined by their nationality, ethnicity, gender, socioeconomic background and educational level) informs their proximity to the participants, which then has critical implications for the power relations between researcher and research participants (Hamdan 2009; Doucet & Mauthner 2012; Anyan 2013; Leung 2015). The need to consider how, where and when power may influence knowledge production is an especially pertinent one for this study because, as a Singaporean Chinese, I occupy a particular status as I am part of the population that employs women migrant domestic workers. Having relatives who have employed women migrant domestic workers, I have had the opportunity to observe the experience of having a domestic worker in the home, and the relationships that form and the tensions that arise as a result. Having such 'insider knowledge' has made me conscious of the larger socio-historical and familial context in which the employment of women migrant domestic workers occurs. Yet this 'insider knowledge' is significantly constrained as I am not a migrant domestic worker and I have come to this research after having been exposed to largely Western models of feminism through my studies in Australia. As much as my upbringing in Singapore has led me to question the images of the oppressed and exploited migrant domestic worker often represented in Western academic discourse, the concepts of gender, exploitation and power that I have learned to interpret through a Western feminist paradigm have caused me to interrogate my own thinking about female migrant domestic labour. In many ways, this has been a very uncomfortable and difficult journey, not least because scrutinising the experiences of women migrant domestic workers also meant critiquing the socio-cultural norms and customs of my country, friends and family. However, as Pillow (2010) states, practising reflexivity means that one must scrutinise, question and deconstruct what is most hegemonic in our lives, to reflect on our unconscious categories of thought that precondition our practices.

At the same time, Pillow points out that in practising reflexivity, it is insufficient to merely acknowledge the existence of researcher subjectivity and privilege. This runs the risk of further perpetuating an unequal power relationship and misrepresenting the other's situation (Pillow 2003). In particular, she cautions against simply treating reflexivity as a methodological exercise and that it 'cannot be a simple story of subjects, subjectivity and transcendence or self-indulgent tellings' (Pillow 2003, p. 192). In this research, my identity matters because I am asking questions that are of personal, academic and political significance to me; however, I agree with Pillow (2003) in that there is a danger in assuming that coming to know oneself will aid in knowing, understanding and witnessing the other. She suggests that researchers engage in what she terms 'uncomfortable reflexivity' and continually question how one 'can keep grounded in collective struggle, mindful of the politics of representation and critical of the concealment of power in the construction of the discourse of a crisis of representation' (Villenas 1996, p. 91 as cited in Pillow 2003). Thus, working within an 'uncomfortable reflexivity' involves problematising my understandings and position as a researcher to resist complicity in adopting a linear framing of women migrant domestic workers' experiences through the lens of either victimisation or resistance, or (unintentionally) regenerating the mainstream discourse, which minimises harms to workers.

For this research, engaging in uncomfortable reflexivity meant that I had to be rigorous in thinking about *how* I am analysing, writing about and re-presenting the participants' experiences and voices. An important aspect of this process was the deconstruction of my initial focus on exploitation to centre security instead. Scrutinising my insider–outsider biases and unpacking my prejudices is an ongoing process. For example, in conducting the interviews with workers, it was important for me to think about how the workers would perceive the purpose of my research and the questions I asked. Acknowledging that power imbalances exist is important. Yet it was also important to remind myself that, in opting to speak to me, these workers have power, just as they have power in their workplace because of the work they do, while at the same time recognising that this power is mediated by other factors. As an Australian-based native Singaporean researcher, my multiple subjectivities cannot be erased, just as the power disparities between the researcher and the participants cannot be completely eliminated. However, that is also precisely why it is essential to practise reflexivity, to be mindful of acknowledging my biases and becoming 'vigilantly subjective' (Hamdan 2009, p. 392).

Translating, Interpreting and Presenting the Participants' Voices

Given that more than half of the participants in this study did not speak English as a first language,[2] one of the key challenges was the translation of the interviews, which convey the participants' subjective expressions. The quality and validity of translation has been identified by many qualitative and feminist researchers as fundamental to producing ethical and rigorous qualitative research (Hennink 2008; Berman & Tyyskä 2011; Kim 2012). Bearing in mind the impact that language intermediaries can have on research processes and outcomes, I chose a trilingual former migrant domestic worker as the most appropriate interpreter for this research, as she was familiar not only with the language but also with the socio-cultural nuances. However, as it turned out, in spite of the methodological preparations for cultural translation, her actual role in the interview process was very minimal as the worker-participants preferred to communicate directly with me in English as much as possible. Being a trilingual researcher (English, Mandarin Chinese and Cantonese) also meant that I could 'switch'[3] across languages when either the participant or I felt that a particular point was not being conveyed accurately during the interview. This allowed me to circumvent many of the possible problems arising from the use of an interpreter (such as the selective representation of participants' experiences or knowledge), although my approach presented other issues.

In transcribing the interviews, I decided to maintain the local accents and colloquialisms that were used during the interviews rather than transcribe them into formal standard Australian English. Although the majority of the participants spoke English and did not require translation or the assistance of a language intermediary, this research was conducted in Singapore and Hong Kong, where English is spoken differently from the standard English spoken in Australia. Moreover, more than half of the participants did not speak English as a first language. Therefore, to capture the diversity of participant voices, I chose to retain their original phrasing as much as possible. For some of the quotes, where required, clarifications have been added in brackets. Where non-English phrases were used, I have included both the original and translated quotations, to help the reader better understand the subtle nuances of the participants' statements. This is intended to reflect the methodological realities and challenges of including diverse (non-standard English) voices. Bringing attention to these issues within the knowledge-creation process highlights the fact that the inclusion of non-English-speaking voices within English-language research requires assistance or mediation. This is not to suggest that such diverse voices are less valid or hold less authority, but rather to recognise that certain voices – in particular, those of marginalised communities – can only be included and heard with assistance (Ham 2017).

While I sought to retain the participants' original phrasing and expressions as much as possible in the transcription and quotes, I faced another translation dilemma in relation to the gap between the everyday words and expressions used by the participants to explain their perceptions and the terms used in academic text or language in human rights and legal documents. Specifically, a key focus of this research was to examine how exploitation is defined, experienced and responded to in female migrant domestic labour. Yet none of the workers or employers used the word 'exploitation' when talking about their experiences. When I probed further by asking what they considered to be 'exploitation', the answers provided were about severe physical or sexual violence, which pointed to a disjuncture between academic or legal language and the reality of women's lives. DeVault (1990, p. 97) notes that this lack of fit between women's lived experiences and the words available to describe those experiences is not uncommon yet 'presents real difficulties for ordinary women's self-expression in their everyday lives'; and as a result, 'for women who want to talk of their experiences, [they] must "translate", either saying things that are not quite right, or working at using the language in non-standard ways'. To ensure that as feminist researchers we do not further silence or marginalise women's experiences, it is imperative to apply ethical interpretive listening that captures the complexities and ambiguities present in their everyday accounts, which requires us to go around and beyond words (DeVault 1990; Temple 2005; Kim 2012). The implications of this approach extend beyond linguistic issues including translation techniques; how we describe and represent the problems that women face has ramifications for what are considered to be appropriate solutions and responses to those problems. A critical concern for my research, then, is whether the continued use of the term 'exploitation' is suitable or will be a distortion of the participants' perceptions and lived experiences. These tensions are examined in further detail in the Conclusion, where I propose that there is a need to reconfigure our understanding of exploitation to better account for women migrant domestic workers' lives. With the methodological aspects of the book established, in the remainder of this introductory chapter I lay out the historical, economical and socio-cultural context that has produced the contemporary demand for women migrant domestic workers in Singapore and Hong Kong.

Migration and Domestic Labour in Singapore and Hong Kong: Past and Present

Statistics from Singapore's Ministry of Manpower (MOM) and Hong Kong's Immigration Department demonstrate that as of December 2021 there were 247,400 and 339,000 migrant domestic workers employed in Singapore and Hong Kong, respectively. This means that approximately one in five[4] Singaporean households employs a live-in migrant domestic worker (Islam et al. 2016). Hong Kong reflects similar ratios, with an estimated one in eight[5] Hong Kong households employing a live-in migrant domestic worker (Chan 2014). While the COVID-19 pandemic and state measures to prevent importation of virus cases have led to temporary border restrictions and therefore a decrease in the number of women migrant domestic workers,[6] it is expected that these numbers will again increase[7] with the growing aging population in both city-states. The shortage of labour to assist with caregiving needs in Singapore and Hong Kong during the pandemic has also prompted the implementation of processes to facilitate the entry of smaller numbers of women migrant domestic workers (Choo 2021; Menon 2021; Sun 2022). The above data indicate a significant formalised reliance on women migrant domestic workers' provision of domestic and care labour for families in Singapore and Hong Kong. Referring to this as a 'maid dependency syndrome', Devasahayam (2010, p. 48) argues that the high numbers of migrant domestic workers reflect not only a reliance on women migrant domestic workers to fill the gendered labour gap in individual households but equally a structural dependency on migrant women's labour in the domestic sphere to sustain public welfare and economic systems.

In Singapore and Hong Kong, the practice of employing migrant women for full-time, live-in domestic and care labour has existed since 1920s, as part of the British colonial era and is a longstanding and culturally ingrained practice within both societies. Historical records dating back to the 1930s indicate that a large number of 'unattached and illiterate' women from Guangdong Province in Mainland China emigrated to Hong Kong and Malaya (present-day Singapore and Malaysia) to work as domestic workers for wealthy Chinese families and their British colonial masters (Gaw 1991; Ooi 1992). Commonly referred to as 'amahs',[8] these women were employed to help the women of wealthy and elite families in three main areas of domestic activity: housework, cooking, and caring for young children (Gaw 1991; Ooi 1992; Wickramasekera 2000). Due to the nature of their work, most of the amahs were employed in a live-in capacity, not unlike the current system for contemporary women migrant domestic workers, where the place of employment and lodging is one and the same. In their review of the roles and functions of amahs, both Gaw (1991) and Ooi (1992) explain that in the families they worked for, amahs were generally well respected and regarded not as hired servants but as members of the family. At the same time, closely tied to the familial inclusion of amahs was the gendered description of them as selfless, dedicated and devoted to the family (Gaw 1991; Ooi 1992). The establishment of amahs has had a profound influence on the social norms underpinning the cultural acceptance of and expectations towards the employment of live-in women migrant domestic workers in Singapore and Hong Kong (Constable 1997; Lee 2016; Peng 2018). However, in the late 1960s, the social and economic upheavals in Asia that occurred after World War II, coupled with stricter immigration conditions, led to a sharp decline in the emigration of Chinese amahs. This diminishing population of Chinese amahs alongside rapid industrialisation in Singapore and Hong Kong produced a gradual transition from the employment of Chinese amahs to employing women migrant domestic workers from Southeast Asia (Huang & Yeoh 1996). By the late 1970s, the domestic worker population in Singapore and Hong Kong was constituted entirely of migrant women from neighbouring Southeast Asian countries such as the Philippines, Indonesia, Thailand, Myanmar and Sri Lanka (Constable 1996; Huang & Yeoh 1996).

The global economic restructuring that occurred in the 1970s and 1980s led to unprecedented economic growth in both Singapore and Hong Kong, which resulted in a heightened demand for local women's participation in the paid labour force (Leung 1995; Poon 2009). Improved educational attainment, expanded job opportunities, growing economic pressures and women's rising personal ambitions sparked a change in social attitudes. Women were encouraged to continue working after marriage and pregnancy (Pearson & Leung 1995; Wong 1996; Cortés & Pan 2013). Notwithstanding these changing political and socioeconomic circumstances, domestic and care work in the home, such as cleaning, cooking, washing and caring for the young and elderly, remain firmly gendered – construed as the domain of wives and mothers (Lee 2002; Choi & Ting 2009; Lyons 2017). To fill the domestic and care deficits, households have turned to the employment of transnational women migrants as a solution (Huang & Yeoh 1998; Parreñas 2000; Lan 2006; Labadie-Jackson 2008). Migrating from economically impoverished nations to richer nations, these women provide a relatively inexpensive[9] and highly convenient option to support local women's housekeeping and care responsibilities (Yeoh, Huang & Devasahayam 2004; Chan 2005; Choi & Ting 2009; Cortés & Pan 2013).

However, in addition to persistent gendered expectations around the division of domestic responsibilities, the market demand for women migrant domestic workers also needs to be understood against two other key factors. One is the absence of a comprehensive welfare system and lack of affordable care alternatives for households (Teo & Piper 2009; Tan 2010; Lyons 2017). While there is a basic system of social security in Singapore and Hong Kong, there remains a limited investment in long-term welfare and care services.[10] Instead, the provision of care for the young, the elderly and other dependants is largely regarded by the two states as a private familial (and female) affair (Ochiai 2009; Hill, Ford & Baird 2017). This is supported by policies that promote the development of an informal, non-familial care workforce (that is, of women migrant domestic workers) over a formal care infrastructure, thus making the choice of employing a live-in worker more 'sensible' and cost efficient[11] than other forms of public care services (Hill, Ford & Baird 2017; Ogawa et al. 2018; Peng 2018). The other contributing factor relates to cultural perceptions of the home as a safe haven that is the most suitable site for the care of the family (Rahman, Yeoh & Huang 2005; Lan 2006; Lyons 2017). In her study with Taiwanese employers, Lan (2006, p. 96) observed that the 'live-in' aspect of this labour made women migrant domestic workers a more appealing option than other non-home-based solutions as it 'approximates the ideal of stay-at-home motherhood'. Similarly, in other studies on elderly care in Singapore and Hong Kong (see Chan et al. 2012; Wee et al. 2015; Chan & Wong 2018), researchers have found that families generally favoured home-based care over external care providers because of the association with genuine concern and personalised attention to both bodily care and emotional needs. Quality paid care is thus not only seen as requiring care for the physical body (such as bathing, dressing, feeding and administering medications) but must also include an emotional or intimate component whereby the worker is 'genuinely' devoted and attentive to the well-being of the care recipient (Boris & Parreñas 2010; Cranford & Miller 2013; Marchetti 2015). These perceptions of home-based care and expectations of emotional commitment, which are beyond standard employment conventions, are particularly consequential for women migrant domestic workers as they translate into expectations of how and what care should be provided, while also defining appropriate behaviour for these workers (Marchetti 2015; Johnson et al. 2019).

Yet, in spite of the structural dependency on women migrant domestic workers, their residency in Singapore and Hong Kong is premised on the idea of 'permanent temporariness', easy repatriation and exclusion from full access to labour rights (Baas 2017; Platt et al. 2017). Both city-states are considered globally to have liberal foreign labour policies; and there is no set limit on the number of visas that can be issued to migrant domestic workers (Justice Centre Hong Kong 2016). However, the labour migration regime in both jurisdictions is structured to produce and maintain their liminal position as simultaneously necessary, yet undesirable. Under the current labour migration policies of each state, women migrant domestic workers enter Singapore and Hong Kong on a renewable two-year work contract, but their right to remain and work in these city-states is dependent on continued employment by the employer-sponsor (Constable 2003; Sim 2009). This tied-visa system essentially enlists employers (and private employment agencies) to oversee and control female migrant bodies. This ought to be understood as part of the state's efforts to mitigate risks around the permanent settlement of 'undesirable' migrant workers (Demetriou 2015; Elias 2018; Chin 2019). This situation, which for workers produces a nexus of legal and economic dependency on employers, is exacerbated by specific clauses in labour migration regulations that preclude migrant workers from permanent settlement, family reunion, and circulating in the local labour market and accessing new work (for example, by changing employment sector or employer) (Constable 2009; Tan 2010). Singapore-based migrant domestic workers are also prohibited from becoming pregnant and marrying a Singaporean resident or national – the consequence of which is immediate deportation (Kaur 2010). Border controls thus create what scholars have termed 'differential inclusion' (Andrijasevic & Anderson 2009; Mezzadra & Neilson 2013), where women migrant domestic workers are 'managed as a temporary and controlled phenomenon' who are filling specific labour shortages rather than contributing desired skills that would benefit the nation over the long term (Yeoh, Huang & Devasahayam 2004, p. 19). In this way they are discursively and legally constructed as *just* workers, not as persons, and as (permanently) temporary subjects, not long-term residents (Constable 2009; Tan 2010; Parreñas 2015). As will be discussed in later chapters, the intersecting dimensions of border controls and labour regulations in Singapore and Hong Kong have contributed to the reproduction of marginality and everyday insecurity for women migrant domestic workers; a situation that has been exacerbated during the pandemic.

These historical, gendered and socio-political conventions support the significant market for the services of women migrant domestic workers in Singapore and Hong Kong. However, the outmigration of women for domestic labour also needs to be understood in relation to the structural problems and labour export policies of labour-sending countries.

Emigration of Women into Domestic Labour: Role of the State and the Private Sector

In tandem with the growing market demand for domestic and care labour, unequal global economic development has progressively made migration for work an economic necessity or a 'survival strategy' for a substantial proportion of women from 'Third World' countries (Sassen 2000; Yeoh, Huang & Devasahayam 2004; Jagori 2012; Piper, Rosewarne & Withers 2016). Within Asia, the Philippines and Indonesia in particular have seen an active government-driven promotion of temporary emigration for low-wage labour since the 1970s. Both nations were significantly negatively impacted by the structural adjustment requirements implemented by the International

Monetary Fund and the World Bank. It is within this context that the Philippines, and later, Indonesia, began encouraging the labour outmigration of its women into domestic work as a response to escalating levels of national debt, declining local livelihoods and domestic unemployment (see Tyner 1996; Guevarra 2010; Tigno 2014; Palmer 2016; Piper, Rosewarne & Withers 2016). Overseas employment subsequently became central to these countries' programs of development, and women migrant domestic workers were (and continue to be) hailed as national heroes who are invaluable to the development and improvement of both the nation-state *and* their families (Guevarra 2010; Chan 2014; Tigno 2014; Parreñas 2015).

Underpinning this state narrative of 'national heroism', however, is the ideal of domesticated femininity, grounded in women's gendered and moral responsibilities to be good mothers, daughters and wives by financially supporting their families (Ford 2003; Silvey 2007; Guevarra 2010; Chan 2014; Yeoh et al. 2017; Platt 2018). Notwithstanding the emancipatory potential of labour emigration,[12] it has also reinforced and reproduced the existing gender order and social hierarchies. In her study on Indonesia's state representation of women migrant domestic workers, Chan (2014, p. 6957) found that the country's emigration policy for women was underpinned by notions of a 'national feminine ideal of the sacrificial family-oriented citizen'. This was echoed in other studies on the Philippines and Indonesia that found that state-driven policies and practices essentialise Filipina and Indonesian women as ideal domestic workers by emphasising and promoting their sexual purity, feminine docility, obedience, loyalty and responsibility to the family (Silvey 2007; Guevarra 2014; Yeoh 2014). In several studies on pre-employment training for women migrant domestic workers, the findings reveal that in addition to being taught to display 'proper' female moral discipline (for example, not displaying promiscuous behaviour), workers are 'educated' in a manner that encourages the suppression of negative emotions and self-adjustment in response to conflict with employers (see Rudnyckyi 2004; Liang 2011; Constable 2014; Guevarra 2014; Prusinski 2017; Chang 2018; Platt 2018). Rudnyckyi (2004) uses the term 'technologies of servitude' to describe these disciplinary and regulatory technologies employed by placement agents to elicit a performance of docility, obedience and other 'proper' attitudes expected of a woman migrant domestic worker. In this manner, Indonesian and Filipina women's economic and migratory capacity is constructed within a value-laden framework that emphasises *and* encourages feminine ideals of self-sacrifice and prioritisation of family over self (Oishi 2005; Platt 2018). These discursive constructions of women migrant domestic workers in turn produce gendered and moral expectations of what makes a 'good' or 'bad' worker (Ford 2003; Silvey 2007). Such expectations have significant implications for these workers' employment experiences and expectations of work, as well as for the broader migration and labour law infrastructure that provides the formal scaffolding around their work, life and migration (Chan 2014; Guevarra 2010, 2014; Platt 2018).

A central actor tasked with the reproduction of such gendered moralities *and* the facilitation of migrant mobilities more broadly is the cross-border network of employment intermediaries, which includes licensed recruitment and placement agencies, training centres and informal village-level recruiters (Lindquist 2010; Goh, Wee & Yeoh 2017). Notwithstanding the role of states in facilitating and regulating migrant mobility via labour migration policies and regulations, the coordination of contemporary migration in Asia (and globally) has become increasingly decentralised, organised via a complex migration infrastructure involving a large network of both state *and* non-state actors (Lindquist, Xiang & Yeoh 2012; Xiang & Lindquist 2014; Anderson & Franck 2019). However, extant work on migrant mobilities and governance has tended to focus on countries of origin and destination, with comparatively less attention paid to the role of private migration intermediaries, also commonly referred to as brokers. A significant proportion of older research on migration brokers has attended to their contribution to the exploitation of low-wage migrant workers through excessive recruitment fees, misrepresenting working conditions, withholding or modifying travel documents, and driving up migration costs (Kaur 2010; Fudge 2011; Xiang 2013). Yet, as recent studies in the Asian context demonstrate, the reductionist vilification of migration brokers assumes troubling dichotomies of legality vs. illegality and profit orientation vs. altruism (Lindquist, Xiang & Yeoh 2012), which leaves little room to capture the ambivalence and diversity in brokerage practices (see Lindquist 2010; Lindquist, Xiang & Yeoh 2012; McKeown 2012; Xiang & Lindquist 2014; Goh, Wee & Yeoh 2017).

In analysing the role and operations of private migration intermediaries, scholars have observed that they do not only assist employers and workers in navigating the labyrinth of migration-related logistical administrative processes, laws and regulations. Recruitment and placement agents have two further key functions. The first is in shaping migrant domestic workers' subjectivities through technologies of gendered and moral discipline (Rudnyckyi 2004; Lan 2006; Liang 2011; Guevarra 2014). Specifically, the pre-employment training sessions for women migrant domestic workers mentioned above are overwhelmingly run by employment agencies, illuminating how brokers coproduce and reinforce the gendered and cultural essentialisation of these workers *and* the domestic labour industry in tandem with the state. The second function is in providing advice and 'counsel' to employers and workers on how to manage employment relationships and arbitrating conflict where necessary (Goh, Wee & Yeoh 2017). It is within this context that placement agents produce and compound the precarity experienced by women migrant domestic workers, as the legal frameworks in labour-receiving states allow considerable space (and power) for agents to interpret and enact state regulations and guidelines (Kaur 2010; Constable 2013; Goh, Wee & Yeoh 2017; Elias 2018). The recognition that brokers have considerable power and control over the terms and conditions of employment for women migrant domestic workers, especially those on their first contracts, should not be understated and remains an important challenge in policy and practice. There is increasing recognition that brokers are deeply imbricated in the global and national structure of labour markets and the broader policy context, as they are reflexive agents who actively respond to and mitigate the exploitative effects of infrastructure but are also constrained by the regulatory infrastructure and the gendered relational context of domestic labour (Lindquist, Xiang & Yeoh 2012; McKeown 2012; Meehan & Plonski 2017; Goh 2018). Rather than continuing to reproduce the narrative of the exploitative broker and the victimised migrant, a more generative conversation on the extent and kinds of responsibilities brokers have in facilitating or constraining women migrant domestic workers' everyday security will better inform policy and practice by redirecting our gaze to the structural and relational factors that shape workers' negotiation of safe work.

The question of safe work and women migrant domestic workers' everyday security sits at the centre of this book. The decision to shift away from a narrower lens designed to examine the utility of legal protections in responding to the exploitation of these workers enabled the analysis of the connections between the motivations of workers and employers, the gendered and relational context of domestic labour, and the institutional structures of migration and labour laws, and in turn the implications for women migrant domestic workers' experiences and negotiation of security. This process was necessarily mediated by methodological limitations and embodied epistemologies. However, I have focused on capturing women migrant workers' voices, experiences and priorities. The women I interviewed talked about their objective of being in paid employment and their navigation of employer–employee relations when describing what mattered to their everyday working and living conditions. In this book, I have sought to reflect their accounts of the conditions that enable or constrain safe and sustainable work.

Notes

1 The term 'city-state' is defined as 'an autonomous state consisting of a city and surrounding territory' (Merriam-Webster n.d.). As a sovereign island in Southeast Asia, Singapore can be described as a city-state. Although Hong Kong is part of the People's Republic of China, it is one of China's two Special Administrative Regions. Enshrined under the Sino-British Joint Declaration is the constitutional framework of 'one country, two systems' (Alsford 2019), which authorises Hong Kong to enjoy a 'high degree of autonomy except in foreign and defence affairs' (Constitutional and Mainland Affairs Bureau 2007). Currently, Hong Kong possesses its own government and independent[1] executive, legislative and judicial power, and it is responsible for implementing its own policies, including labour and immigration policies (Constitutional and Mainland Affairs Bureau 2007). In consideration of these factors, both Singapore and Hong Kong can be referred to as city-states.

2 English is not the first language for women migrant domestic workers and employers in Hong Kong, where Cantonese is the more commonly spoken language.

3 In this process, no deliberate signal was ever used to indicate the switch; rather, this occurred 'naturally' over the course of our conversation. For example, in one of the interviews with employers, we had been talking in Mandarin Chinese, yet when the employer was describing her frustration at the perceived unfairness of the pregnancy legislation in Hong Kong, she could not find the right vocabulary to explain her opinions so had to switch over to Cantonese. This switching of languages occurred in all of the interviews with the Hong Kong–based employers and in some interviews with women migrant domestic workers.
4 There are no official figures on the total number of employers of domestic workers in Singapore. This estimate is based on the statistics released by MOM in 2010, when the number of female migrant domestic workers stood at 201,000.
5 According to the Hong Kong Legislative Council (2017), one in three households with children employs a full-time migrant worker.
6 At the end of 2019, the number of women migrant domestic workers in Singapore and Hong Kong had peaked at 261,800 and 400,000, respectively.
7 In 2017, the Hong Kong Legislative Council projected that the number of migrant domestic workers would increase to 600,000 over the subsequent 30 years.
8 'Amah' is used in general reference to Chinese domestic workers from Canton (present-day Guangdong). However, Constable (1996, p. 452) explains that, in practice, depending on the tasks relegated to them (e.g., cooking, cleaning, washing), amahs were referred to by different names.
9 Research in Singapore and Hong Kong interrogating the affordability of hiring a migrant domestic worker to meet a household's care needs has indicated that it remains expensive and uneconomical for low-income families (see Teo 2016; Cheung 2021). While a recent study in Hong Kong documents a shifting trend towards lower-income families employing women migrant domestic workers to cope with heavy work and childcare responsibilities, doing so is costly, which then has negative implications for the working and living conditions of these workers.
10 In Singapore and Hong Kong, the state's focus is primarily on economic development, while welfare policies are supported with the proviso that they do not hinder economic growth or create excessive social expenditure (Holliday 2000; Teo & Piper 2009; Chan 2011; Ogawa et al. 2018).
11 In Singapore, for approximately SGD600 a month, a family can have childcare and/or elderly care plus basic domestic chores such as cleaning, cooking and washing performed by one person in the home (Teo & Piper 2009; Devasahayam 2010; Teo 2013). In addition, the current 'maid levy' scheme, which offers substantial concessions for employers with young children, elderly and/or disabled relatives, encourages Singaporean households with caregiving needs to hire a woman migrant domestic worker. In Hong Kong, the monthly cost for full-time care in a government-subsidised childcare centre is approximately HKD5200 (Lo 2017), while the monthly wage of a full-time, live-in female migrant domestic worker is HKD4630, with an additional HKD1173 food allowance to be provided to the worker if the employer does not provide food (Gov HK 2021). In this situation, the employment of women migrant domestic workers, which is an affordable expense for Hong Kong's middle- to high-income households, is often the only viable choice, especially for dual-income families that have heavy work and care responsibilities (Chan 2006; Cortés & Pan 2013; Chan & Wong 2018).
12 Empirical studies with women migrant domestic workers have established that labour emigration is a means for women to escape oppressive marriages, gain economic independence and improve their social position by becoming self-sufficient earners *and* breadwinners for their families (see Parreñas 2000, 2012; Piper 2013; Yeoh 2016). For some women, working overseas has reshaped their self-identity and challenged the power dynamics within their families (Constable 2007; McKay 2007).

References

Ackerly, B & True, J (2008), 'Reflexivity in practice: Power and ethics in feminist research on international relations', *International Studies Review*, 10(4): 693–707.

Allen, M (2011), 'Violence and voice: Using a feminist constructivist grounded theory to explore women's resistance to abuse', *Qualitative Research*, 11(1): 23–45.

Alsford, NJP (2019), 'Hong Kong: Why the 'one country two systems' model is on its last legs', *The Conversation*, 19 June, viewed 10 Dec, https://theconversation.com/hong-kong-why-the-one-country-two-systems-model-is-on-its-last-legs-118960

Anderson, B (2010), 'Migration, immigration controls and the fashioning of precarious workers', *Work, Employment and Society*, 24(2): 300–317.

Anderson, JT & Franck, AK (2019), 'The public and the private in guestworker schemes: Examples from Malaysia and the US', *Journal of Ethnic and Migration Studies*, 45(7): 1207–1223.

Andrijasevic, R & Anderson, B (2009), 'Conflicts of mobility: Migration, labour and political subjectivities', *Subjectivity*, 29: 363–366.

Anyan, F (2013), 'The influence of power shifts in data collection and analysis stages: A focus on qualitative research interview', *The Qualitative Report*, 18(18): 1–9.

Baas, M (2017), 'Temporary labour migration', in G Liu-Farrer & BSA Yeoh (eds.), *Routledge Handbook of Asian Migrations*, Routledge, New York, pp. 51–63.

Barua, P, Haukanes, H & Waldrop, A (2016), 'Maid in India: Negotiating and contesting the boundaries of domestic work', *Forum for Development Studies*, 43(3): 415–436.

Berman, RC & Tyyskä, V (2011) 'A critical reflection on the use of translators/interpreters in a qualitative cross-language research project', *International Journal of Qualitative Methods*, 10(1): 178–190.

Blackett, A (2012), 'The decent work for domestic workers convention and recommendation, 2011', *American Journal of International Law*, 106(4): 778–794.

Boris, E & Parreñas, RS (2010), 'Introduction', in E Boris & RS Parreñas (eds.), *Intimate Labors: Cultures, Technologies and the Politics of Care*, Stanford University Press, California, pp. 1–12.

Campbell, K (2004), 'The promise of feminist reflexivities: Developing Donna Haraway's project for feminist science studies', *Hypatia*, 19(1): 162–182.

Chang, AS (2018), 'Producing the self-regulating subject: Liberal protection in Indonesia's migration infrastructure', *Pacific Affairs*, 91(4): 695–716.

Chan, AHN (2005), 'Live-in foreign domestic workers and their impact on Hong Kong's middle-class families', *Journal of Family and Economic Issues*, 26(4): 509–528.

Chan, AHN (2006), 'The effects of full-time domestic workers on married women's economic activity status in Hong Kong: 1981-2001', *International Sociology*, 21(1): 133–159.

Chan, CK (2011), *Social security policy in Hong Kong: From British colony to China's Special Administrative Region*, Lexington Books, UK.

Chan, CLW, Ho, AHY, Leung, PPY, Chochinov, HM, Neimeyer, RA, Pang, SMC & Tse, DMW (2012), 'The blessings and the curses of filial piety on dignity at the end of life: Lived experience of Hong Kong Chinese adult children caregivers', *Journal of Ethnic & Cultural Diversity in Social Work*, 21: 227–296.

Chan, RKH & Wong, PYK (2018), 'The double burden of care in Hong Kong: Implications for care policies and arrangements', in R Ogawa, RKH Chan, AS Oishi & LR Wang (eds.), *Gender, Care and Migration in East Asia*, Palgrave Macmillan, Singapore, pp. 25–46.

Chan, T (2014), 'Forced labour laws in Hong Kong: A comparative analysis', *Journal of Law, Technology and Public Policy*, 1(1): 87–114.

Cheung, AKL (2021), 'Re-examining the middle-class thesis: Class profiles of families employing migrant domestic workers in Hong Kong', *Asian and Pacific Migration Journal*, 10.1177/01171968211069697.

Chin, BN (1998), *In Service and Servitude: Foreign Domestic Workers and the Malaysian "Modernity" Project*, Columbia University Press, New York.

Chin, C (2019), 'Precarious work and its complicit network: Migrant labour in Singapore', *Journal of Contemporary Asia*, 49(4): 528–551.

Choi, SYP & Ting, KF (2009), 'A gender perspective on families in Hong Kong', in FM Cheung & E Holroyd (eds.), *Mainstreaming gender in Hong Kong society*, The Chinese University Press, Hong Kong, pp. 159–180.

Choo, YT (2021), 'Pilot scheme to facilitate entry of more maids into S'pore amid Covid-19', 14 Jul, viewed 1 Feb, https://www.straitstimes.com/singapore/pilot-programme-to-kick-off-for-more-foreign-domestic-workers-to-enter-singapore

Chuang, JA (2010), 'Achieving accountability for migrant domestic worker abuse', *North Carolina Law Review*, 88(5): 1627–1656.

Constable, N (1996), 'Jealousy, chastity and abuse: Chinese maids and foreign helpers in Hong Kong', *Modern China*, 22(4): 448–479.

Constable, N (1997), 'Sexuality and discipline among Filipina domestic workers in Hong Kong', *American Ethnologist*, 24(3): 539–558.

Constable, N (2003), 'A transnational perspective on divorce and marriage: Filipina wives and workers', *Identities: Global Studies in Culture and Power*, 10(2): 163–180.

Constable, N (2007), *Made to Order in Hong Kong: Stories of Migrant Workers*, Cornell University Press, New York.

Constable, N (2009), 'Migrant workers and the many states of protest in Hong Kong', *Critical Asian Studies*, 41(1): 143–164.

Constable, N (2013), 'Migrant workers, legal tactics, and fragile family formation in Hong Kong', *Oñati Socio-Legal Series*, 3(6): 1004–1022.

Constable, N (2014), *Born Out of Place*, University of California Press, California.

Cortés, P & Pan, J (2013), 'Outsourcing household production: Foreign domestic workers and native labor supply in Hong Kong', *Journal of Labor Economics*, 31(2): 327–371.

Cranford, CJ & Miller, D (2013), 'Emotion management from the client's perspective: The case of personal home care', *Work, Employment & Society*, 27(5): 785–801.

Crawford, A, & Hutchinson, S (2016). 'Mapping the contours of 'everyday security': Time, space and emotion'. *British Journal of Criminology*, 56(6): 1184–1202.

Demetriou, D (2015), '"Tied visas" and inadequate labour protections: A formula for abuse and exploitation of migrant domestic workers in the United Kingdom', *Anti-Trafficking Review*, 5: 69–88.

Devasahayam, TW (2010), 'Placement and/or protection? Singapore's labour policies and practices for temporary women migrant workers', *Journal of the Asia Pacific Economy*, 15(1): 45–58.

DeVault, ML (1990), 'Talking and listening from women's standpoint: Feminist strategies for interviewing and analysis', *Social Problems*, 37(1): 96–116.

Doucet, A & Mauthner, N (2012), 'Qualitative interviewing and feminist research', in P Alasuutari, L Bickman & J Brannen (eds.), *The SAGE Handbook of Social Research Methods*, SAGE Publications Ltd., London, pp. 328–343.

Elias, J (2018), 'Governing domestic worker migration in Southeast Asia: Public-private partnerships, regulatory grey zones and the household', *Journal of Contemporary Asia*, 48(2): 278–300.

Ford, M (2003), 'Beyond the femina fantasy: The working-class woman in Indonesian discourses of women's work', *RIMA: Review of Indonesian and Malaysian Affairs*, 37(2): 83–113.

Ford, M & Piper, N (2007), 'Southern sites of female agency: Informal regimes and female migrant labour resistance in East and Southeast Asia', in JM Hobson & L Seabrooke (eds.), *Everyday Politics of the World Economy*, Cambridge University Press, UK, pp. 63–80.

Fudge, J (2011), 'Global care chains, employment agencies and the conundrum of jurisdiction: Decent work for domestic workers in Canada', *Canadian Journal of Women and the Law*, 23(1): 235–264.

Gaw, K (1991), *Superior servants: The legendary Cantonese amahs of the Far East*, Oxford University Press, Singapore.

Goh, JMC (2018), Agents as migration infrastructure: Circulating debt and channelling Indonesian domestic workers in Singapore, Master's Thesis, National University of Singapore, Singapore.

Goh, JMC, Wee, K & Yeoh, BSA (2017), 'Migration governance and the migration industry in Asia: Moving domestic workers from Indonesia to Singapore', *International Relations of the Asia Pacific*, 17(3): 401–433.

Gottfried, H (ed.) (1996), *Feminism and Social Change: Bridging Theory and Practice*, University of Illinois Press, Chicago.

Guevarra, AR (2010), *Marketing dreams, manufacturing heroes: The transnational labour brokering of Filipino workers*, Rutgers University Press, New Brunswick.

Guevarra, AR (2014), 'Supermaids: The racial branding of global Filipino care labour', in B Anderson & I Shutes (eds.), *Migration and Care Labour: Theory, Policy and Politics*, Palgrave Macmillan, New York, pp. 130–150.

Ham, J (2017), *Sex Work, Immigration and Social Difference*, Routledge, London.

Ham, J, Segrave, M & Pickering, S (2013), 'In the eyes of the beholder: Border enforcement, suspect travellers and trafficking victims', *Anti-Trafficking Review*, 2: 51–66.

Hamdan, AK (2009), 'Reflexivity of discomfort in insider-outsider educational research', *McGill Journal of Education*, 44(3): 377–404.

Hennink, MH (2008), 'Language and communication in cross-cultural qualitative research', in P Liamputtong (ed.), *Doing Cross-Cultural Research: Ethical and Methodological Perspectives*, Springer, Melbourne, pp. 21–34.

Hess, S (2005), 'Feminized transnational spaces – or the interplay of gender and nation', *Anthropological Journal on European Cultures*, 14: 227–246.

Hill, E, Ford, M & Baird, M (2017), 'Work/care regimes in the Asia-Pacific: A feminist framework', in M Baird, M Ford & E Hill (eds.), *Women, Work and Care in the Asia-Pacific*, Routledge, New York, pp. 1–22.

Holliday, I (2000), 'Productivist welfare capitalism: Social policy in East Asia', *Political Studies*, 48(4): 706–723.

Huang, S & Yeoh, BSA (1996), 'Ties that bind: State policy and migrant female domestic helpers in Singapore', *Geoforum*, 27(4): 473–493.

Huang, S & Yeoh, BSA (1998), 'Maids and ma'ams in Singapore: Constructing gender and nationality in the transnationalisation of paid domestic work', *Geography Research Forum*, 18: 22–48.

Huckerby, J (2015), 'Same, but different: Assessing the interaction of the migrant workers' rights and anti-trafficking regimes under international law', *Journal of International Law and Politics*, 47(3): 593–645.

International Labour Organization (ILO) (2021), 'Making decent work a reality for domestic workers; Progress and Prospects ten years after the adoption of the Domestic Workers Convention, 2011 (no. 189)', viewed 1 Feb, https://www.ilo.org/global/publications/books/WCMS_802551/lang--en/index.htm

Islam, MR & Cojocaru, S (2015), 'Migrant domestic workers in Asia: Transnational variations and policy concerns', *International Migration*, 54(1): 48–63.

Islam, MR, Cojocaru, S, Rahman, ZA, Siti Hajar, AB & Arnakim, LYB (2016), 'Story behind the closed doors: Decent work practice among the migrant domestic workers in Singapore and Italy', *Revista de Cercetare si Interventie Sociala*, 53: 304–325.

Jacobsen, K & Landau, LB (2003), 'The dual imperative in refugee research: Some methodological and ethical considerations in social science research on forced migration', *Disasters*, 27(3): 185–206.

Jagori, (2012), 'Migration, trafficking and sites of work: Rights and vulnerabilities', in K Kempadoo, J Sanghera & B Pattanaik (eds.), *Trafficking and Prostitution Reconsidered: New perspectives on migration, sex work and human rights*, Paradigm Publishers, New York, pp. 159–174.

Johnson, M, Lee, M, McCahill, M & Mesina MR (2019), 'Beyond the "all seeing eye": Filipino migrant domestic workers' contestation of care and control in Hong Kong', *Ethnos: Journal of Anthropology*, 10.1080/00141844.2018.1545794.

Justice Centre Hong Kong (2016), *Coming clean – The prevalence of forced labour and trafficking for forced labour amongst migrant domestic workers in Hong Kong*, Justice Centre Hong Kong, Hong Kong.

Kaur, A (2010), 'Labour migration in Southeast Asia: migration policies, labour exploitation and regulation', *Journal of the Asia Pacific Economy*, 15(1): 6–19.

Killias, O (2018), *Follow the Maid: Domestic Worker Migration In and From Indonesia*, NIAS Press, Copenhagen.

Kim, YJ (2012), 'Ethnographer location and the politics of translation: Researching one's own group in a host country', *Qualitative Research*, 12(1): 131–146.

Kobayashi, A (2003), 'GPC ten years on: Is self-reflexivity enough?', *Gender, Place & Culture*, 10(4): 345–349.

Labadie-Jackson, G (2008), 'Reflections on domestic work and the feminization of migration', *Campbell Law Review*, 31(1): 67–90.

Lan, PC (2006), *Global Cinderellas: Migrant domestics and newly rich employers in Taiwan*, Duke University Press, Durham.

Lee, PWY & Petersen CJ (2006), 'Forced labour and debt bondage in Hong Kong: A study of Indonesian and Filipina migrant domestic workers', *Centre for Comparative and Public Law*, Occasional Paper No. 16, June.

Lee, SSY (2016), *Between worlds: Filipino domestic workers in Hong Kong, 1970-2005*, PhD thesis, SOAS University of London, London.

Lee, WKM (2002), 'Gender ideology and the domestic division of labor in middle-class Chinese families in Hong Kong', *Gender, Place and Culture*, 9(3): 245–260.

Leung, BKP (1995), 'Women and social change: The impact of industrialization on women in Hong Kong', in V Pearson and BKP Leung (eds.), *Women in Hong Kong*, Oxford University Press, UK, pp. 22–46.

Leung, MWH (2015), '"Talk to her, she is also Chinese": A reflection on the spatial-temporal reach of co-ethnicity in migration research', *Forum: Qualitative Social Research*, 16(2): art. 13.

Liang, LF (2011), 'The making of an "ideal" live-in migrant care work: Recruiting, training, matching and disciplining', *Ethnic and Racial Studies*, 34(11): 1815–1534.

Lindquist, J (2010), 'Labor recruitment, circuits of capital and gendered mobility: Reconceptualising the Indonesian migration industry', *Pacific Affairs*, 83(1): 115–132.

Lindquist, J, Xiang, B & Yeoh, BSA (2012), 'Introduction: Opening the black box of migration: Brokers, the organization of transnational mobility and the changing political economy in Asia', *Pacific Affairs*, 85(1): 7–19.

Lo, KW (2017), *Intergenerational ambivalence and family exchanges: Exploring grandparents childcare in Hong Kong and East Asia*, PhD thesis, Monash University, Melbourne.

Longhurst, R (2010), 'Semi-structured interviews and focus groups', in N Clifford, S French & G Valentine (eds.), *Key Methods in Geography*, SAGE Publications Ltd, London, pp. 103–115.

Lutz, H (2010), 'Gender in the migratory process', *Journal of Ethnic and Migration Studies*, 36(10): 1647–1663.

Lyons, L (2007), 'Dignity overdue: Women's rights activism in support of foreign domestic workers in Singapore', *Women's Studies Quarterly*, 35(3-4): 106–122.

Lyons, L (2017), 'Singapore: Contradictions in the work/care regime', in M Baird, E Hill & M Ford (eds.), *Women, Work and Care in the Asia-Pacific*, Routledge, London, pp. 55–70.

Mantouvalou, V (2012), 'Human rights for precarious workers: The legislative precariousness of domestic labor', *Comparative Labour Law & Policy Journal*, 34(1): 133–165.

Marchetti, S (2015), ' "Mum seems happy". Relatives of dependent elders and the difficult task to employ a migrant care-giver', in A Triandafyllidou & S Marchetti (eds.), *Employers, Agencies and Immigration: Paying for Care*, Routledge, New York, pp. 93–110.

Marshall, J (1992), 'Researching women in management as a way of life', *Management Education and Development*, 23(30): 281–289.

Mason, G & Stubbs, J (2012), 'Feminist approaches to criminological research', in D Gadd, S Karstedt & S Messner, (eds.), *Criminological Research Methods*, SAGE, UK, pp. 486–499.

McKay, D (2007), 'Sending dollars shows feelings: Emotions and economies in Filipino migration', *Mobilities*, 2(2): 175–194.

McKeown, A (2012), 'How the box became black: Brokers and the creation of the free migrant', *Pacific Affairs*, 85(1): 21–45.

Meehan, P & Plonski, S (2017), 'Brokering the margins: A review of concepts and methods', *ESRC Borderlands, Brokers and Peacebuilding Project*, 589, Working Paper 1.

Menon, M (2021), 'More maids to be allowed into S'pore from Nov 1; they could still take 3 to 6 months to enter', *The Straits Times*, 5 Oct, viewed 1 Feb, https://www.straitstimes.com/singapore/parliament-more-maids-to-be-allowed-into-singapore-from-nov-1-but-entry-approval-only-for

Mezzadra, S & Neilson B (2013), *Border as Method, or, the Multiplication of Labor*, Duke University Press, Durham.

Mullally, S (2015), 'Introduction: Decent work, domestic work: Gendered borders and limits', in S Mullally (eds.), *Care, Migration and Human Rights: Law and Practice*, Routledge, London, pp. 1–10.

Noaks, L & Wincup, E (2004), *Criminological Research*, SAGE Publications Ltd, London.

Ochiai, E (2009), 'Care diamonds and welfare regimes in East and South-east Asian societies: Bridging family and welfare sociology', *International Journal of Japanese Sociology*, 18(1): 60–78.

O'Connell Davidson, J & Anderson, B (2006), 'The trouble with "trafficking"', in CL van den Anker & J Doomernik (eds.), *Trafficking and Women's Rights*, Palgrave Macmillan, New York, pp. 11–26.

Oishi, N (2005), *Women in Motion: Globalization, State Policies and Labor Migration in Asia*, Stanford University Press, California.

Ogawa, R, Chan, RKH, Oishi, A & Wang, LR (2018), 'Introduction: Situating gender, care, and migration in East Asia', in R Ogawa, RKH Chan, A Oishi & LR Wang (eds.), *Gender, Care and Migration in East Asia*, Palgrave Macmillan, London, pp. 1–22.

Ooi, KG (1992), 'Domestic servants par excellence: The black and white amahs of Malaya and Singapore with special reference to Penang', *Journal of the Malaysian Branch of the Royal Asiatic Society*, 65(2): 69–84.

Palmer, W (2016), *Indonesia's Overseas Labour Migration Programme 1960–2010*, Brill Publishing, Boston.

Palumbo, L & Sciurba, A (2015), 'Vulnerability to forced labour and trafficking: The case of Romanian women in the agricultural sector in Sicily', *Anti-Trafficking Review*, 5: 89–111.

Pande, A (2012), 'From "balcony talk" and "practical prayers" to illegal collectives: Migrant domestic workers and meso-level resistances in Lebanon', *Gender and Society*, 26(3): 382–405.

Parreñas, RS (2000), 'Migrant Filipina domestic workers and the international division of reproductive labor', *Gender and Society*, 14(4): 560–580.

Parreñas, RS (2012), 'The reproductive labor of migrant workers', *Global Networks*, 12(2): 269–275.

Parreñas, RS (2015), *Servants of Globalization: Migration and Domestic Work* (2nd edition), Stanford University Press, California.

Pearson, P & Leung, BKP (1995), *Women in Hong Kong*, Oxford University Press, Hong Kong.

Peng, I (2018), 'Shaping and reshaping care and migration in East and Southeast Asia', *Critical Sociology*, 44(7-8): 1117–1132.

Pickering, S (2014), 'Floating carceral spaces: Border enforcement and gender on the high seas', *Punishment and Society*, 16(2): 187–205.

Platt, M (2018), 'Migration, moralities and moratoriums: Female labour migrants and the tensions of protectionism in Indonesia', *Asian Studies Review*, 42(1): 89–106.

Platt, M, Baey, G, Yeoh, BSA, Khoo, CY & Lam, T (2017), 'Debt, precarity and gender: Male and female temporary labour migrants in Singapore', *Journal of Ethnic and Migration Studies*, 43(1): 119–136.

Pillow, W (2003), 'Confession, catharsis or cure: Rethinking the uses of reflexivity as methodological power in qualitative research', *International Journal of Qualitative Studies in Education*, 16(2): 175–196.

Pillow, W (2010), 'Dangerous reflexivity/Rigour, responsibility and reflexivity in qualitative research', in P Thomson & M Walker (eds.), *The Routledge Doctoral Student's Companion: Getting to Grips with Research in Education and the Social Sciences*, Routledge, London, pp. 270–282.

Piper, N (2013), 'International migration and gendered axes of stratification: Introduction', in N Piper (ed.), *New perspectives on gender and migration: Livelihood, rights and entitlements*, Routledge, New York, pp. 1–19.

Piper, N, Rosewarne, S & Withers, M (2016), 'Redefining a rights-based approach in the context of temporary labour migration in Asia', *UNRISD Working Paper* 11. UNRISD, Switzerland, pp. 1–21.

Poon, A (2009), 'Maid visible: Foreign domestic workers and the dilemma of development in Singapore', *Crossroads: An Interdisciplinary Journal of Southeast Asian Studies*, 17(1): 1–28.

Prusinski, E (2017), 'Becoming siap mental: Education for transnational labour migration', *Ethnography and Education*, 12(3): 329–346.

Rahman, NA, Yeoh, BSA, & Huang, S (2005), 'Dignity overdue: Transnational domestic workers in Singapore', in S Huang, BSA Yeoh & NA Rahman (eds.), *Asian Women as Transnational Domestic Workers*, Marshall Cavendish Academic, Singapore, pp. 233–261.

Reininger, B, Marin, DW, Ross, M, Pamela Smith, S & Dinh-Zarr, T (2005), 'Advancing the theory and measurement of collective empowerment: A qualitative study', *International Quarterly of Community Health Education*, 25(3): 211–238.

Rudnyckyi, D (2004), 'Technologies of servitude: Governmentality and Indonesian transnational labour migration', *Anthropology Quarterly*, 77(3): 407–434.

Sassen, S (2000), 'Women's burden: Counter-geographies of globalization and feminization of survival', *Journal of International Affairs*, 53(2): 503–524.

Scott, S & Geddes, A (2016), 'Ethics, methods and moving standards in research on migrant workers and forced labour', in D Siegel & RD Wildt (eds.), *Ethical Concerns in Research on Human Trafficking*, Springer International, Switzerland, pp. 117–135.

Segrave, M (2009), 'Order at the border: The repatriation of victims of trafficking', *Women's Studies International Forum*, 32(4): 251–260.

Segrave, M & Powell, R (2015), 'Victimisation, citizenship and gender: Interrogating state responses', in D Wilson & S Ross (eds.), *Crimes, Victims and Policy: International Contexts, Local Experiences*, Palgrave Macmillan, UK, pp. 53–83.

Sharapov, K (2015), 'Traffickers and their victims: Anti-trafficking policy in the United Kingdom', *Critical Sociology*, 43(1): 1–21.

Silvey, R (2007), 'Unequal borders: Indonesian transnational migrants at immigration control', *Geopolitics*, 12(2): 264–279.

Sim, A (2009), 'Women versus the state: Organizing resistance and contesting exploitation in Indonesian labor migration to Hong Kong', *Asian and Pacific Migration Journal*, 18(1): 47–75.

Sulaiman-Hill, CMR & Thompson, SC (2011), 'Sampling challenges in a study examining refugee settlement', *BMC International Health and Human Rights*, 11(1): 1–11.

Sun, Y (2022), 'Hong Kong faces domestic worker shortage in push for Covid zero', *Bloomberg CityLab + Equality*, 25 January, viewed 1 Feb, https://www.bloomberg.com/news/features/2022-01-25/hong-kong-push-for-covid-zero-creates-a-labor-shortage

Tan, EKB (2010), 'Managing female foreign domestic workers in Singapore: Economic, pragmatism, coercive legal regulation or human rights', *Israel Law Journal*, 43: 99–125.

Temple, B (2005), 'Nice and tidy: Translation and representation', *Sociological Research Online*, 10(2): 45–54.

Teo, YY (2013), 'Support for deserving families: Inventing the anti-welfare familialist state in Singapore', *Social Politics*, 20(3): 387–406.

Teo, YY (2016), 'Not everyone has "maids": Class differentials in the elusive quest for work-life balance', *Gender, Place & Culture*, 23(8): 1164–1178.

Teo, YY & Piper, N (2009), 'Foreigners in our homes: Linking migration and family policies in Singapore', *Population, Space and Place*, 15(2): 147–159.

Tigno, JV (2014), 'At the mercy of the market?: State-enabled, market-oriented labor migration and women migrants from the Philippines', *Philippine Political Science Journal*, 35(1): 19–36.

Tyner, J (1996), 'The gendering of Philippine labor migration', *The Professional Geographer*, 48(4): 405–416.

Varia, N (2011), 'Sweeping changes? A review of recent reforms on protections for migrant domestic workers in Asia and the Middle East', *Canadian Journal of Women and the Law*, 23(1): 265–287.

Wickramasekera, P (2000), 'Asia labour migration: Issues and challenges in an era of globalization', *Report and Conclusions: ILO Asia Pacific Regional Symposium for Trade Union Organizations on Migrant Workers*, International Labour Office: Bureau of Worker Activities, Bangkok, http://www.ilo.org/global/topics/labour-migration/publications/WCMS_201784/lang--en/index.htm

Wijers, M (2015), 'Purity, victimhood and agency: Fifteen years of the UN trafficking protocol', *Anti-Trafficking Review*, 4: 56–79.

Wee, SL, Hu, AJ, Yong, J, Chong, WF, Raman, P & Chan, A (2015), 'Singaporeans' perceptions of and attitudes towards long-term care services', *Qualitative Health Research*, 25(2): 218–227.

Wong, D (1996), 'Foreign domestic workers in Singapore', *Asia and Pacific Migration Journal*, 5(1):117–138.

Xiang, B (2013), 'Multi-scalar ethnography: An approach for critical engagement with migration and social change', *Ethnography*, 14(3): 282–299.

Xiang, B & Lindquist, J (2014), 'Migration infrastructure', *International Migration Review*, 48(1): 122–148.

Yeoh, BSA (2014), 'Asia(ns) on the move: Globalisation, Migration and Development', *TRaNS: Trans-Regional and -National Studies of Southeast Asia*, 2(2): 157–162.

Yeoh, BSA (2016), 'Migration and gender politics in Southeast Asia', *Migration, Mobility & Displacement*, 2(1), 10.18357/mmd21201615022.

Yeoh, BSA, Huang, S & Devasahayam, TW (2004), 'Diasporic subjects in the nation: Foreign domestic workers, the reach of law and civil society in Singapore', *Asian Studies Review*, 28(1): 7–23.

Yeoh, BSA, Platt, M, Khoo, CY, Lam, T & Baey, G (2017), 'Indonesian domestic workers and the (un)making of transnational livelihoods and provisional futures', *Social & Cultural Geography*, 18(3): 415–434.

Chapter 2

Women Migrant Domestic Workers in the Home: Tensions Surrounding Intimacy and Labour

Unwaged and Waged Domestic and Care Labour in the Home

The story of how domestic and care responsibilities have been transferred from middle-income women to women of lesser social and economic means is now well-established (Hochschild 2000; Maher & Staab 2005). Changes to economic markets and social conditions brought on by globalisation and industrialisation processes have led to increased employment opportunities within the formal labour force for women in economically advanced states. This development, however, has not translated into a more egalitarian division of domestic and care work in the home, as previously predicted (Lan 2006; Cortés & Pan 2013; Michel & Peng 2017). Instead, persistent gendered divisions of domestic labour, which construe duties in the home as a 'woman's domain', alongside the lack of state welfare and care support, have enabled a situation where the burgeoning class of middle-income women are solely responsible for finding a domestic worker to assume responsibility for the management of housekeeping chores and caring for children and the elderly (Anderson 2000; Ogawa et al. 2018). Paying for a domestic worker has thus become the most viable means for middle-income women to enter the labour market, representing a necessary survival strategy and coping mechanism within patriarchal society (Parreñas 2000; Lan 2006; Labadie-Jackson 2008). This has arguably afforded many middle-income women the opportunity to pursue a role in the 'productive' economy. Yet the commodification or subcontracting of domestic and care labour in the home has been problematised by feminist scholars, who argue that it not only reproduces the demeaning and sexist aspects of housework but also further entrenches unequal race and class relations as domestic labour is largely performed by poor women, women of colour or immigrant women (Nakano Glenn 1992; Anderson 2000; Hondagneu-Sotelo 2001; Parreñas 2001; Romero 2002; Das Gupta 2008). However, others (see Himmelweit 1995; Moras 2008; Barker 2012; Palmer & Eveline 2012) have argued that the problem is not in the commodification of reproductive labour or care work per se, but that this work is perceived to be of low value

DOI: 10.4324/9781003250364-2

and is poorly paid. In this regard, the marginalisation and devaluation of waged domestic workers and other care workers more broadly must be understood in terms of the interrelations between *who* is primarily responsible for this work, *what* is conventionally defined as 'work' in contemporary society and *where* this work is performed. The next section draws on interdisciplinary research across gender studies, sociology of work and feminist economic studies to explore the gendered construction of and continuities between unwaged and waged domestic and care labour in the home.

Domestic and Care Labour as 'Love' Work: Implications for Waged Domestic Workers

The historical undervaluation of women's domestic and care labour needs to be discussed in relation to the gendered logic that presents such labour as 'natural' to women. This is critical to the question of who does the work and how such work is defined. In the context of what is deemed to be a 'natural' role, caring becomes a woman's trait rather than a skill that is valued and requires training. Therefore, critically, such work is defined as non-labour, or 'non-genuine' work that does not deserve an economic return (Folbre 1995; Himmelweit 1995; Albanese 2007; Barker 2012; Palmer & Eveline 2012). Indeed, underpinning the delivery of care services is the gendered, familial notion that quality care work is done for reasons of altruism, affection or social norms of obligation and respect, rather than for money; and the appropriate 'reward' for care work is thus emotional fulfilment, not professional prestige or financial or other market-based rewards (Badgett & Folbre 1999; England, Budig & Folbre 2002; Palmer & Eveline 2012). Barker (2012) refers to this as the 'paradox of caring labour', whereby those engaged in care work, including domestic workers, are penalised with low pay and low status, while simultaneously being valorised for the essential role they play in sustaining the social reproduction of families, and national and global economies. The long-standing exclusion of subsistence activities undertaken by women to support the well-being of families (such as domestic and care labour in the home) from the formal labour market also serves to reinforce 'society's undervaluation of women and of their contribution to social well-being' (Benería 1999, p. 186).

Notwithstanding the marketisation of domestic and care labour in the home, contemporary arrangements governing waged domestic labour relations mirror and reproduce the normative gendered expectations surrounding women's work in a largely uncontested fashion (Hill, Ford & Baird 2017). In addition to maintaining the traditional sexual division of labour, there is a transference of social and gendered expectations onto the waged worker by the employer (Rollins 1986; Lan 2006). In a number of empirical studies with employers of women migrant domestic workers, many employers expected that even with minimal training, migrant domestic workers, as women, should be *naturally* able to complete their domestic and caring responsibilities

(Huang & Yeoh 2007; Ogawa et al. 2018). By that same logic, the everyday management and evaluation of women migrant domestic workers predominantly fall on the shoulders of mothers and wives (Chin 1998; Lan 2006). This draws attention to a critical feature of paid domestic labour that women migrant domestic workers are essentially employed to serve as a surrogate for or 'menial' extension of their female employers, to help them complete their wifely or motherly duties, particularly the responsibilities associated with dirt and disorder (see Hondagneu-Sotelo 1999; Duffy 2005; Lan 2006).

Embedded in this framing is the conceptualisation of domestic labour as a 'labour of love', which obfuscates the divisions between work, adequate compensation and labour exploitation, on the one hand, and gender, moral and filial obligations, on the other (Lutz 2002; Gottfried & Chun 2018). This characterisation of domestic labour, which stems in part from the cultural construction of motherhood (England, Budig & Folbre 2002), underpins how we make sense of our treatment of domestic work, such that even when performed in exchange for money, is not considered 'genuine work', but is instead seen as 'love work' performed as 'part of the natural female role'. This has also supported the idea that domestic workers can be held to the same standard of selflessness and self-sacrifice as housewives are (Fitzpatrick & Kelly 1998; Marchetti 2015). Such hegemonic conceptualisations of domestic labour as natural love labour are reflected in labour laws, in which formal definitions of exploitation, harm and unacceptable employment conditions remain strongly entwined with gendered logics of reproductive labour and familial obligation (see Albin 2012; Fudge 2014; Rodgers 2016; Elias 2018; Romero 2018). Most tellingly, most of what would be considered unacceptable labour standards in other employment contexts – such as excessively long working hours, exclusion from minimum pay and mandatory rest days, and irregular salary payments – has been normalised within the context of domestic work in many states (Anderson 2007; Chuang 2010; Cox 2013; Chan 2014; Demetriou 2015). For example, the Ministry of Manpower (MOM) in Singapore has consistently affirmed the impracticality of regulating specific aspects of domestic work, including hours of work and work on rest days and public holidays as 'they [domestic workers] work in a home environment and the habits of households vary' (as cited in Teo & Piper 2009, p. 151). This has served to shape the regulatory environment, such that even in jurisdictions where domestic work is formally established as a type of waged labour, domestic workers continue to be excluded from full labour rights (Cox 2013; Fudge 2014; Johnson & Wilcke 2015; Elias 2018). However, it is not only the gendered dynamics of domestic and care labour that legitimise or render invisible the everyday forms of harm and exploitation faced by women migrant domestic workers. As discussed in the following section, the location of the workplace in the private home, too, produces enduring and significant challenges in policy and practice, not least because of the reluctance of governments to directly interfere in matters within the household, even if domestic work is (indirectly) governed by labour, migration and family regulations and legislations.

Homes as Public Workplaces

The discussion on the significance of homes as formalised workplaces is closely intertwined with feminist debates on the role and position of women in the private household. In particular, contesting how the 'home' is often imagined as *the* positive site of love, safety and support, feminist research on domestic violence has pointed out that the home can be as much a location of oppression, violence and resistance for women (McDowell 1999; Warrington 2001). Building on feminist analyses of power and violence in the home, Huang and Yeoh (2007, p. 198) note that in the context of domestic work, the home 'often falls short of its idealised construction as a place of safety and support, and instead becomes a place of spatial restriction, abuse and violence'. Specifically, as a consequence of 'live-in' requirements, for domestic workers, 'home' is not just a place for rest but also a place of work, which blurs the boundaries between 'work' and 'non-work' and has in many cases led to workers being continuously on call and/or in a position where they need to repeatedly renegotiate their working conditions (Lutz 2011; Akalin 2015; Islam & Cojocaru 2015). The two or so years since the start of the COVID-19 pandemic, which have seen the imposition of increased spatial restrictions and exacerbation of boundaryless working time,[1] have brought to fore the impacts of 'live-in' requirements and the ambivalence of 'home' as a safe space (Chan & Latham 2021; Lui et al. 2021). For live-in women domestic workers, the paradox of the home space being at once a site of positive familial emotions and a place of work is further compounded by the nature of domestic work, where employers' expectations extend beyond 'task-based' responsibilities to include the performance of emotional and affective labour (Huang & Yeoh 2007; Akalin 2015; Marchetti 2015). That is to say, women domestic workers are not only expected to complete housework and caring tasks; they are also expected to do so with an appropriate affective state that reflects authentic concern, obedience and the suppression of negative emotions (Ahmed 2001; Huang & Yeoh 2007; Akalin 2015). In this respect, the 'home' is not a safe or inclusive place for a woman domestic worker (or women in general), whose labour demands that she must constantly manage and to some extent, suppress her body and emotions (Huang & Yeoh 2007; Johnson et al. 2019).

Research on the exploitation (that is, unlawful and substandard employment conditions) experienced by women migrant domestic workers emphasises how the employment location enables exploitation to flourish in two key ways. First, the relative isolation of working alone in a private household constrains domestic workers' access to information, assistance, collective organisation as well as privacy (Human Rights Watch 2006; Barrientos, Kothari & Phillips 2013; Rodgers 2016). Second, the principle of inviolability of the private home has often been used as an excuse to justify the absence of labour laws and/or of the enforcement of regulations (Constable 1997; Yeoh, Huang & Devasahayam 2004; Chen 2011; Demetriou 2015; Johnson & Wilcke 2015). This discursive construction of the private/public dichotomy has long been problematised by feminist scholarship on domestic violence (Schneider 1994; Price 2002). One of the main concerns of this scholarship relates to how this spatial dichotomy of private/public spheres, which is deeply gendered, shapes how we think about and respond to violence against women. Feminist scholars such as MacKinnon (1989), Gavison (1992), Schneider (1994), Goldfarb (2000) and Warrington (2001) emphasise how the construct of 'privacy' delineates the domestic sphere as a space in which love and affection, rather than law or money, hold currency. This has allowed for a wide range of behaviours and relations within the domestic sphere to be exempt from legal regulation and scrutiny. Implicit in this view is the assumption that violence that occurs in the home is an individual problem, which conceals not just unequal power relations and the insecurity they create but also the public significance of such violence – that is, the extent to which gendered patterns and violence in the domestic sphere mirror and fortify larger social patterns of inequality in society (MacKinnon 1989; Gavison 1992; Schneider 1994; Goldfarb 2000). The impact of legal nonintervention (that is, reluctance to intervene, lack of legal regulation and selective application of the law) in violence against women is well-documented, and this research reveals that this extends to labour law violations in the domestic work context.

As discussed above, there is a persistent perception that conventional labour regulations cannot be enforced within the home, as associated procedures, such as labour inspections, would be difficult to implement and compliance would be difficult to monitor (Chuang 2010; Chen 2011; Cox 2013). The full or partial exclusion of women migrant domestic workers from protective labour legislation has been described as creating 'legislative precariousness', which disadvantages workers and limits their ability to negotiate personal security in the domestic workplace (Albin & Mantouvalou 2012; Mantouvalou 2012). Critical scholarship on workplace relations suggests that such justifications disregard how employment within the private sphere greatly exacerbates the risk of exploitation and abuse for women migrant domestic workers (Parreñas 2007; Cox 2013; Demetriou 2015). In particular, they fail to account for the nature of the employer–worker relationship in this context, which is often predicated upon asymmetrical power dynamics that are produced and sustained by state migration and care labour regimes (Lutz 2011; Cox 2013; Anderson 2016).

The reluctance to lay down standard rules regarding specific employment conditions for such work suggests a decontextualised assumption that women migrant domestic workers are fully autonomous subjects who have the capacity to substantively challenge and negotiate their terms of employment (Yeoh, Huang & Devasahayam 2004; Cheng 2014). To be clear, women migrant domestic workers are not victims who passively submit to their employment conditions. Indeed, empirical literature has documented the ways that women migrant domestic workers utilise individual and collective strategies of subversion, resistance or submission to secure their well-being and livelihood (Rollins 1986; Lan 2006; Ford & Piper 2007; Pande 2012; Parreñas 2015; Blackett 2019). However, as Kabeer (1999) notes, the perceived utility of strategies is shaped by women's social location, available resources and perceived consequences or outcomes of strategies. The context, nature and location of their employment, where they are constantly in close proximity to employers who have much power over their job and right to remain in the country, necessarily means that for women migrant domestic workers, negotiating terms of employment, even when it is within their right, is a challenging terrain to navigate.

In examining homes within the context of paid domestic and care labour, some scholars have noted that the home is a politicised site of employment where private/public boundaries *and* employer–worker relationships are constantly being shaped, negotiated and contested (Momsen 1999; Yeoh & Huang 1999; Davidoff 2003; Triandafyllidou & Marchetti 2015). Blunt and Dowlings (2006) describe homes as places where state-based practices and discourse are reproduced. The home is also a site where workplace relations are embedded in and influenced by wider networks in society (Strauss & McGrath 2017). Thus, in this context, multiple actors including placement agents, state apparatuses, foreign embassies and other household members have an influence on the employer–worker relationship, and the home can be understood as the place where the struggle of both employers and workers for security and safety is articulated, negotiated and enacted. From this perspective, homes are not just static spaces of oppression for socially and legally marginalised workers but also sites where power relations play out and are reshaped over time. Importantly, this suggests that the power relations between employer and worker may be more dynamic and fluid than is indicated in the existing scholarship, which has tended to emphasise a linear and binary construction whereby the employer holds absolute power while the woman migrant domestic worker is powerless (Dickney 2000; Hondagneu-Sotelo 2001; Parreñas 2015; Anderson 2016; Blackett 2019 being key exceptions).

Employer–Domestic Worker Relationship

Given the intimacy and ambiguous boundaries of the home space, the maintenance of a desired working situation and safe work requires careful attention to workplace relations. The emphasis on asymmetrical power relations is useful for highlighting how employers have more power than women migrant domestic workers to dictate the terms and conditions of employment. However, in the context of live-in domestic work, the employer–worker relationship, particularly that between mothers and female domestic workers, has also been identified as one that is characterised by ambivalent feelings of anxiety and insecurity. In a number of studies with employers, scholars have identified the paradoxical relationship that female employers share with their women migrant domestic workers (Constable 1996; Dickney 2000; Lan 2006; Anderson 2007; Poon 2009). On the one hand, the employer's dependency on the worker to perform domestic and intimate labour in the private home in and of itself requires a relationship of trust as it involves the sharing and safeguarding of intimate knowledge (Dickney 2000; Ruijter, van der Lippe & Raub 2003; Zelizer 2010; Yeoh et al. 2021). On the other hand, interviews with employers revealed mixed feelings, including mistrust and perceptions of female migrant domestic workers as backward, unhygienic and morally suspect individuals with poor work ethics (Lan 2006; Marchetti 2015; Anderson 2016; Lee 2016; Shi 2017).

Research with female employers who hire migrant domestic workers to care for their children reveals another area of tension. Often, these employers expect an investment of emotional labour by workers when providing care for children (Lan 2006; Moras 2008). In other words, even though such work is a form of waged labour, it is imbued with emotional demands whereby workers are expected to be 'proto-mothers' and perform their responsibilities not only with certain skills but also with affection and a degree of self-sacrifice (Moras 2008; Gutiérrez-Rodríguez 2010; Yelland et al. 2013; Shahvisi 2018). It is not sufficient for workers to simply mechanically complete tasks and produce specific results (such as a clean child or a well-fed elder); the worker needs to display genuine care for those whose well-being is entrusted to them (Barker 2012; Yeoh et al. 2021). Yet, at the same time, other studies with female employers demonstrate that women become concerned and uneasy when they notice their children developing an emotional attachment to the domestic worker, perceiving it to be a threat to their 'motherly status' (Lan 2006). These perceptions and feelings of insecurity are observed to have an impact on how employers carry out measures of control and surveillance over workers' actions, both inside and outside the home (see Johnson et al. 2019) – a situation also identified in the employer interviews in the research underpinning this book.

These tensions around intimacy between female employers and workers, alongside the construction of domestic and care labour as a job in which social relationships play an essential role, more broadly point to how the worker–employer relationship (and norms) within the domestic workplace is different from that in the formal labour market (Anderson 2016; Chiu 2018; Blackett 2019; Yeoh et al. 2021). In particular, there is a stronger emphasis on bonds of trust, affection and the relationship between the domestic worker and household members (Ehrenreich & Hochschild 2002; Lan 2006; Yeoh et al. 2021). A 'fictive kin' relationship is identified as a social relationship model that characterises employer–worker dynamics in live-in domestic work (Anderson 2016; Chiu 2018). In several studies, researchers note that both employers and workers use terms such as 'part of the family' to describe their employment relationship, reflecting the sense of intimacy and affective relations they feel

(Hondagneu-Sotelo 2001; Lan 2006; Parreñas 2015; Anderson 2016; Chiu 2018). However, in the domestic labour literature fictive kinship is traditionally regarded as an exploitative relationship model that disregards women migrants' status as workers and allows employers to continually add on tasks and extract excessive labour, which workers are expected to complete out of a sense of emotional obligation (Ibarra 2010; Anderson 2016). A number of researchers argue that fictive kinship is fundamentally an employment model that is more favourable to the interests of employers (see, for example, Lan 2003; Anderson 2016). For example, Lan (2003, p. 536) posits that the language of 'familial inclusion' is used to secure workers' commitment to the household and ensure the 'authenticity and sincerity of their emotional labour'. In another example, interviews with Thai and Malaysian employers revealed that familial relations in the context of live-in domestic work are predicated on asymmetrical power relations whereby inclusion can be selectively invoked and withdrawn at the employer's discretion (Anderson 2016). It is therefore not surprising that there have been calls to improve professionalisation and formalisation of the employer–worker relationship in domestic labour.

Recognition of the power differentials inherent to the employer–worker relationship in the domestic workplace cannot go unheeded and addressing it remains an important challenge in policy and practice. Yet, a general representation of fictive kinship may not capture all of the accounts and experiences of fictive kinship of migrant women in domestic work. Women migrant domestic workers have discussed the emotional and financial costs that come with fictive kinship but have also been frank about their active and consistent deployment of the fictive kinship model in this context (see Hondagneu-Sotelo 2001; Ibarra 2010; Parreñas 2015; Anderson 2016; Chiu 2018). This suggests that 'being part of the family' is critical to workers' employment experiences. Some scholars have explained this with reference to the notion of an exchange perspective, where workers' development and maintenance of fictive kinship with the families they work for is motivated by their desire for the material and immaterial rewards they can gain (Mendez 1998; Hondagneu-Sotelo 2001; Lan 2006), such as appreciation of their efforts, their employer's respect for them as people, or obtaining personal favours when needed. In other contexts, Parreñas (2015) describes how women migrant domestic workers employ fictive kinship and relations of intimacy as a tactic to subvert and challenge the authority and control of employers within their everyday routines. In addition to these transactional and subversive aspects, Chiu (2018) argues that there are also interactive and emotional aspects, which are developed and reinforced within the overall context of the working environment. Employing this conceptualisation of fictive kinship may allow for a relational analysis of the employer–worker relationship; one that is not just about employers' compliance with labour standards but also explains the subjective feelings of reciprocity, acceptance, care and trust that develop through the day-to-day interaction between employer and worker. The assumed value and exercise of fictive kinship will vary across the domestic work sector. Migrant women's social locations and the specific country's broader labour migration regime that structures the nature of their employment may also influence the perceived utility or significance of the fictive kinship model. However, an important opportunity for understanding women migrant domestic workers' evaluations of value and labour is lost if the exploitation of victimised workers by their employers remains the sole focus. Rather than continuing to apply a reductive lens to fictive kinship, and to the employer–worker relationship more generally, there is perhaps greater utility in exploring questions such as the following: What does a fictive kin relationship mean for women migrant domestic workers, especially in terms of defining their experience and managing their own security? What resources does it offer and what complications does it produce that impact workers' pursuit of safety and security in their everyday work? Asking these questions, and thereby permitting a relational and contextual analysis, can help to illuminate what workers define and understand as exploitation as well as the implications for their negotiation of safe work. In addition to an approach that captures the significance of context and relational factors, an analytical approach that attends to structural factors is also crucial for understanding how workers navigate their everyday working and living conditions, as they develop strategies and responses within the framework of labour and migration regulations that have the conflicting aims of containment, management and protection. To examine these tensions, an outline of the national labour and criminal law systems in Singapore and Hong Kong is provided below.

Gender, Domestic Work and Migration: Regulatory Intersections

To redress the insecurities and exploitation faced by women migrant domestic workers, advocacy efforts have focused on facilitating the formal recognition of waged domestic labour by states and the introduction of employment contracts in this sphere. The objective of these formalisation and inclusion processes is for migrant domestic workers to become recognised as 'genuine workers' in the formal labour economy and to possess equal contractual or labour rights to those of other workers (see Anderson 2007; Cox 2013; Fudge 2014; Fudge & Mundlak forthcoming). The primary contention underpinning such efforts is that a clear and comprehensive legal premise that defines domestic work and the boundaries of what is acceptable in the workplace (including what constitutes exploitation or abuse) will enhance protection and access to justice for women migrant domestic workers. Legal definitions of exploitation or unacceptable conditions of work and the imposition of employers' duties will ensure that there is a formal standard against which these workers can compare their working conditions to identify whether and how conditions are in breach of the law, as well as reducing the risks posed by arbitrary treatment or informal rules implemented by employment agencies or employers (Mantouvalou 2012; Oelz 2014).

In the context of Singapore and Hong Kong, there is formal recognition of the entry and labour of migrant domestic workers, and both jurisdictions have instituted a temporary contract labour migration scheme to proactively facilitate the entry of South and Southeast Asian women into the labour market (Lan 2006; Ogawa et al. 2018). Although, as discussed in Chapter 1, the domestic worker visa is designed to ensure these women's transient status as disposable workers who can easily be repatriated, in both Singapore and Hong Kong this visa does guarantee certain employment rights and benefits for women migrant domestic workers. Table 2.1 outlines the key provisions included and excluded under Singapore's Employment of Foreign Manpower Act (EFMA) and Hong Kong's Standard Employment Contract (SEC).

Table 2.1 Key provisions under Singapore's EFMA and Hong Kong's SEC

Singapore	*Hong Kong*
Key provisions *included* under EFMA • Punctual payment of wages[i] • Mandatory personal accident and medical insurance • Mandatory weekly rest day (or compensation-in-lieu) • Providing 'adequate' food, rest and medical treatment • Ensuring 'safe' working conditions[ii] • Cover all financial costs for repatriation of worker upon cancellation of her work permit (e.g., transport costs and sustenance during travel)	Key provisions *included* under SEC • Mandatory personal accident and medical insurance • Mandatory weekly rest day (or compensation-in-lieu) • Providing food (or food allowance) • Statutory entitlement to sickness allowance • Statutory entitlement to severance payment and long service payment • Cover travel costs incurred for repatriation of worker upon cancellation of her contract • Protection against dismissal when pregnant, during childbirth[iii] or when medically unwell • Statutory entitlement to public holidays, annual leave and sick leave • Minimum allowable wage (MAW)[iv]
Provisions *excluded* from EFMA • Limitations on hours of work • Statutory entitlement to public holidays, annual leave and sick leave • Minimum wage	Provisions *excluded* from SEC • Limitations on hours of work

i Employers are required to pay their domestic worker no later than seven days after the last day of the salary period. As of 1 January 2019, employers are also prohibited from keeping their workers' salary, bank book or bank card (MOM 2019).

ii Under Part I of the Fourth Schedule in the EFMA, 'safe working conditions' refers specifically to restrictions on the cleaning of the exterior of windows, in order to ensure that the 'life or personal safety of the foreign employee is not endangered during and in the course of employment'. Restrictions on cleaning the exterior of windows were put in place after a spate of work-related fatalities (MOM 2012).

iii The Sex Discrimination Ordinance further prohibits placement agencies from limiting the transfer and/or training options of migrant domestic workers (MDWs) who are pregnant or returning from maternity leave (Truong, Marin & Quesada-Bondad 2014).

iv As of October 2018, the Minimum Allowable Wage had been set at HKD4520. This amount is adjusted annually.

While there are a number of differences between their respective labour and immigration policies, Singapore's EFMA and Hong Kong's SEC offer systematic institutional support through employment guidelines, minimum standards and employer responsibilities, which operate alongside the labour law and criminal justice framework to establish legal standards of acceptable employment, as well as poor working conditions and harms that are formally recognised as unlawful behaviour or criminal offences. In Singapore, the government has also made it mandatory for first-time employers and women migrant domestic workers to attend targeted educational programs, which are designed to provide information on relationship management, and ensure a basic understanding of the legal issues and guidelines related to the employment of a migrant domestic worker. In Hong Kong, information kiosks are set up on weekends to handle inquiries from workers and to distribute labour rights information kits (Paul & Neo 2018). In addition, the Home Affairs Department stations information ambassadors who speak English, Tagalog, Bahasa Indonesia and Thai at the airport to give newly arrived workers a brief introduction on Hong Kong and/or answer any questions they may have (Paul & Neo 2018). While potentially useful, these interactions are, however, dependent on women migrant domestic workers being aware of, and proactively accessing them.[2] Table 2.2 outlines the employment practices that are deemed unlawful and substandard in Singapore and Hong Kong.

Singapore

In Singapore, the EFMA, overseen by MOM, functions as the principal legislative and regulatory instrument governing the work conditions of women migrant domestic workers, including applications for and cancellations of work permits, medical insurance, workers' levies and repatriation (MOM 2012). It establishes the responses to reported labour law violations while the Penal Code defines labour law violations, criminal abuse and ill-treatment.[3] In 1998, the Penal Code was amended to increase the penalties[4] for employers found guilty of physical abuse, and the Singapore Government presented this amendment[5] as a sign of its recognition of the vulnerabilities of female migrant domestic workers due to their live-in status *and* of its commitment to protecting these workers and reducing the prevalence of abuse by their employers (Yeoh, Huang & Devasahayam 2004; Human Rights Watch 2005). Despite the recognition that women migrant domestic workers 'work isolated from society' and 'face a different situation from other workers' (Lee as cited in Yeoh, Huang & Devasahayam 2004, p. 14), the EFMA governs migrant domestic labour at a distance,[6] such that employment conditions or relations are to be negotiated via individual arrangements, reflecting the rationale of keeping state support and intervention in household matters at a minimum (Chin 2019). For example, MOM stipulates that employers are required to provide 'adequate' shelter, including 'basic needs such as a bed or mattress,

Table 2.2 Laws and recommendations in Singapore and Hong Kong

	Singapore	*Hong Kong*
Punishable by law **(i) Work conditions**	• Less than a weekly rest day • No payment in-lieu of work on rest day • Denial of salary • Dangerous chores • Identity documents taken without consent/not returned upon request • Impediments to movement • Deceptive recruitment: different work location, different *non-domestic* tasks, different employers and different salary than agreed upon	• Less than a weekly rest day and/or no substitution of rest day • No payment in lieu of annual leave • Denial of salary or lower than MAW • Dangerous chores • Identity documents taken without consent/not returned upon request • Impediments to movement • Deceptive recruitment: different work location, different *non-domestic* tasks, different employers and different salary than agreed upon • No arrangement of alternative holiday for statutory holidays • Illegal dismissal: termination of contract while worker is on sick leave, or due to worker's pregnancy, participation in trade union activities, injury at work and/or legal proceedings • No standard employment contract signed • Non-payment of food and travel allowance
(ii) Accommodation conditions	• Inadequate sleeping space • Nutritional neglect	
(iii) Violence and abuse	• Physical, sexual and psychological violence	• Physical, sexual and psychological violence
(iv) Employment guidelines (not punishable by law)	• Recommended to work less than 12 hours daily • Working on rest day • No employment contract signed • Restrictions on communication • Different sleeping space than agreed upon	• Recommended to work less than 12 hours daily • Working on rest day[i] • Different sleeping space than agreed upon

i Under the Hong Kong Employment Ordinance, it is illegal for the employer to compel the migrant domestic worker to perform duties on her rest day; however, the worker may work voluntarily on her rest day (Hong Kong Labour Department 2022).

blanket, towels and bathroom amenities', 'sufficient' ventilation, 'sufficient' space and privacy, and to ensure that the food provided 'includes a mix of rice, meat, vegetables and fruit'. There are, however, no formal specifications as to what constitutes 'adequate' and 'sufficient' and it is expected that these details will be negotiated between employers and workers – a stance that has been criticised for overestimating women migrant domestic workers' capacity and power to negotiate an equitable contract (Yeoh, Huang & Devasahayam 2004; Human Rights Watch 2005; Teo & Piper 2009; Chin 2019). Exacerbated by the inconsistent enforcement[7] of labour laws, the situation faced by women migrant domestic workers in Singapore is such that they are thus caught in an undefined sphere of uncertain formal employment regulations and dependence on individual employers.

If there is a breakdown in the employment relationship, women migrant domestic workers can opt to transfer to a new employer while remaining in Singapore – either independently (that is, without the assistance of an employment agency) or, more commonly, through the mediation of an employment agency, which will likely incur additional costs for the worker[8] (Goh 2018). To change employers, however, the worker is also required to secure an issuance declaration from her current employer, which indicates their agreement to her transfer (MOM 2019). Further, employers are required to give 'reasonable notice' for repatriation. However, the lack of clarification with regard to what constitutes 'reasonable notice' means that in practice employers have the power to unilaterally cancel their worker's work permit and repatriate her, even against her wishes (Wessels, Ong & Daniel 2017). Although workers can challenge and stop their forced repatriation by approaching MOM representatives or police officers stationed at the airport, there is no formalised or systematic safety net.[9] Against this backdrop of inadequate enforcement of regulations, the Singapore state has thus rendered women migrant domestic workers almost entirely dependent on their employers for their employment and legal status, food, accommodation, medical care and privacy.

Labour migration policies also effectively positions employers as agents of the state by making them legally responsible for the bodies and conduct of their workers. This is realised through the security bond scheme, which requires employers to put up a SGD5000 security bond that may be forfeited if they or their domestic worker violates labour regulations and conditions (MOM 2019). There is no publicly available data regarding how often bond forfeiture happens in practice, although studies on the work conditions of Singapore-based domestic workers have found that the *threat* of bond forfeiture has produced a situation where employers have a tendency to excessively police workers' lives through measures such as withholding their identification documents, inspecting their personal belongings, monitoring their mobile phone usage and restricting their social activities (Human Rights Watch 2005; Poon 2009; Tan 2010; Constable 2019). This reflects how migration regimes and legal infrastructures can indirectly shape employers' insecurities, which in turn directly affects the everyday negotiations between employer and worker. By placing the responsibility for workers on individual employers, Singapore's labour policies and regulations place employers and workers in positions of co-dependency and potential conflict, and, as examined in Chapter 5, this has significant implications for day-to-day employer–worker relations.

Hong Kong

The principal legislation stipulating the employment rights of women migrant domestic workers in Hong Kong is the Employment Ordinance, which sets the obligations and basic entitlements of all employers and employees in Hong Kong (Chiu 2002). In conjunction with the Employment Ordinance, workers in Hong Kong are covered under the Employee's Compensation Ordinance, Occupational Health and Safety Ordinance, Disability Discrimination Ordinance, Race Discrimination Bill and Sex Discrimination Ordinance (Lee & Petersen 2006; Truong, Marin & Quesada-Bondad 2014). Offences of assault and harassment are broadly covered under the Crimes Ordinance (Amnesty International 2013). Employers convicted of criminal offences or labour law breaches may also be ineligible to employ a migrant domestic worker 'for a period of time' (Hong Kong Immigration Department 2022). The governance and operation of the Employment Ordinance is further specified under the SEC, which sets out the employer responsibilities and minimum working conditions (Hong Kong Immigration Department 2022). Although the SEC offers more comprehensive legal protections than the EFMA, it also has some disadvantages in regard to working hours, as it does not specify fixed hours of work or offer genuine recourse for workers to redress grievances concerning long working hours. This omission ultimately reinforces the situation whereby it is difficult for women migrant domestic workers to refuse working long hours, on rest days and/or on holidays if requested by their employer. However, in comparison with other Asian and Middle Eastern or Gulf regions, Hong Kong is commonly considered by scholars and labour rights advocates to be an exemplary place in which to work, as it has one of the most comprehensive labour protection frameworks for women migrant domestic workers (Truong, Marin & Quesada-Bondad 2014; Constable 2015). These workers are also able to exercise their civil liberties, such as freedom of speech and the right to associate. Further, women migrant domestic workers in Hong Kong are not only legally safeguarded against dismissal and termination of contract on the basis of pregnancy, they are also entitled to paid maternity leave (Truong, Marin & Quesada-Bondad 2014). Although the extent to which these concessions can be substantively accessed is limited (see Constable 2014; Paul & Neo 2018), this policy nonetheless compares favourably with Singapore's stance of immediate repatriation upon confirmation of pregnancy.

However, these labour rights and protections are overshadowed by immigration policies and rules under the New Conditions of Stay (Immigration Ordinance). Introduced in 1987, the New Conditions of Stay (NCS) stipulates a number of immigration conditions with which workers are required to comply. These include:

- abiding by the 'two-week rule'
- no changing of employment in the first two years of the employment contract
- not being allowed to submit a new and valid employment contract without repatriation if worker breaks her contract
- no switching to non-domestic employment
- no obtaining of permanent residence.

The NCS were justified on the basis of protecting the local labour force and combatting the allegedly prevalent 'job-hopping[10] and moonlighting' of female migrant domestic workers (Lee 2016). Under the SEC, both workers and employers have the right to early termination of a contract as long as a one-month notice period (or payment in lieu of notice) is provided (Hong Kong Immigration Department 2022). Nonetheless, concerns around job-hopping have led to greater scrutiny of new visa applications for women migrant domestic workers and those considered to have terminated their contracts simply to find another job may be denied a new visa[11] (Hong Kong Immigration Department 2021). There are, however, no clear guidelines as to what differentiates a job-hopping application from a genuine one, and as the chapters in this book reveal, these structural uncertainties can have significant implications for workers' negotiation of their employment situation. In addition, the 'two-week rule', which stipulates that workers have 14 days to find a new employer upon expiry or termination of their contract, further compounds their precarious migration status as it provides an extremely short window[12] within which workers must find new employment. Although this rule does not preclude migrant domestic workers from applying for a new visa in the future, they are caught in an undesirable situation where they must either remain in Hong Kong to look for a new employer and risk overstaying their visa or return to their country of origin and incur high financial costs associated with re-migration while having no income during the process (Amnesty International 2013; Constable 2014). Consequently, even though Hong Kong's labour migration regime does not ascribe these responsibilities to employers of these workers in the same way as Singapore's system does (Constable 2019), migrant domestic workers in Hong Kong remain extremely dependent on their employers.

Conclusion

The intersection of domestic work and labour migration regulations in both Singapore and Hong Kong speak to gendered logics that inform the legal premise that defines work and the boundaries of what is deemed acceptable and unacceptable practices in the workplace. In particular, the structurally embedded reluctance, or even refusal, to lay down rules in regard to certain terms of employment, such as working hours or definitions of the tasks and services to be provided, is strongly tied to gendered notions of mothering as 'love work' that never ends. Although women migrant domestic workers in both jurisdictions are formally recognised as 'genuine' workers and are protected, in part, by regulatory and legal frameworks, they are simultaneously kept invisible by policies that frame domestic work as a 'private matter' to be sorted through individual arrangements in respective households.

Central to this study is the interrogation of the employment experiences of women migrant domestic workers in Singapore and Hong Kong and how these workers negotiate with employers and various formal and informal mechanisms to enable their everyday security. To do this requires analysing a range of women's experiences of employment relations and conditions that may fall outside the dominant categories and understandings of labour that persist in criminological research and public discourse. Overall, it is within this terrain characterised by the simultaneous devaluation of reproductive labour *and* this labour's gendered associations with personal relationships of love and obligation that the woman domestic worker is employed. At the same time, as discussed in Chapter 1, for the woman *migrant* domestic worker, her migration status determines her right to remain in the nation-state and can act as an additional technology of control. Having considered how women migrant domestic workers' experience of labour migration is influenced by a range of socio-structural factors, the development of an appropriate conceptual framework that can attend to the links between these contextual and relational aspects of domestic labour and state systems is now necessary to analyse how these workers negotiate their work situation and ensure their own security. This framework is discussed in the following chapter.

Notes

1 A joint survey by Asian Migrants' Coordinating Body, Mission for Migrant Workers and the Asia Pacific Mission for Migrants found that workers reported a significant increase in workload, with workers being required to work even on their weekly rest days (Wang 2021).

2 There is no publicly available information on the extent to which this service is accessed, and it is reported that many workers begin work in Hong Kong with very little or no information on their legal entitlements and protections (Paul & Neo 2018).

3 Under Chapter III, Section 73, of the Penal Code (2019), this includes causing hurt or grievous hurt (i.e., physical, psychological or sexual abuse), use of criminal force, and wrongful confinement.

4 Convicted employers would be 'liable to face punishment one and a half times the amount to which they would have otherwise been liable for those specific offenses. Convicted employers and their spouses would also be permanently banned from employing another FDW' (MOM 2015).

5 During the second reading of the Penal Code (Amendment) Bill in Parliament, the then Minister of Home Affairs, Wong Kan Seng, stated that the harsher penalties 'are intended to send a strong signal to those employers who have a tendency to abuse their domestic maids and that we [the government] take a very stern view against such abuse' (as cited in Yeoh, Huang & Devasahayam 2004, p. 14).

6 MOM has introduced new safeguards aimed at improving detection of signs of abuse. One of these is the new home visit scheme, where MOM officers will meet women migrant domestic workers and employers in the domestic workplace to check on the working and living conditions of workers, and to discuss safe working conditions and channels for support (Menon 2021). Officers are also 'trained to look signs of distress and if they are withholding information', which would be followed up by MOM (Low 2021; Menon 2021). This measure supplements the existing initiative of randomly selecting first-time arrivals for in-person interviewing to find out how they are adjusting to work in Singapore. However, there is a lack of publicly available data or information to evaluate how effective these initiatives are.

7 Data from HOME indicates that, despite commonly receiving complaints of insufficient food and poor living conditions, the organisation is only aware of one conviction against an employer for providing insufficient food (HOME & TWC2 2017).

8 Employment agencies in Singapore are legally allowed to charge women migrant domestic workers a 'transfer fee' of up to two months' worth of salary deductions. Under the Employment Agency Act, in cases where the employment contract is terminated within six months of no fault of the migrant domestic worker, agencies are obligated to refund her one month's worth of service fees. However, Goh (2018) notes that this clause is open to interpretation and only loosely enforced.

9 Information about this provision is not widely publicised and was not known by the workers in this study. Of the 21 Singapore-based workers interviewed in this study, only one stated that she was aware of this provision. In addition, Singapore-based NGO staff members observed that access to worker protection via this provision is not always guaranteed. Instead, it is dependent on the discretion of the immigration officer.

10 In a press release by Hong Kong's secretary for Labour and Welfare (2018), job-hopping is cited in reference to migrant domestic workers who 'abuse the arrangements for premature contract termination in order to change employers'.

11 A 2022 press release by the Hong Kong SAR Government indicates that 2833 visa applications were rejected in 2021 due to suspected job-hopping.

12 A 2013 study by Amnesty International with immigration officers in Hong Kong found that applications for a visa normally take around four to six weeks to process.

References

Ahmed, S (2001), 'Communities that feel: Intensity, difference and attachment', in A Kolvunen & S Paasonen (eds.), *Conference Proceedings for Affective Encounters: Rethinking Embodiment in Feminist Media Studies, Series A*, vol. 49, University of Turku, http://www.utu.fi/hum/mediatutkimus/affective.proceedings.pdf

Akalin, A (2015), 'Motherhood as the value of labour', *Australian Feminist Studies*, 30(83): 65–81.

Albanese, P (2007), '(Under)valuing care work: The case of child care workers in small-town Quebec', *International Journal of Early Years Education*, 15(2): 125–139.

Albin, E (2012), 'From "domestic servant" to "domestic worker"', in J Fudge, S McCrystal & K Sankaran (eds.), *Challenging the Legal Boundaries of Work Regulation*, Hart Publishing, Oxford, pp. 231–250.

Albin, E & Mantouvalou, V (2012), 'The ILO Convention on domestic workers: From the shadows to the light', *Industrial Law Journal*, 41(1): 67–78.

Amnesty International (2013), *Exploited for Profit, Failed by Governments: Indonesian Migrant Domestic Workers Trafficked to Hong Kong*, Amnesty International Ltd., London.

Anderson, B (2000), *Doing the Dirty Work?: The Global Politics of Domestic Labour*, Zed Books, New York.

Anderson, B (2007), 'Motherhood, apple pie and slavery: Reflections on trafficking debates', *Centre on Migration, Policy and Society, Working Paper*, no. 48.

Anderson, B (2016), *Worker, helper, auntie, maid?: Working conditions and attitudes experienced by migrant domestic workers in Thailand and Malaysia*, International Labour Organisation, Asia Pacific, https://www.ilo.org/wcmsp5/groups/public/---asia/---ro-bangkok/---sro-bangkok/documents/publication/wcms_537808.pdf

Badgett, M & Folbre, N (1999), 'Assigning care: Gender norms and economic outcomes', *International Labour Review*, 138(3): 311–326.

Barker, DK (2012), 'Querying the paradox of caring labor', *Rethinking Marxism: A Journal of Economics, Culture & Society*, 24(4): 574–591.

Barrientos, S, Kothari, U & Phillips, N (2013), 'Dynamics of unfree labour in the contemporary global economy', *The Journal of Development Studies*, 49(8): 1037–1041.

Benería, L (1999), 'The enduring debate over unpaid labour', *International Labour Review*, 138(3): 287–309.

Blackett, A (2019), *Everyday Transgressions: Domestic Workers' Transnational Challenge to International Labor Law*, Cornell University Press, Ithaca.

Blunt, A & Dowlings, R (2006), *Home*, Routledge, New York.

Chan, HHY & Latham, A (2021), 'Working and dwelling in a global city: Going-out, public worlds and the intimate lives of migrant domestic workers in Hong Kong', *Journal of Ethnic and Migration Studies*, 10.1080/1369183X.2021.2000854

Chan, T (2014), 'Forced labour laws in Hong Kong: A comparative analysis', *Journal of Law, Technology and Public Policy*, 1(1): 87–114.

Chen, MA (2011), 'Recognizing domestic workers, regulating domestic work: Conceptual measurement and regulatory challenges', *Canadian Journal of Women and the Law*, 23(1): 167–184.

Cheng, SJA (2014), 'State and immigration regulations: Shared experiences of foreign domestics in Singapore, Saudi Arabia and Canada', *Transnational Social Review*, 4(2-3): 259–268.

Chin, BN (1998), *In Service and Servitude: Foreign Domestic Workers and the Malaysian "Modernity" Project*, Columbia University Press, New York.

Chin, C (2019), 'Precarious work and its complicit network: Migrant labour in Singapore', *Journal of Contemporary Asia*, 49(4): 528–551.

Chiu, CCH (2002), *Labour relations and regulation in Hong Kong: Theory and Practice*, City University of Hong Kong: Working Paper Series no. 37, Southeast Asia Research Centre, Hong Kong.

Chiu, MYL (2018), 'Familization of Indonesian domestic workers in Singapore', in R Ogawa, RKH Chan, AS Oishi & LR Wang (eds.), *Gender, Care and Migration in East Asia*, Palgrave Macmillan, Singapore, pp. 97–116.

Chuang, JA (2010), 'Achieving accountability for migrant domestic worker abuse', *North Carolina Law Review*, 88(5): 1627–1656.

Constable, N (1996), 'Jealousy, chastity and abuse: Chinese maids and foreign helpers in Hong Kong', *Modern China*, 22(4): 448–479.

Constable, N (1997), 'Sexuality and discipline among Filipina domestic workers in Hong Kong', *American Ethnologist*, 24(3): 539–558.

Constable, N (2014), *Born Out of Place*, University of California Press, California.

Constable, N (2015), 'Migrant motherhood, "failed migration" and the gendered risks of precarious labour', *TRaNS: Trans-Regional and -National Studies of Southeast Asia*, 3(1): 135–151.

Constable, N (2019), 'Tales of two cities: Legislating pregnancy and marriage among foreign domestic workers in Singapore and Hong Kong', *Journal of Ethnic and Migration Studies*, 10.1080/1369183X.2019.1592403.

Cortés, P & Pan, J (2013), 'Outsourcing household production: Foreign domestic workers and native labor supply in Hong Kong', *Journal of Labor Economics*, 31(2): 327–371.

Cox, R (2013), 'House/work: Home as a space of work and consumption', *Geography Compass*, 7(12): 821–831.

Das Gupta, M. (2008), 'Housework, feminism and labor activism: Lessons from domestic workers in New York', *Signs: Journal of Women in Culture and Society*, 33(3): 532–537.

Davidoff, L (2003), 'Gender and the "great divide": Public and private in British gender history', *Journal of Women's History*, 15(1): 11–26.

Demetriou, D (2015), '"Tied visas" and inadequate labour protections: A formula for abuse and exploitation of migrant domestic workers in the United Kingdom', *Anti-Trafficking Review*, 5: 69–88.

Dickney, S (2000), 'Permeable homes: Domestic service, household space and the vulnerability of class boundaries in urban India', *American Ethnologist*, 27(2): 462–489.

Duffy, M (2005), 'Reproducing labor inequalities: Challenges for feminists, conceptualising care at the intersections of gender, race and class', *Gender & Society*, 19 (1): 66–82.

Ehrenreich, B & Hochschild, AR (2002), *Global Woman: Nannies, Maids and Sex Workers in the New Economy*, Metropolitan Books, New York.

Elias, J (2018), 'Governing domestic worker migration in Southeast Asia: Public-private partnerships, regulatory grey zones and the household', *Journal of Contemporary Asia*, 48(2): 278–300.

England, P, Budig, M & Folbre, N (2002), 'Wages of virtue: The relative pay of care work', *Social Problems*, 49(4): 455–473.

Fitzpatrick, J & Kelly RK (1998), 'Gendered aspects of migration: Law and the female migrant', *Hastings International & Competition Law Review*, 22: 47–112.

Folbre, N (1995), 'Holding hands at midnight: The paradox of caring labor', *Feminist Economics*, 1(1): 73–92.

Ford, M & Piper, N (2007), 'Southern sites of female agency: Informal regimes and female migrant labour resistance in East and Southeast Asia', in JM Hobson & L Seabrooke (eds.), *Everyday Politics of the World Economy*, Cambridge University Press, UK, pp. 63–80.

Fudge, J (2014), 'Feminist reflections on the scope of labour law: Domestic work, social reproduction and jurisdiction', *Feminist Legal Studies*, 22(1):1–23.

Fudge, J & Mundlak, G (forthcoming), 'Law and gendered labour market segmentation', *International Labour Review*, 10.1111/ilr/12339

Gavison, R (1992), 'Feminism and the private-public distinction', *Stanford Law Review*, 45: 1–46.

Goh, JMC (2018), Agents as migration infrastructure: Circulating debt and channelling Indonesian domestic workers in Singapore, Master's Thesis, National University of Singapore, Singapore.

Goldfarb, S (2000), 'Violence against women and the persistence of privacy', *Ohio State Law Journal*, 61(1): 1–87.

Gottfried, H & Chun, JJ (2018), 'Care work in transition: Transnational circuits of gender, migration and care', *Critical Sociology*, 44(7-8): 997–1012.

Gutiérrez-Rodríguez, E (2010), *Migration, Domestic Work and Affect: A Decolonial Approach on Value and the Feminization of Labor*, Routledge, New York.

Hill, E, Ford, M & Baird, M (2017), 'Work/care regimes in the Asia-Pacific: A feminist framework', in M Baird, M Ford & E Hill (eds.), *Women, Work and Care in the Asia-Pacific*, Routledge, New York, pp. 1–22.

Himmelweit, S (1995), 'The discovery of "unpaid work": The social consequences of the expansion of "work"', *Feminist Economics*, 1(2): 1–19.

Hochschild, A (2000), 'Global care chains and emotional surplus value', in T Giddens & W Hutton (eds.), *On the Edge: Globalization and the New Millennium*, Sage Publishers, London, pp. 130–146.

HOME & TWC2 (2017), *Convention on the elimination of all forms of discrimination against women (CEDAW) shadow report for Singapore*, HOME & TWC2, Singapore.

Hondagneu-Sotelo, P (1999), 'Introduction: Gender and contemporary US immigration', *American Behavioural Scientist*, 42(4): 565–576.

Hondagneu-Sotelo, P (2001), *Domestica: Immigrant Workers Cleaning and Caring in the Shadow of Affluence*, University of California Press, Los Angeles.

Hong Kong Immigration Department (2021), *Press release: Problem of job-hopping by foreign domestic helpers*, The Government of Hong Kong Special Administrative Region, Hong Kong, viewed 11 Nov, https://www.info.gov.hk/gia/general/202201/19/P2022011900499.htm

Hong Kong Immigration Department (2022), *Guidebook for the Employment of Domestic Helpers from Abroad*, viewed 1 Feb, https://www.immd.gov.hk/eng/forms/forms/id-e-969.html

Hong Kong Secretary for Labour and Welfare (2018), *Press release: Combating job-hopping acts of foreign domestic helpers*, The Government of the Hong Kong Special Administrative Region, Hong Kong, viewed 11 Nov, https://www.info.gov.hk/gia/general/201812/12/P2018121200629.htm

Hong Kong Labour Department (2022), *A Concise Guide to the Employment Ordinance*, viewed 1 Feb, https://www.labour.gov.hk/eng/public/ConciseGuide.htm

Huang, S & Yeoh, BSA (2007), 'Emotional labour and transnational domestic work: The moving geographies of "maid abuse" in Singapore', *Mobilities*, 2(2): 195–217.

Human Rights Watch (2005), *Maid to order: Ending abuses against migrant domestic workers in Singapore*, 17(10) Human Rights Watch, Singapore.

Human Rights Watch (2006), *Swept under the rug: Abuses against domestic workers around the world*, Human Rights Watch, https://www.hrw.org/news/2006/07/27/domestic-workers-abused-worldwide

Ibarra, ML (2010), 'My reward is not money: Deep alliances and end-of-life care among Mexicana workers and their wards', E Boris & RS Parreñas (eds.), *Intimate labours: Culture, technologies and the politics of care*, Stanford University Press, California, pp. 117–131.

Islam, MR & Cojocaru, S (2015), Migrant domestic workers in Asia: Transnational variations and policy concerns, *International Migration*, 54(1): 48–63.

Johnson, M & Wilcke, C (2015), 'Caged in and breaking loose: Intimate labor, the state and migrant domestic workers in Saudi Arabia and other Arab countries', in SL Friedman & P Mahdavi (eds.), *Migrant encounters: Intimate labor, the state and mobility across Asia*, University of Pennsylvania Press, Pennsylvania, pp. 135–159.

Johnson, M, Lee, M, McCahill, M & Mesina MR (2019), 'Beyond the "all seeing eye": Filipino migrant domestic workers' contestation of care and control in Hong Kong', *Ethnos: Journal of Anthropology*, 10.1080/00141844.2018.1545794

Kabeer, N (1999), 'Resources, agency, achievements: Reflections on the measurement of women's empowerment', *Development and Change*, 30(3):435–464.

Labadie-Jackson, G (2008), 'Reflections on domestic work and the feminization of migration', *Campbell Law Review*, 31(1): 67–90.

Lan, PC (2003), 'Negotiating social boundaries and private zones: The micropolitics of employing migrant domestic workers', *Social Problems*, 50(4): 525–549.

Lan, PC (2006), *Global Cinderellas: Migrant domestics and newly rich employers in Taiwan*, Duke University Press, Durham.

Lee, PWY & Petersen CJ (2006), 'Forced labour and debt bondage in Hong Kong: A study of Indonesian and Filipina migrant domestic workers', *Centre for Comparative and Public Law*, Occasional Paper No. 16, June.

Lee, SSY (2016), *Between worlds: Filipino domestic workers in Hong Kong, 1970-2005*, PhD thesis, SOAS University of London, London.

Low, YJ (2021), *MOM conducting house visits, more interviews of first-time maids to ensure their well-being*, Channel NewsAsia, April 26, https://www.todayonline.com/singapore/mom-conducting-house-visits-more-interviews-first-time-maids-ensure-their-well-being

Lui, ID, Vandan, N, Davies, SE, Harman, S, Morgan, R, Smith, J, Wenham, C, & Grépin, KA (2021), '"We also deserve help during the pandemic": The effect of the COVID-19 pandemic on foreign domestic workers in Hong Kong', *Journal of Migration and Health*, 3:100037.

Lutz, H (2002), 'At your service madam! The globalization of domestic service', *Feminist Review*, 70:89–104.

Lutz, H (2011), *The New Maids: Transnational Women and the Care Economy*, Zed Books, London.

MacKinnon, C (1989), *Towards a Feminist Theory of the State*, Harvard University Press, Cambridge.

Maher, KH & Staab, S (2005), 'Nanny politics', *International Feminist Journal of Politics*, 7(1): 71–89.

Mantouvalou, V (2012), 'Human rights for precarious workers: The legislative precariousness of domestic labor', *Comparative Labour Law & Policy Journal*, 34(1): 133–165.

Marchetti, S (2015), '"Mum seems happy". Relatives of dependent elders and the difficult task to employ a migrant care-giver', in A Triandafyllidou & S Marchetti (eds.), *Employers, Agencies and Immigration: Paying for Care*, Routledge, New York, pp. 93–110.

McDowell, L (1999), *Gender, Identity and Place: Understanding Feminist Geographies*, Polity Press, Cambridge.

Mendez, J (1998), 'Of mops and maids: Contradictions and continuities in bureaucratized domestic work', *Social Problems*, 45(1): 114–135.

Menon, M (2021), *Manpower Ministry starts new house visits scheme to check on welfare of maids*, The Straits Times, 26 April, https://www.straitstimes.com/singapore/manpower-ministry-starts-new-house-visits-scheme-to-check-on-welfare-of-maids

Michel, S & Peng, I (2017), 'Introduction', in S Michel & I Peng (eds.), *Gender, Migration and the Work of Care: A Multi-Scalar Approach to the Pacific Rim*, Palgrave Macmillan, Cham, pp. 3–22.

Ministry of Manpower (MOM) (2012), *Informal consolidation of Work Permit Pass conditions*, Government Gazette, Singapore, viewed 7 Sep, https://www.mom.gov.sg/-/media/mom/documents/services-forms/passes/wpspassconditions.pdf

Ministry of Manpower (MOM) (2015), *Employer's guide: When an FDW employer can be debarred*, Ministry of Manpower, Singapore, viewed 9 Oct, https://www.mom.gov.sg/passes-and-permits/work-permit-for-foreign-domestic-worker/employers-guide/when-employers-can-be-debarred

Ministry of Manpower (MOM) (last updated 2019), *Work permit for foreign domestic worker: Transfer an FDW to a new employer*, Ministry of Manpower, Singapore, viewed 9 Oct, https://www.mom.gov.sg/passes-and-permits/work-permit-for-foreign-domestic-worker/transfer-to-a-new-employer

Momsen, J (ed.) (1999), *Gender, Migration and Domestic Service*, Routledge, London.

Moras, A (2008), 'The private home as a public workplace: Employing paid domestic labour', *Journal of Workplace Rights*, 13(4): 377–400.

Nakano Glenn, E (1992), 'From servitude to service work: Historical continuities in the racial division of paid reproductive labor', *Signs*, 18(1): 1–43.

Oelz, M (2014), 'The ILO's domestic worker convention and recommendation: A window of opportunity for social justice', *International Labour Review*, 153(1): 143–172.

Ogawa, R, Chan, RKH, Oishi, A, & Wang, LR (2018), 'Introduction: Situating gender, care, and migration in East Asia', in R Ogawa, RKH Chan, A Oishi & LR Wang (eds.), *Gender, Care and Migration in East Asia*, Palgrave Macmillan, London, pp. 1–22.

Palmer, E & Eveline, J (2012), 'Sustaining low pay in aged care work', *Gender, Work and Organization*, 19(3): 254–275.

Pande, A (2012), 'From "balcony talk" and "practical prayers" to illegal collectives: Migrant domestic workers and meso-level resistances in Lebanon', *Gender and Society*, 26(3): 382–405.

Parreñas, RS (2000), 'Migrant Filipina domestic workers and the international division of reproductive labor', *Gender and Society*, 14(4): 560–580.

Parreñas, RS (2001), *Servants of Globalization: Women, Migration and Domestic Work*, Stanford University Press, California.

Parreñas, RS (2007), 'The gender ideological clash in globalization: Women, migration and the modernization building project of the Philippines', *Social Thought & Research*, 28: 37–56.

Parreñas, RS (2015), *Servants of Globalization: Migration and Domestic Work* (2nd edition), Stanford University Press, California.

Paul, AM & Neo, P (2018), 'Am I allowed to be pregnant? Awareness of pregnancy protection laws among migrant domestic workers in Hong Kong', *Journal of Ethnic and Migration Studies*, 44(7): 1195–1213.

Poon, A (2009), 'Maid visible: Foreign domestic workers and the dilemma of development in Singapore', *Crossroads: An Interdisciplinary Journal of Southeast Asian Studies*, 17(1): 1–28.

Price, JM (2002), 'The apotheosis of home and the maintenance of spaces of violence', *Hypatia*, 17(4): 39–70.

Rodgers, L (2016), *Labour Law, Vulnerability and Precarious Work*, Edward Elgar Publishing, Cheltenham.

Rollins, J (1986), *Between Women: Domestics and Their Employers*, Temple University Press, Philadelphia.

Romero, M (2002), 'Global woman: Nannies, maids and sex workers in the new economy', *British Journal of Industrial Relations*, 42(4): 747–755.

Romero, M (2018), 'Reflections on globalized care chains and migrant women workers', *Critical Sociology*, 44(7-8): 1179–1189.

Ruijter, E, van der Lippe, T & Raub, W (2003), 'Trust problems in household outsourcing', *Rationality and Society*, 15(4): 473–507.

Schneider, E (1994), 'The violence of privacy', in MA Fineman & R Mykitiuk (eds.), *The Public Nature of Private Violence: Women and the Discovery of Abuse*, Routledge, New York, pp. 36–58.

Shahvisi, A (2018), 'Hermeneutical injustice and outsourced domestic work', *Women's Studies International Forum*, 69: 18–25.

Shi, W (2017), 'Cultural politics of emotions in households: Migrant domestic workers in Macau', *Inter-Asia Cultural studies*, 18(4): 464–481.

Strauss, K & McGrath, S (2017), 'Temporary migration, precarious employment and unfree labour relations: Exploring the "continuum of exploitation" in Canada's Temporary Foreign Worker Program', *Geoforum*, 78: 199–208.

Tan, EKB (2010), 'Managing female foreign domestic workers in Singapore: Economic, pragmatism, coercive legal regulation or human rights', *Israel Law Journal*, 43: 99–125.

Teo, YY & Piper, N (2009), 'Foreigners in our homes: Linking migration and family policies in Singapore', *Population, Space and Place*, 15(2): 147–159.

Triandafyllidou, A & Marchetti, S (2015), 'The employers' perspective on paid domestic and care work', in A Triandafyllidou & S Marchetti (eds.), *Employers, Agencies and Immigration: Paying for Care*, Routledge, New York, pp. 1–17.

Truong, TD, Marin, MLS & Quesada-Bondad, A (2014), 'Intersectionality, structural vulnerability, and access to sexual and reproductive health services: Filipina domestic workers in Hong Kong, Singapore and Qatar', in TD Truong, D Gasper, J Handmaker & SI Bergh (eds.), *Migration, Gender and Social Justice: Perspectives on Human Insecurity*, Springer, Heidelberg.

Wang, V (2021), *'For Hong Kong's domestic workers during COVID, discrimination is its own epidemic'*, New York Times, May 18, https://www.nytimes.com/2021/05/18/world/asia/hong-kong-domestic-worker-discrimination.html

Warrington, M (2001), '"I must get out": The geographies of domestic violence', *Transactions of the Institute of British Geographers*, 26(3): 365–382.

Wessels, A, Ong, M & Daniel, D (2017), 'Bonded to the system: Labour exploitation in the foreign domestic work sector in Singapore', *Research Across Borders*, https://www.researchgate.net/profile/Anja_Wessels/publication/321298753_Bonded_to_the_system_Labour_exploitation_in_the_foreign_domestic_work_sector_in_Singapore/links/5a23672a4585155dd41cc58b/Bonded-to-the-system-Labour-exploitation-in-the-foreign-domestic-work-sector-in-Singapore.pdf

Yelland, N, Yarrow, A, Blaise, M & Chan, YO (2013), '"We spend more time with the children than they do ...": Education, care and the work of foreign domestic workers in Hong Kong', *Globalisation, Societies and Education*, 11(4): 443–458.

Yeoh, BA, Liew, JA, Ho, E & Huang, S (2021), 'Migrant domestic workers and the household division of intimate labour: Reconfiguring eldercare relations in Singapore', *Gender, Place & Culture*, 10.1080/0966369X.2021.1956435.

Yeoh, BSA & Huang, S (1999), 'Singapore women and foreign domestic workers: Negotiating domestic work and motherhood', in JH Momsen (ed.), *Gender, Migration and Domestic Service*, Routledge, London, pp. 277–300.

Yeoh, BSA, Huang, S & Devasahayam, TW (2004), 'Diasporic subjects in the nation: Foreign domestic workers, the reach of law and civil society in Singapore', *Asian Studies Review*, 28(1): 7–23.

Zelizer, VA (2010), *Economic Lives: How Culture Shapes the Economy*, Princeton University Press, New Jersey.

Chapter 3

Gender, Exploitation and Everyday Security

Defining and Responding to Exploitation

One of the key elements of human trafficking, 'exploitation' sits at the core of interventions, laws and policies to address human trafficking, modern slavery and other efforts to define and deliver 'decent work'[1] (Coghlan & Wylie 2011; Gallagher 2015). While most often used in relation to work targeting human trafficking and modern slavery, the concepts of 'exploitation' and 'exploitative labour practices' have also been invoked in reference to employment practices, such as low wages, substandard working conditions and situations of unfree, forced and coerced labour (Skrivankova 2010; Strauss & McGrath 2017). The International Labour Organization (ILO) (2012, p. 53) has proposed an understanding of labour exploitation as something that occurs along a 'continuum' from *decent work* (non-exploitative and free labour), to *substandard work* (exploitative work that is not forced), and finally to *extreme and forced labour* (exploitative work that is forced). However, in both policy and practice, exploitation and exploitative labour practices are often defined and identified more narrowly through the confines of law, specifically, according to what is constituted as illegal in criminal and/or labour law within a particular jurisdiction (Scott 2017). As discussed in Chapter 2, in both Singapore and Hong Kong migrant domestic workers are de jure or at least partly covered under legislative and criminal justice frameworks, which outline labour provisions, employers' obligations and the range of substandard, unlawful or criminal employment practices. Determinations of harm, abuse and exploitative employment practices are thus established through these extant frameworks, which are used to establish whether labour law breaches or criminal offences have taken place. These baselines also inform responses and interventions, whereby support and assistance for women migrant domestic workers who encounter work-related problems or disputes privilege legal and criminal justice processes and outcomes – that is, prosecution, conviction and punishment. In Singapore and Hong Kong, the identification of exploitation, acknowledgement of victimhood and access to redress and protection mechanisms occur only when women migrant domestic workers lodge a formal complaint or claim with the authorities, provide sufficient evidence *and* process

DOI: 10.4324/9781003250364-3

their cases through the labour law or criminal justice system. This places the burden of enforcement on the worker, and, as is characteristic of legal and criminal justice responses, interventions are primarily reactive, responding to harms and exploitation *after* the fact. While Singapore has introduced the proactive measure of home visits, where labour officers conduct house visits to check on the working and living conditions of women migrant domestic workers,[2] Hong Kong's approach to securing worker protection and well-being remains steadfastly embedded in reactive models of law and legal process.

These efforts reflect a degree of commitment by the two city-states to protect women migrant domestic workers and address the work-related harms and exploitation to which these workers are subjected. Specifically, in defining certain employment conditions as exploitative or harmful, criminalisation and regulation have ideological importance and can appear to provide a degree of human security (Fudge & Mundlak forthcoming). Yet, as Mullally (2015) and Romero (2018), among many others, remind us, the presence of legal provisions and regulatory standards does not necessarily translate into de facto protection or security, especially for vulnerable populations who sit across the many axes of power and difference. Indeed, critical human trafficking and modern slavery research has shown that law and criminal justice systems tend to fall short of their promise to provide protection for low-waged, temporary migrant workers in two key ways, which are outlined below.

First, labour law and criminal justice approaches, which frame labour exploitation and poor working conditions as a straightforward issue to be negotiated by employer and worker, effectively distance all the structural inequalities that are the foundation of the problem (Sharapov 2015; Segrave 2017). For example, in Singapore and Hong Kong, there are legal sanctions ensuring that aberrant employers are punished for criminal offences and labour law breaches. However, the underlying structural factors that are conducive to unlawful employment practices – such as restrictive conditions of entry and stay, or the 'live-in' requirement, 'employer-tied' visa scheme, and the gendered devaluation of domestic labour – are left intact (Yeoh, Huang & Devasahayam 2004; Lan 2006; Amnesty International 2013; Clarke 2013; Constable 2014; Justice Centre Hong Kong 2016). Implicit in this response, then, is a narrow, individualised understanding of exploitation and abuse as something that 'bad egg' employers do to innocent women. By characterising the exploitation of women migrant domestic workers as the actions of deviant employers, the employer thus becomes the problem to be targeted by legislative and regulatory efforts, which operate on the basis that regulating and punishing the pathologised behaviour of such individuals will reduce workers' vulnerability to exploitation and improve protection (Anderson 2010; Chan 2014). Yet this framing obfuscates the systemic and relational context of live-in domestic labour. Scholars researching in both Singapore and Hong Kong note that this has created a situation where only the most serious criminal and labour offences are identified, leaving the bulk of 'everyday' forms of exploitation invisible and unaddressed (see Yeoh, Huang &

Devasahayam 2004; Lowe 2007; Tan 2010; Chan 2014; Constable 2014). Employers are held directly responsible for and benefit from the exploitation of women migrant domestic workers; however, critical studies on human trafficking, modern slavery and domestic labour have established that individual offenders do not represent the whole problem (see Albin & Mantouvalou 2012; Marshall & Thatun 2012; Rosewarne 2013; Boris & Fish 2014; Segrave & Powell 2015). Instead, broader processes of neoliberal capitalist labour relations and uneven global development that enable the exploitation of migrant workers (Segrave & Powell 2015; Strauss & McGrath 2017; Simeone & Piper 2021), restrictive labour and immigration laws and policies that enforce temporariness and produce precarious working and living conditions (Anderson 2010; Segrave 2019; Lee 2021), and unequal gender dynamics that underpin waged domestic labour and shape socio-legal norms and expectations (Fudge 2014; Rodgers 2016; Elias 2018) facilitate and sustain exploitative, precarious employment contexts for low-wage migrant workers. While investments in enhancing regulatory, legal and criminal justice mechanisms are important, in that the absence of legal rights has very real impacts for excluded groups, legal and policy change is inadequate when it fails to contest or alter the cultural, economic and political structures that produce insecurity and precarity (Wonders & Jones 2021; Fudge & Mundlak forthcoming).

Second, law and order responses to labour exploitation often display little regard for or understanding of the complex needs and desires of workers (Davies & Davies 2008; Palumbo & Sciurba 2015; Segrave 2017). While this is most visible in the case of victims of labour trafficking in countries where law and order outcomes are prioritised over victims' desire to remain and work in the destination country (Segrave 2009; Jagori 2012; Milivojevic & Pickering 2013), research on migrant domestic work in Singapore and Hong Kong has revealed a similar failure to account for workers' complex motivations and the pressures they face (Devasahayam 2010; Chan 2014; Constable 2014). For example, in her analysis of Singapore's labour policies and practices, Devasahayam (2010, p. 53) notes that while the criminal justice system may be effective for penalising errant employers, it offers little to no compensation for victims and 'drastically falls short in protecting the FDW [foreign domestic worker]'. In Singapore and Hong Kong, a worker is only permitted to take on alternative employment while undergoing case investigations or legal proceedings on a restrictive case-by-case basis. For workers who have migrated to provide financial support for their families, the prospect of not earning an income for an extended period of time renders the option of filing a formal complaint untenable (Anderson 2007; Kempadoo 2012; Romero 2018). As Paul and Neo (2018, p. 1198) explain,

> An MDW [migrant domestic worker], whose employer does not follow the letter of the law, must decide if her employer's infraction is serious enough to warrant the lodging of an official complaint as this could result

in a lengthy court case, the loss of immediate income and/or a black mark on the worker's employment record whether or not she wins.

There is thus little incentive (and often limited capacity) for a migrant domestic worker whose autonomy is significantly constrained by her economic responsibilities, precarious migration status and dependency on her employer to come forward to report workplace exploitation (Briones 2008; Anderson 2016; Demetriou 2015; Mullally 2015; Segrave 2017; Romero 2018). When mechanisms of protection and intervention sit alongside policies and laws that maintain workers' structural precarity *and* labour immobility, together these factors reinforce workers' dependency on employers, which in turn significantly reduces their power to negotiate or seek redress for exploitation or abuse (Lan 2006; Ueno 2009; Herrera Vivar 2012; Anderson 2016; Parreñas & Silvey 2018). As many scholars have rightly pointed out, in a context where a worker's right to employment and residence is bound to an individual employer, the risk of losing their legal status and right to work significantly deters them from accessing formal mechanisms of protection or redress (Fitzpatrick & Katrina 1998; Mantouvalou 2012; Fudge & Strauss 2014; Johnson & Wilcke 2015). Yet, as mentioned above, labour law and criminal justice responses rely largely on workers coming forward to report their victimisation.

This situation highlights a pressing concern surrounding the current labour regulatory frameworks in Singapore and Hong Kong; that the needs of victims/workers are often relegated to secondary status, with little consideration of whether the interventions introduced are needed or even welcomed by these workers, meaning that efforts to combat labour exploitation do not give the victims involved any meaningful agency (Davies & Davies 2008; Timoshkina 2014; Segrave & Powell 2015). In examining existing state interventions, including prevention and protection efforts, critical scholars note that they are largely based on misplaced assumptions about victims' needs and how to reduce victims' vulnerability to exploitation (Chapkis 2003; Segrave 2009; Milivojevic & Segrave 2012; Timoshkina 2014). In the context of female migrant domestic labour, these measures have primarily taken the form of awareness-raising and professionalisation/upskilling campaigns, which rest on the assumption that if workers are informed of their rights and possess professional or enhanced technical capabilities, they will be able to improve their autonomy in the workplace and protect themselves from exploitation and abuse (Guevarra 2014; Chang 2018). This suggests that within the labour migration context, vulnerability to exploitation is associated with a lack of education, professional skills or awareness of labour rights and complaint procedures (Chang 2018). Implicit in this logic is also an understanding of 'vulnerability' as an attribute of particular groups (that is, based on gender, class, educational level and occupational status). This again embraces an individualised focus on the pathologies of women migrant domestic workers and displaces attention away from the ways in which social and political structures intersect to create or intensify the risks these workers face and hinder their ability to access help and support (Chang 2018; Maher & Segrave 2018).

The pursuit of prosecutions and convictions is not in and of itself inappropriate, and indeed this is a necessary response as it punishes errant employers and may provide a sense of justice to victims (Anderson & Rogaly 2005; Segrave 2009). However, in practice, this approach has limited capacity to provide genuine protection and security for women migrant domestic workers (Yeoh, Huang & Devasahayam 2004; Lobasz 2009; Segrave 2009; Bhabha 2015; Marks & Olsen 2015). Significantly, all of the above issues underscore a very serious limitation of current approaches: that both the experience of exploitation and the expectation of security have been largely defined and responded to by policymakers. The experiences and voices of women migrant domestic workers remain largely unheard and/or are represented by a very narrow faction – those who have been impacted by unlawful acts *and* whose cases have been processed through formal mechanisms. There are significant ramifications of this absence of victims' voices. The most important of these is that attention is diverted away from the multidimensional nature of the problem, in particular, how human insecurity is a structural component of the contemporary labour markets and migration regimes in both Singapore and Hong Kong. This, in turn, has enabled a reductive form of national policymaking that is unable to prevent or even respond effectively to exploitation.

ILO Domestic Worker Convention: Recognising Domestic and Care Work as 'Real' Work

On the supra-national level, networks of labour activism – national and transnational migrant rights organisations in particular – have campaigned and mobilised for greater coherence of migrant workers' rights and welfare, in response to the institutional failures of global and national bodies (Yamanaka & Piper 2003; Piper, Rosewarne & Withers 2016). Primarily led by migrant domestic workers, these non-governmental organisations have campaigned around a number of claims, based on locally framed labour rights and the global struggle for human and labour rights (Constable 2009; Piper, Rosewarne & Withers 2016; Lee 2021). However, at the heart of migrant advocacy and solidarity movements is the recognition of migrant domestic workers as *workers*, and a global agenda promoting the concept of decent work, which allows for a more encompassing understanding of the complex motivations and pressures that characterise women domestic workers' experience of exploitation (Rosewarne 2013; Boris & Fish 2014; Oelz 2014; Parreñas & Silvey 2017). In 2011, the global dialogue on women's paid labour in private households finally led to the passage of the ILO's *Domestic Workers Convention* (C189) and Recommendation, which formally acknowledges domestic workers' right to fair labour conditions (Albin & Mantouvalou

2012; Boris & Fish 2014). This was seen as a transformative step towards dislodging the norms and inequalities that have perpetuated the subordination and servitude of domestic workers, which have been reinforced and extended by state-based laws (Blackett 2019). In the preamble to the Convention, there is formal recognition of the undervaluing and invisibility of domestic labour and the need for a gendered approach to domestic labour regulation (Albin & Mantouvalou 2012; Blackett 2012). Broadly, the Convention seeks to ensure substantive equality for all domestic workers by advocating their inclusion within standard labour codes and access to full employment rights and social protections (Blackett 2012; Oelz 2014; Mullally 2015). More specifically, in recognition of the sectoral disadvantages that domestic workers face, there is special reference to issues such as the need to ensure that domestic workers are informed of their employment terms and conditions (Article 7); that there is a system of labour inspection in place (Article 17(2)); and that specific attention is given to the issue of work and leisure time, particularly for live-in domestic workers (Article 10), among others (Albin & Mantouvalou 2012). In addition, the Convention (2011) acknowledges the issue of effective access to legal protection and highlights the need for 'effective access to courts, tribunals or other dispute resolution mechanisms under conditions that are not less favourable than those available to workers generally' (Article 16). In their analysis of the Convention, Albin and Mantouvalou (2012, p. 73) note that it is sensitive to the 'special challenges of the public/private divide that characterise the domestic labour relation', thus offering a more nuanced and precise way to address the sectoral disadvantages faced by domestic workers.

However, in spite of its intentions and potentially progressive outcomes, the impact of the Convention in practice has been widely debated as it has been dependent upon its implementation at the national level (Piper, Rosewarne & Withers 2016). Currently, the Convention has extremely low ratification rates,[3] and both Singapore and Hong Kong have yet to ratify the document. In addition to concerns around its practical impact, the other key issue pertains to its failure to call into question the systematic reliance on temporary migration programs (Blackett 2019). These present significant obstacles to implementing and enforcing operational responses to exploitation. Notwithstanding these implementation challenges in national contexts, possible advancements enabled by the Convention and its potential to improve protection and enable 'decent work' for women migrant domestic workers has been the subject of several studies (see Albin & Mantouvalou 2012; Rosewarne 2013; Visel 2013; Oelz 2014; Carter & Aulette 2016; Marchetti 2018; Blackett 2019). However, these theoretical and empirical assessments of the Convention to redress sectoral disadvantages and poor employment practices prevalent in domestic labour industry, have tended to focus on the need for legal inclusion of domestic workers in labour regulatory frameworks and shifting the structure of labour law. One of the key emphasis in the Convention (and the international labour movement) thus remains on improving legal and regulatory frameworks as the means to unsettle or even correct the marginalisation of women migrant domestic workers and to ensure better working and living conditions for them.

The premise that legal systems and reforms can effect meaningful structural change that ensures the safety and security of women in private spaces is one that critical feminists in criminology, sociology and socio-legal studies have long identified as deeply flawed (Mahoney 1991; Snider 1994; Coker 2001; Bailey 2011; Walklate, Fitz-Gibbon & McCulloch 2018; Pividori & Degani 2019). For women experiencing violence in private homes, legal interventions and the justice system can be an important resource for responding to such violence (Dobash & Dobash 1992; Lewis et al. 2001). However, as discussed in the following section, the capacity of legal interventions to offer protection to women, support them in managing their safety and respond to their needs is limited.

Public Laws to Address 'Private' Violence against Women

As established in Chapter 2, domestic labour is a form of gendered labour, performed overwhelmingly by women in private spaces. Therefore, the analysis of female migrant domestic labour and its relationship with the migration regime must consider these gendered dimensions (Anthias & Yuval-Davis 1992; Lutz 2010). An important consequence of this insight is that our evaluation of the utility of law and policy in protecting women migrant domestic workers similarly needs a paradigm shift – away from an examination of the experiences of labour migrants in general towards an analysis that foregrounds gender and the experiences of *women* migrants working in the private sphere. As Walklate, Fitz-Gibbon and McCulloch (2018) and many other feminists have identified, the capacity to 'see' gender is especially salient for understanding women's everyday experiences of security and violence, as well as the relationship between their needs, their negotiation of the choices available to them and their responses to violence (see also Mahoney 1991; Minaker 2001). A review of the literature on state responses to violence against women offers an important yet under-utilised lens with which to examine and challenge the reliance on the law and legal processes in responding to the needs of women migrant domestic workers. In this section, insights are primarily drawn from broader critical feminist research on domestic violence, in which scholars have identified the myriad reasons why the legal response, precisely because of its structural basis, is not capable of accounting for women's motivations or the complexities of their lives and decisions (Minaker 2001; Lewis 2004; Johnson & Conners 2018; Walklate, Fitz-Gibbon & McCulloch 2018). Relevant to this book are the following two key reasons: for this failure of the legal system (1) legal systems do not recognise that women's experiences of violence are not the result of isolated incidents, but rather form part of a dynamic 'process' occurring within the everyday context, and (2) the system adopts the neoliberal construction of women as 'atomistic, mobile individuals' rather than as interconnected to others. Each of these reasons is discussed in turn next.

First, regulatory and legal systems are largely incident focused. They operate on the basis of responding to discrete episodes of violence and are not designed to account for or capture the complex and intersecting relations of power in both the public and private spheres that sustain gendered violence (Minaker 2001; Stubbs 2002; Velonis 2016; Walklate, Fitz-Gibbon & McCulloch 2018). When violence or abuse is framed in this limited context, it is considered an isolated event with a discernible beginning and end, reflecting an assumption that safety for women means responding to and stopping physically violent behaviours (Fitz-Gibbon & Maher 2015). Yet critical research on violence against women shows that this understanding minimises women's lived experience of violence, as it fails to recognise that, for many women, such incidents of violence are not separate and distinct events but represent a pervasive, ongoing part of their lives and relationships, sustained by myriad forms of intimidation, abuse, control and relations of power (Minaker 2001; Lewis 2004; Douglas 2012; Walklate 2018; Walklate, Fitz-Gibbon & McCulloch 2018). The failure to recognise and address the ordinary, 'everyday' nature of women's insecurity and fear born of the threat of violence is in part associated with the legal system's need for a precise and rigid definition of violence, which can in turn obfuscate other, non-physical harms that women may face (Pividori & Degani 2019). In her analysis of law in practice, Douglas (2012, p. 126) points out that one implication of this is that some forms of violence will fall outside legal remit and be situated instead within the 'private sphere of love and communication'. Other scholars have similarly noted that the gap between what is legally constituted and recognised as 'violence' and harm and what is not, reflects a disjuncture with women's realities, which then impacts legal interpretations of the circumstances that contribute to violence against women and the measures that are necessary to meet women's needs and ensure their safety (Smart 1989; Mahoney 1991; Stubbs 2002; Dobash & Dobash 1992; Weissman 2007). This private/public distinction, and the resultant minimisation of certain harms, similarly frames migrant domestic labour, where certain harmful employment practices are legally defined as unacceptable and unlawful, while others are simply discouraged, despite being identified by migrant women as highly harmful (an issue further discussed in Chapter 6).

Second, legal and regulatory systems construct women as 'atomistic', mobile victims living in a social vacuum, thus failing to recognise that they are also mothers, daughters, spouses and workers who are highly interconnected with others (Minaker 2001; Stubbs 2002). The problem with this reductive framing, as Minaker (2001) points out, is how these relationships and the corresponding responsibilities that women shoulder have direct implications for their immediate and longer-term concerns and welfare as well as their material and intangible needs. These relationships and responsibilities in turn produce certain constraints, which limit women's choices and ability to negotiate their own safety and protection (Minaker 2001; Bailey 2011). Further complicating the issue is that, while legal and regulatory systems emphasise survivors' responsibility to participate in formal processes to protect themselves and hold abusers accountable, there are few provisions to ensure women's immediate or longer-term material security (Mahoney 1991; Coker 2001). Yet access to material resources has a significant influence on women's decisions, as they must consider whether they can afford to prioritise legal interventions over more immediate material concerns such as those around food, employment and child or elderly care services (Mahoney 1991; Coker 2001; Minaker 2001; Bailey 2011). This highlights the complex factors influencing protection and safety for women, wherein, for some women, safety is not only about freedom from physical violence and harm but is also embedded within the broader context of their lives (Coker 2001; Minaker 2001; Walklate, Fitz-Gibbon & McCulloch 2018). As Minaker (2001) observes, women's assessment of risk and safety, as well as their response to violence, involves a continuous negotiation between their expectations, needs, roles and responsibilities.

In view of these issues, some critical feminist scholars have argued that legislative changes or criminal justice reforms do not necessarily translate into qualitative benefits for women (Goodmark 2015; Walklate, Fitz-Gibbon & McCulloch 2018). On the one hand, it is recognised that legal and regulatory reforms, alongside effective implementation of existing laws, can be an important tool, particularly as legal interventions do offer women resources to address violence and have enabled many women to obtain relief and remedy (Stubbs 2002; Raphael 2004). The symbolic power of law can inspire ideological change as it sends a strong message about what is or is not acceptable behaviour and, importantly, can valorise the private experiences of women, enabling them to be heard and taken seriously within legal settings. On the other hand, as Wells (2004, p. 508) posits, law 'sits in a framework that ... is sustained by webs of practices and beliefs that perpetuate micro cultures'. That is to say, legal interventions and strategies have limited capacity to effect structural change to the systemic gendered and heteronormative attitudes and values that underpin the control, violence and exploitation of women (Snider 1994; Walklate, Fitz-Gibbon & McCulloch 2018). Instead, they are more likely to uphold or perpetuate the inequalities in relationships, and they offer no real empowerment to women (Weissman 2007; Blackett 2019). All of these difficulties raise broader issues around the degree to which legal and criminal justice interventions can remedy violence against women and improve the protection or safety of women. The next section builds a framework through which to transform how we think about and respond to women migrant domestic workers' employment experiences.

The Intersection of Law, Gender and Women Migrants' Security

The discussion above locates the gendered impacts of legal and criminal justice responses to migrant domestic worker exploitation and violence against women more broadly, at the centre of this inquiry. An important question that emerges from this discussion is: how can women migrant domestic workers' experiences of labour and exploitation be understood and adequately responded to, when regulatory and legal systems have not been designed to recognise the systemic and gendered aspects of women's experiences? Tracing the challenges and limitations of current protection and intervention efforts reveals that a rethinking and reshaping of the socio-cultural understanding of the concepts of safety and protection for women is necessary. Critical feminist and anti-trafficking scholarship has charted how legal interventions inevitably individualise the problem, wherein responsibility and blame are attributed to an identifiable subject, while failing to acknowledge and account for the role and impact of immigration controls. Of significance here is the way labour laws intersect with migration controls to produce insecurities and risks for transnational migrant subjects, particularly women. And feminist criminological work has highlighted how violence against women is as much a social problem as a legal one. Thus, alongside legal reforms, a rethinking and reshaping of the socio-cultural understanding of the concepts of safety and protection for women is necessary (Mahoney 1991; Snider 1994; Fitz-Gibbon & Maher 2015).

Empirically, this book is aimed at challenging conventional understandings of and responses to women migrant domestic workers' experiences, and this shift in focus requires a different sensibility, one that looks beyond the frames of resistance and legal responses to exploitation and instead centres and prioritises the perspectives, experiences, expectations and everyday security of women migrant domestic workers.

Gendering Human Security

The debate around 'security' has for a long time been predicated upon a top-down, hegemonic framing that privileges the state and state sovereignty (Tripp 2013). The concept of 'human security' represents a paradigmatic shift away from this state-centric focus, to one that privileges individual human beings as the referent object of security. While the concepts and 'range of threats' within the purview of human security are disputed, the core concern is the prioritisation of the protection of human beings from threats to life and dignity over the securitisation of state territory or borders against external military threats (Marhia 2012; Gasper 2013; Tadjbakhsh 2013). These debates on security have primarily emerged from international relations and security studies; however, they have also been increasingly taken up within criminology alongside the changing trends in the criminal justice system. In particular, there has been a shift towards a pre-emptive approach to security that seeks to mitigate the risk of harms before they occur *and* towards the integration of national security agendas (for example, to address the threat of terrorism) into the criminal justice system (see also McCulloch & Pickering 2009; Zedner 2009; Valverde 2010; Walklate et al. 2019). Some scholars have suggested that even though the *language* used to describe security has changed, security defined specifically as 'freedom from interpersonal harms' has long been a core disciplinary concern in criminology (Froestad, Shearing & Van Der Merwe 2015, p. 177). However, criminology has primarily engaged with security as a 'big noun', where the focus is on issues such as the characterisation of a security problem and the implementation of security projects. In this context, institutional actors are often imagined as the primary and most effective providers of 'security' for a society's citizens and residents (Crawford & Hutchinson 2016; Walklate et al. 2019). Yet the security of the state, as many scholars have argued, does not necessarily correlate with the security of all individuals living within that state; rather, the pursuit of state security has consequences that can sometimes be to the detriment of certain groups and communities (Newman 2001; Bellamy & McDonald 2002; Gasper 2013; Walklate et al. 2019). Further, within a state-centric approach, security has very specific connotations based upon state interests, which do not necessarily equate with the protection of all individuals and their interests (Jolly 2013; Tadjbakhsh 2013). For example, the punitive and exclusionary impacts on irregular and temporary migrants produced by migration control and border securitisation practices have been widely documented in the criminological literature on the border (see, for example, Weber 2007).

Where the emphasis is on protecting state interests, economically and socially undesirable migrants fall between the gaps and are expected to cope with a number of insecurities, uncertainties and even inequalities, such as having variable access to healthcare and housing services, limited options for redress and inadequate protection measures (Bosniak 2006; Castles 2010; Bauböck 2011; Tazreiter et al. 2016). Consequently, while the state may be the central provider of security in ideal circumstances, it can also produce insecurity, particularly as the state's responsibility often extends only to its citizens. As established in the Introduction, in the context of migrant domestic labour, state labour migration regulatory frameworks have contributed significantly to maintaining precarious everyday working and living conditions for women migrant workers. The assumption that the state is a protector of women has also been problematised by critical feminist scholars, who argue that the reliance on the 'ungendered' human being as the referent for human security has produced a situation where the everyday security threats posed to women are left largely unacknowledged and unaddressed (Tripp 2013; Walklate et al. 2019). Where violence against women is recognised as a security concern, it has typically been conceived as 'isolated' or 'exceptional' events that rupture the fabric of normal life (such as armed conflicts, terrorism, large-scale crises and emergencies), rather than being normalised and embedded in everyday experience (Marhia 2012; True 2012). It is for this reason that some critical feminist scholars have called for a reconceptualisation of human security to privilege context, relationality and individual subjectivities (Hudson 2005; Hoogensen & Stuvøy 2006). Shifting the focus to individuals and foregrounding their lived experiences as the foundation for defining security allows for a recognition and interrogation of the role of states and structures in producing and reinforcing insecurities (McDonald 2002; Crawford & Hutchinson 2016; Walklate et al. 2019). As discussed in the following section, bringing to the fore the human dimensions of migratory controls and liminal citizenship as experienced by various actors, particularly those from marginalised groups, creates new empirical and theoretical spaces for examining how social and power relations are reproduced and sustained.

The concept of human security further lends itself to the concerns of critical feminist research because it offers possibilities for conceptualising human experiences and the (re)production of (in)securities in relation to systemic frameworks and global governance structures (Hudson 2005; Gasper 2013). The need to incorporate a structural analysis is especially pertinent for this research as the migration and domestic labour scholarship has consistently demonstrated how exclusionary labour and migration laws, gendered power relations and ethnic hierarchies converge to produce a labour migration regime that renders women migrant workers structurally vulnerable to exploitation (Anderson 2010; Rodgers 2016; Baas 2017; Elias 2018). Legal admission into state territory does not automatically translate into individual security and protection, nor does it preclude migrant women from being perceived and managed as 'risky subjects' who are necessary yet socially undesirable (Elias 2018; Constable 2019). Instead, labour migration policies that maintain their low-skilled and permanently temporary status have resulted in a lack of substantive protections for women migrant domestic workers and thereby compromised their safety. To understand women migrant workers' experiences and how these women ensure their own safety, a human security framework that is sufficiently broad to consider the structural contexts and systematic patterns of (in)securities is thus necessary. This broader, more fluid understanding of human security also encompasses the messier and subtler lived realities of migrant workers (Schuilenburg, van Steden & Breuil 2014; Gasper & Sinatti 2016; Tazreiter et al. 2016). My use of a broad approach is not meant to generate abstract or unworkable conceptualisations of threat (Tadjbakhsh 2013); rather, this choice is based on the need to acknowledge these interlocking effects of relational and structural factors that shape women migrant domestic workers' experiences of (in)securities in the domestic workplace (as discussed in Chapter 2). While there may be value in narrowing and hierarchising insecurities and threats so as to develop practical solutions, such a perspective imagines threats as something exceptional that emerges from outside and beyond our normal, everyday life, which fails to acknowledge the interconnections and continuities between public and private forms of violence. As Tadjbakhsh (2013, p. 46) notes, 'to hierarchize and prioritize among human insecurities may be a futile exercise, as threats are interdependent and the eradication of any one of them in isolation is of little effect'. For women migrant domestic workers, security is indeed associated with the extent to which their legal status classifies them as 'real' workers who are fully protected by labour laws and entitlements. Yet, as discussed in Chapter 2, the determinants and women's perceptions of security and insecurity are also associated with emotive and subjective factors within the domestic workplace. Only by developing a contextualised understanding of workers' assessment of risk and efforts to ensure their own safety that is based on individual experiences can we adopt more appropriate and effective responses that genuinely address people's needs and help them obtain security in their day-to-day work (Jolly 2013; Tripp 2013). A critical part of this process is the shift away from the ungendered human being as the primary referent for human security to instead centre gender in our theoretical and empirical engagement with security.

Feminist scholars argue that to account for women's realities, we first need to recognise that security and insecurity are differentially experienced by men and women, which challenges the presumption of universality and neutrality that underpins the mainstream security and justice frameworks (Hudson 2005; Hoogensen & Stuvøy 2006; Tripp 2013; Truong, Gasper & Handmaker 2014). To be sure, human security should be for everyone. However, the failure to account for gender differences and what security looks like for women has meant that there is only a partial understanding of security issues and concerns as experienced by women (Hudson 2005; Tripp 2013). And this failure has led to a sidelining and normalisation of the violence and insecurities that women face (Tripp 2013). For example, domestic and sexual violence, which have been identified as having a substantial impact on the everyday security of women, are not recognised as 'security' concerns (Walklate et al. 2019). In undertaking a gendered analysis, one of the objectives is to address women's invisibility and bring attention to how women's security needs and experiences of violence have often been overlooked because the underlying expectations and parameters of security have not traditionally accounted for, or considered the realities of women's lives (Hoogensen & Rottem 2004; Hudson 2005; Walklate et al. 2019). Analysing human security through a gendered lens opens up different framings and emphases, particularly in relation to other axes of power and differentiation (along the lines of race, class, disability and migration status, among others). As Blanchard (2003) notes a gendered analysis is not simply about adding women into the equation, rather it requires a fundamental re-evaluation of the relationships of power that structure our societies. To problematise what is recognised as a security issue and what is not, we need first to identify which power relations and structures determine what is accepted as normal, important and valuable. In asking '*who* decides what is human security?', gendered analyses have shown that the hierarchisation and prioritisation of securities and threats is often based on men's perceptions and understandings, without fully appreciating the linkages between 'macro' and traditionally conceived forms of conflict and violence and 'micro' forms of interpersonal violence that occur 'in private' and most often impact women (Hoogensen & Rottem 2004; Hudson 2005; Tripp 2013). A gendered perspective allows for, as Hoogensen and Stuvøy (2006, p. 225) explain, 'an articulation of security and insecurity from the relational and power positions of various identities'. By drawing upon women's life experiences, the feminist rethinking of human security reveals the complexities of lived experiences and perspectives that inform women's diverse securities (Hoogensen & Rottem 2004). In doing so, it highlights the role of existing political, economic, social and cultural systems in creating and reproducing insecurity for women through structures such as the gendered division of labour; the devaluation of work in the home; unequal access to resources, services and opportunities; and the designation of domestic (and sexual) violence as a 'private' issue (Hudson 2005; Hoogensen & Stuvøy 2006; Tripp 2013; Truong, Gasper & Handmaker 2014). For the concept of human security to be of utility to women (and other marginalised groups), then, it must account for the social relations and structural challenges these groups face, in line with Hudson's (2005) call. It is thus imperative to recognise how security for individuals and groups is context specific and structurally dependent. Without acknowledging or responding to context, we cannot fully comprehend how women generate conceptions and perceptions of security (Hoogensen & Stuvøy 2006; Tripp 2013). The present research responds to this call by examining women migrant domestic workers' security against the background of national labour and migration laws and regulations and gender-based inequalities, including their insecure citizenship in the destination country and the gendering of the household, which strongly influences the legitimacy of behaviours, expectations and norms in defining women migrant workers' work and working conditions.

However, the work of intersectional theorists reminds us of the risks of invoking 'women' as a homogenous or incontestable category. Their analysis illuminates how gender is not the only identity factor relevant to the individual and collective security of women (Crenshaw 1989; Hudson 2005; Ham 2017). While assumptions of gender neutrality serve to conceal the gendered structures that privilege masculinity, the assumption of gendered universality can essentialise women's experiences and disregard how the crosscutting of power relations can situate some women in more privileged positions than others (Hudson 2005; Ferree 2013). Drawing on concepts from intersectional theory, both Hudson (2005) and Ferree (2013) have argued against the false binary of secure oppressor/insecure victim based on gender identity, which erases relationality. Individuals occupy multiple social locations so, accordingly, a human security approach needs to be concerned with the complexity of relationships and how they inflect different axes of inequality, including those based on gender, race, class, generation, ethnicity, nationality and sexuality, among others. For example, a woman migrant domestic worker performs domestic and care work similar to that performed by a mother or a wife, and therefore women from both categories experience a routine and gendered devaluation of their labour as a result of the gendered norms and expectations around women's work in the home. At the same time, workers' day-to-day performance of labour is further intertwined with macro structures related to the economy and migration control in ways that produce vastly different insecurities for workers compared to their female employers. Recognition of the heterogeneity of lives and experiences is particularly pertinent in the context of low-wage female labour migration, where the confluence of gender, class and nationality shapes women migrant workers' experiences of discrimination, non-belonging, resilience and resistance (Truong, Gasper & Handmaker 2014). As detailed above, the legal and regulatory frameworks in Singapore and Hong Kong are inadequate for addressing women migrant domestic workers' needs, as they both adopt a narrow legalistic understanding of exploitation and abuse, without recognising workers' individual and collective identities of gender, worker and primary breadwinner, and the relationships between and within these identity categories. Examining the intersections between live-in domestic worker, liminal resident, primary breadwinner and human security allows for a deeper understanding of the relations of power and dependency that impact these workers, and how this constrains a worker's capacity to ensure their own security via formal mechanisms. The application of an intersectional perspective thus offers a useful framework with which to contextualise women migrant workers' nuanced experiences. For instance, to understand how women migrant domestic workers gauge and negotiate their safety and security in the domestic workspace requires an analysis of how gender intersects with discursive constructions of their work and skills; the legislation regarding their entitlements, employment and residency rights; *and* their relationships with their employers (Chin 1998; Agustín 2003; Anderson 2016). However, since the argument is that an intersectional, gendered perspective recognises the power dynamics and (in)securities inherent to the employment relationship, it follows that the security of women migrant domestic workers cannot be defined by dominant (state) institutions. Instead, understanding of women migrant workers' security must be based on foregrounding their voices and making visible their experiences of power and agency in the everyday workplace, as discussed in the following section.

Human Security 'from Below': Drawing on Everyday Experience

Inspired by Crawford and Hutchinson's (2016) analytic approach, everyday human security provides the conceptual foundation for this book, where 'everyday security' is understood as the lived realities and practices of security experienced by individuals. By speaking in terms of everyday experience, this research is concerned with the 'wide variety of practices, subjects, relations [and] things that usually would not feature in political analysis' (Guillaume & Huysmans 2019, p. 285), as well as employment practices and standards that are not exceptional or unusual. Crawford and Hutchinson have joined a growing number of security scholars and criminologists calling for an examination of how security governance and practices are experienced by individuals and groups 'on the ground' (see Newman 2010; Tadjbakhsh 2013; Walklate & Mythen 2016; Walklate et al. 2019; Quirk, Robinson & Thibos 2020). This is echoed in recent anti-trafficking and modern slavery scholarship that highlights the need for a shift away from established conventions of human trafficking, modern slavery and labour exploitation as these systems have tended to essentialise workers' experiences into reductive binaries of exploitation/not exploitation (Parry-Davies 2020; Quirk, Robinson & Thibos 2020). In failing to challenge the status quo, the everyday nature of the exploitation and insecurities experienced by migrant workers, and the systems that enable this insecurity and exploitation, are normalised and obscured, as is migrant workers' everyday expertise that enables them to de-escalate, evade conflict and attain safety (Parry-Davies 2020; Quirk, Robinson & Thibos 2020). Focusing the analysis on the everyday allows us to make visible how (in)security is experienced, while also providing a crucial vantage point from which to understand how individuals and groups manage and enable their own security. As Crawford and Hutchinson (2016, p. 1189) explain, the value of deploying a notion of the 'everyday' within analyses of human security is in the capacity to attend to the 'normal, regularised and prevailing nature of insecurity for some people in particular environments, while also forcing us to consider the shared and potentially progressive dimensions of the "mundane" and the "routine"'. This approach also reveals the wide variety of practices, relations and experiences that are a regular yet unnoticed part of larger socioeconomic and regulatory structures (Quirk, Robinson & Thibos 2020).

An everyday security approach, in tandem with a critical feminist lens, offers a potentially powerful tool for correcting the tendency to frame acts of violence against women as 'spectacular' or as crisis points, and acknowledges that for many women in economically advanced and politically stable countries, security is about trying to ensure safety for themselves, while living with the routine gendered 'struggles' of everyday life. In this regard, the everyday security framework lends itself to criminological and migrant labour scholarship as well as critical feminist research and methodologies in that it can unpack how structural gender inequalities impact the everyday experiences and realities of women migrant workers (Nussbaum 2005; Robinson 2011; Walklate et al. 2019). An everyday security framework can also interrogate the labour rights issues that these workers face, by bringing forth how various sociocultural and regulatory structures determine women migrant domestic workers' experiences. Previous research on domestic labour has largely focused on women migrant domestic workers' responses to exploitative employment, either via organised collective action or private, individual forms of resistance. There is considerably less discussion of how these workers create and sustain security for themselves in the day-to-day domestic workspace, beyond their responses to isolated incidents. Yet, as Ferree (2013, p. 295) points out, security is not defined purely in terms of the absence or presence of violence. It is not only about the identification and recognition of threats. It is also related to the creation of secure spaces in which people can ensure their own security. For marginalised groups, their lived experiences are characterised by a daily negotiation of security (Cochrane 2016). Exploring the interplay between context and workers' perspectives and negotiations can help us to understand what 'safe work' looks like for women migrant domestic workers, and the security that they are trying to build while negotiating their work conditions

At the same time, the everyday security framework provides an opportunity for criminologists (and this study) to develop a more 'positive' frame of thinking about safety and security, beyond the current dominance of control- and risk-oriented approaches to insecurity and crime, which emphasise mechanisms of punishment (Schuilenburg, van Steden & Breuil 2014). As Schuilenburg, van Steden and Breuil (2014, p. 12) rightly argue, 'governing through crime cannot make us more secure'. Instead, there is a need to consider *what more* is required to support women migrant workers in their efforts to secure and sustain their own safety while living and working within an insecure domestic workplace. Recent scholarship on gender violence similarly suggests that for women in abusive relationships, filing formal reports and seeking legal justice or state support is not often considered by these women to be a viable option for securing their safety or that of their children (Johnson & Conners 2018; Mirza 2018; Walklate 2018). Rather, studies demonstrate that women's decision-making in relation to their safety is a situated and iterative process whereby they must grapple with and negotiate their safety through forms of resistance that are achievable and conceivable at particular times in their life. For example, remaining in an abusive relationship may significantly increase their vulnerability to further harms and attacks. Yet, given the available options, the circumstances of the abuse and other structural or cultural constraints, staying and managing the situation is, for some women, the most viable option for ensuring their safety and security (Mirza 2018). Utilising the everyday security framework thus presents an opportunity to examine the nuances of action and non-action by women migrant domestic workers across different situations, which supports a more inclusive and grounded understanding of how these women attain security in the workplace, even if in complex and sometimes contradictory ways. Paying attention to women's accounts of how they assess their options, resources and limitations is of vital importance (Maher & Segrave 2018; Maher et al. 2018; Mirza 2018). It offers insight into how women's lives and choices are differentially informed by both socio-structural factors and the 'everydayness' of ordinary fears, risks and threats. Emphasising the everyday experience places the interactions and relations between individuals and systems centre stage and recognises emotions as key to experiences of security and to the practices in which people engage to manage their safety (Crawford & Hutchinson 2016). As discussed in Chapter 2, the formation of fictive kinship and emotional attachments is a valued aspect of domestic workers' employment experiences, suggesting that it may play a part in shaping their everyday security (see Anderson 2016; Chiu 2018). Yet the affective and emotive dimensions of women migrant domestic workers' experiences of security are not well understood. Questions therefore also need to be asked about how fictive kinship and emotional attachments impact upon their everyday security practices.

Conclusion

Understandings of exploitation and exploitative employment practices are primarily located in and defined by the broader structures of economic, legal and regulatory systems. The conceptual framework of everyday human security offers an opportunity to broaden discussion about the perspectives, subjectivities and experiences of women migrant domestic workers. In shifting the lens of analysis to 'everyday security', we can challenge rigid ideas of acceptable and unacceptable employment conditions that remain closely tied to legal and criminal justice systems yet have been found to be deficient in accounting for the structural inequalities and gendered realities that shape the lives of these workers. The focus on everyday experience offers a platform from which to 'reveal the sutures that bind the local with the global, the private, with the public in the sphere of labour' (Elias & Rai 2019, p. 207). To do so, Crawford and Hutchinson's (2016) conceptualisation of everyday security is employed for this research, to draw attention to: (1) the normal and regularised risks and threats that are commonly overlooked, downplayed or neglected by state-centric agendas; (2) the everyday security practices through which women migrant domestic workers and their employers seek to ensure their welfare and safety, beyond formal state processes or official authorities; and (3) the contradictory consequences and tensions stemming from migratory controls.

Notes

1 The ILO defines 'decent work' as work that is 'productive, delivers a fair income with security and social protection, safeguards basic rights, offers equality of opportunity and treatment, prospects for personal development and the chance for recognition and to have your voice heard.'
2 It is reported that officers are 'trained to look out for non-verbal cues that could point to violations or unfair working conditions the ministry would then follow up on' (Menon 2021). However, no further information has been provided about implementation efforts or effectiveness of this measure.
3 As of March 2022, only 35 countries have ratified the Convention.

References

Agustín, L (2003), 'Forget victimization: Granting agency to migrants', *Development*, 46(3): 30–39.

Albin, E & Mantouvalou, V (2012), 'The ILO Convention on domestic workers: From the shadows to the light', *Industrial Law Journal*, 41(1): 67–78.

Amnesty International (2013), *Exploited for Profit, Failed by Governments: Indonesian Migrant Domestic Workers Trafficked to Hong Kong*, Amnesty International Ltd., London.

Anderson, B (2007), 'Motherhood, apple pie and slavery: Reflections on trafficking debates', *Centre on Migration, Policy and Society, Working Paper*, no. 48.

Anderson, B (2010), 'Migration, immigration controls and the fashioning of precarious workers', *Work, Employment and Society*, 24(2): 300–317.

Anderson, B (2016), *Worker, helper, auntie, maid?: Working conditions and attitudes experienced by migrant domestic workers in Thailand and Malaysia*, International Labour Organisation, Asia Pacific, <https://www.ilo.org/wcmsp5/groups/public/---asia/---ro-bangkok/---sro-bangkok/documents/publication/wcms_537808.pdf>.

Anderson, B & Rogaly, B (2005), 'Forced labour and migration to the UK, Trades Union Congress', London, <http://www.ituc-csi.org/IMG/pdf/Forced_labour_in_UK_12-2009.pdf>.

Anthias, F & Yuval-Davis, N (1992), *Racialized Boundaries: Race, Nation, Gender, Colour and Class and the Anti-Racist Struggle*, Routledge, London.

Baas, M (2017), 'Temporary labour migration', in G Liu-Farrer & BSA Yeoh (eds.), *Routledge Handbook of Asian Migrations*, Routledge, New York, pp. 51–63.

Bailey, KD (2011), 'Lost in translation: Domestic violence, "the personal is political," and the criminal justice system', *The Journal of Criminal Law & Criminology*, 100(4): 1255–1300.

Bauböck, R (2011), 'Temporary migrants, partial citizenship and hypermigration', *Critical Review of International Social and Political Philosophy*, 14(5): 665–693.

Bellamy, AJ & McDonald, M (2002), '"The utility of human security": Which humans? What security? A reply to Thomas & Tow', *Security Dialogue*, 33(3): 373–377.

Bhabha, J (2015), 'Looking back, looking forward: The UN Trafficking Protocol at fifteen', *Anti-Trafficking Review*, 4: 3–13.

Blackett, A (2012), 'The decent work for domestic workers convention and recommendation, 2011', *American Journal of International Law*, 106(4): 778–794.

Blackett, A (2019), *Everyday Transgressions: Domestic Workers' Transnational Challenge to International Labor Law*, Cornell University Press, Ithaca.

Blanchard, EM (2003), 'Gender, international relations, and the development of feminist security theory', *Signs*, 28(4): 1289–1312.

Boris, E & Fish, JN (2014), '"Slaves no more": Making global labor standards for domestic workers', *Feminist Studies*, 40(2): 411–443.

Bosniak, L (2006), *The Citizen and the Alien: Dilemmas of Contemporary Membership*, Princeton University Press, New Jersey.

Briones, L (2008), 'Beyond trafficking, agency and rights: A capabilities perspective on Filipina experiences of domestic work in Paris and Hong Kong', *Wagadu*, 5: 49–72.

Carter, K & Aulette, J (2016), 'The domestic workers convention is not enough: A postcolonial feminist view of Ethiopian and Filipino domestic workers in Iraqi Kurdistan', *A Journal of Women Studies*, 37(3): 175–203.

Castles, S (2010), 'Understanding global migration: A social transformation perspective', *Journal of Ethnic and Migration Studies*, 36(10): 1565–1586.

Chan, T (2014), 'Forced labour laws in Hong Kong: A comparative analysis', *Journal of Law, Technology and Public Policy*, 1(1): 87–114.

Chang, AS (2018), 'Producing the self-regulating subject: Liberal protection in Indonesia's migration infrastructure', *Pacific Affairs*, 91(4): 695–716.

Chapkis, W (2003), 'Trafficking, migration, and the law: Protecting innocents, punishing immigrants', *Gender and Society*, 17(6): 923–937.

Chin, BN (1998), *In Service and Servitude: Foreign Domestic Workers and the Malaysian "Modernity" Project*, Columbia University Press, New York.

Chiu, MYL (2018), 'Familization of Indonesian domestic workers in Singapore', in R Ogawa, RKH Chan, AS Oishi & LR Wang (eds.), *Gender, Care and Migration in East Asia*, Palgrave Macmillan, Singapore, pp. 97–116.

Clarke, L (2013), 'Behind closed doors: Trafficking into domestic servitude in Singapore', *The Equal Rights Review*, 10: 33–58.

Cochrane, B (2016), Migrant motherhood project: Search for an everyday security, PhD thesis, Monash University, Melbourne.

Coghlan, D & Wylie, G (2011), 'Defining trafficking/denying justice? Forced labour in Ireland and the consequences of trafficking discourse', *Journal of Ethnic and Migration Studies*, 37(9): 1513–1526.

Coker, D (2001), 'Crime control and feminist law reform in domestic violence law: A critical review', *Buffalo Criminal Law Review*, 4(2): 801–860.

Constable, N (2009), 'Migrant workers and the many states of protest in Hong Kong', *Critical Asian Studies*, 41(1): 143–164.

Constable, N (2014), *Born Out of Place*, University of California Press, California.

Constable, N (2019), 'Tales of two cities: Legislating pregnancy and marriage among foreign domestic workers in Singapore and Hong Kong', *Journal of Ethnic and Migration Studies*, 10.1080/1369183X.2019.1592403.

Crawford, A & Hutchinson, S (2016), 'Mapping the contours of 'everyday security': Time, space and emotion', *British Journal of Criminology*, 56(6): 1184–1202.

Crenshaw, K (1989), 'Demarginalizing the Intersection of Race and Sex: A Black feminist critique of antidiscrimination doctrine, feminist theory and antiracist politics', *University of Chicago Legal Forum*, 1(8): 139–167.

Davies, J & Davies, B (2008), 'How to use a trafficked woman. The alliance between political and criminal trafficking organisations', *Recherches Sociologiques et Anthropologiques*, 39(1): 117–135.

Demetriou, D (2015), ''Tied visas' and inadequate labour protections: A formula for abuse and exploitation of migrant domestic workers in the United Kingdom', *Anti-Trafficking Review*, 5: 69–88.

Devasahayam, TW (2010), 'Placement and/or protection? Singapore's labour policies and practices for temporary women migrant workers', *Journal of the Asia Pacific Economy*, 15(1): 45–58.

Dobash, RE & Dobash, RP (1992), *Women, Violence and Social Change*, Routledge, London.

Douglas, H (2012), 'Battered women's experiences of the criminal justice system: Decentring the law', *Feminist Legal Studies*, 20(2): 121–134.

Elias, J (2018), 'Governing domestic worker migration in Southeast Asia: Public-private partnerships, regulatory grey zones and the household', *Journal of Contemporary Asia*, 48(2): 278–300.

Elias, J & Rai SM (2019), 'Feminist everyday political economy: Space, time and violence', *Review of International Studies*, 45(2): 201–220.

Ferree, MM (2013), 'The discursive politics of gendering human security: Beyond the binaries', in A Tripp, MM Ferree & C Ewig (eds.), *Gender, Violence and Human Security*, New York University Press, New York, pp. 285–308.

Fitz-Gibbon, K & Maher, JM (2015), 'Feminist challenges to the constraints of law: Donning uncomfortable robes?', *Feminist Legal Studies*, 23(3): 253–271.

Fitzpatrick, J & Katrina RK (1998), 'Gendered aspects of migration: Law and the female migrant', *Hastings International & Competition Law Review*, 22: 47–112.

Froestad, J, Shearing, C & Van Der Merwe, M (2015), 'Criminology: Reimagining security', in P Bourbeau (ed.), *Security: Dialogue across Disciplines*, Cambridge University Press, Cambridge, pp. 177–195.

Fudge, J (2014), 'Feminist reflections on the scope of labour law: Domestic work, social reproduction and jurisdiction', *Feminist Legal Studies*, 22(1): 1–23.

Fudge, J & Mundlak, G (forthcoming), 'Law and gendered labour market segmentation', *International Labour Review*, 10.1111/ilr/12339.

Fudge, J & Strauss, K (2014), 'Migrants, unfree labour, and the legal construction of domestic servitude: Migrant domestic workers in the United Kingdom', in P Kotiswaran (ed.), *Revisiting the Law and Governance of Trafficking, Forced Labour and Modern Slavery*, Cambridge University Press, Cambridge, pp. 524–555.

Gallagher, A (2015), 'Two cheers for the trafficking protocol', *Anti-trafficking Review*, 4: 14–32.

Gasper, D (2013), 'Human security: From definitions to investigating a discourse', in M Martin & T Owen (eds.), *Routledge Handbook of Human Security*, Routledge, New York, pp. 28–42.

Gasper, D & Sinatti, G (2016), 'Investigating migration within a human security framework', *Revista Migración y Desarrollo*, 14(27): 19–82.

Goodmark, L (2015), ''Law and justice are not always the same': Creating community-based justice forums for people subjected to intimate partner abuse', *Florida State University Law Review*, 42(3): 707–763.

Guevarra, AR (2014), 'Supermaids: The racial branding of global Filipino care labour', in B Anderson & I Shutes (eds.), *Migration and Care Labour: Theory, Policy and Politics*, Palgrave Macmillan, New York, pp. 130–150.

Guillaume, X & Huysmans, J (2019), 'The concept of 'the everyday': Ephemeral politics and the abundance of life', *Cooperation and Conflict*, 54(2): 278–296.

Ham, J (2017), *Sex work, immigration and social difference*, Routledge, London.

Herrera Vivar, MT (2012), 'The right to always wear a smile: Migration policies and the exploitation of domestic workers' labour in Germany', in C van den Anker & I van Liempt (eds.), *Human Rights and Migration: Trafficking for Forced Labour*, Palgrave Macmillan, London, pp. 108–128.

Hoogensen, G & Rottem, SV (2004), 'Gender identity and the subject of security', *Security Dialogue*, 35(2): 155–171.

Hoogensen, G & Stuvøy, K (2006), 'Gender, resistance and human security', *Security Dialogue*, 37(2): 207–228.

Hudson, H (2005), '"Doing" security as though humans matter: A feminist perspective on gender and the politics and human security', *Security Dialogue*, 36(2): 155–174.

International Labour Organization (ILO) (2012), *Facts on decent work*, Geneva.

Jagori, (2012), 'Migration, trafficking and sites of work: Rights and vulnerabilities', in K Kempadoo, J Sanghera & B Pattanaik (eds.), *Trafficking and Prostitution Reconsidered: New Perspectives on Migration, Sex Work and human Rights*, Paradigm Publishers, New York, pp. 159–174.

Johnson, H & Conners, DE (2018), 'Negotiating women's safety: The mandatory charging debate', in K Fitz-Gibbon, S Walklate, J McCulloch & JMM Maher (eds.), *Intimate Partner Violence, Risk and Security: Securing Women's Lives in a Global World*, Routledge, London, pp. 233–250.

Johnson, M & Wilcke, C (2015), 'Caged in and breaking loose: Intimate labor, the state and migrant domestic workers in Saudi Arabia and other Arab countries', in SL Friedman & P Mahdavi (eds.), *Migrant Encounters: Intimate Labor, the State and Mobility across Asia*, University of Pennsylvania Press, Pennsylvania, pp. 135–159.

Jolly, R (2013), 'Security and development: Context specific approaches to human insecurity', in M Martin & T Owen (eds.), *Routledge Handbook of Human Security*, Routledge, London, pp. 139–148.

Justice Centre Hong Kong (2016), *Coming clean – The prevalence of forced labour and trafficking for forced labour amongst migrant domestic workers in Hong Kong*, Justice Centre Hong Kong, Hong Kong.

Kempadoo, K (2012), 'The anti-trafficking juggernaut rolls on', in K Kempadoo, J Sanghera & B Pattanaik (eds.), *Trafficking and Prostitution Reconsidered: New Perspectives on Migration, Sex Work and Human Rights*, Paradigm Publishers, New York, pp. 249–260.

Lan, PC (2006), *Global Cinderellas: Migrant Domestics and Newly Rich Employers in Taiwan*, Duke University Press, Durham.

Lee, M (2021), 'Borders and migrant domestic workers', in L Weber & C Tazreiter (eds.), *Handbook of Migration and Global Justice*, Edward Elgar Publishing, Cheltenham & Northampton, pp. 49–65.

Lewis, R (2004), 'Making justice work: Effective legal interventions for domestic violence', *British Journal of Criminology*, 44(2): 204–244.

Lewis, R, Dobash, RE, Dobash RP & Cavanagh K (2001), 'Law's progressive potential: The value of engagement with the law for domestic violence', *Social Legal Studies*, 10(1): 105–130.

Lobasz, JK (2009), 'Beyond border security: Feminist approaches to human trafficking', *Security Studies*, 18: 319–344.

Lowe, CTL (2007), 'Migrant workers: The excluded 'others' in a globalizing world: The case of Filipino domestic workers in Hong Kong', *3rd Global Conference: Pluralism, Inclusion and Citizenship*, Salzburg, Austria, 16–18 Nov.

Lutz, H (2010), 'Gender in the migratory process', *Journal of Ethnic and Migration Studies*, 36(10): 1647–1663.

Maher, JMM & Segrave, M (2018), 'Family violence risk, migration status and 'vulnerability': Hearing the voices of immigrant women', *Journal of Gender-Based Violence*, 2(3): 503–518.

Maher, JMM, Spivakovsky, C, McCulloch, J, McGowan, J, Beavis, K, Lea, M, Cadwallader, J & Sands, T (2018), *Women, disability and violence: Barriers to accessing justice*, ANROWS Research Report, vol. 2.

Mahoney, M (1991), 'Legal images of battered women: Redefining the issue of separation', *Michigan Law Review*, 90(1): 1–94.

Mantouvalou, V (2012), 'Human rights for precarious workers: The legislative precariousness of domestic labor', *Comparative Labour Law & Policy Journal*, 34(1): 133–165.

Marchetti, S (2018), 'The global governance of paid domestic work: Comparing the impact of ILO Convention No. 189 in Ecuador and India', *Critical Sociology*, 44(7–8): 1191–1205.

Marhia, N (2012), Everyday (In)Security/(Re)securing the everyday: Gender, policing and violence against women in Delhi, PhD thesis, The London School of Economics and Political Science, London.

Marks, E & Olsen, A (2015), 'The role of trade unions in reducing migrant workers' vulnerability to forced labour and human trafficking in the Greater Mekong Subregion', *Anti-trafficking Review*, 5: 111–128.

Marshall, P & Thatun, S (2012), 'Miles away: The trouble with prevention in the Greater Mekong Sub-region', in K Kempadoo, J Sanghera & B Pattaniak (eds.), *Trafficking and Prostitution Reconsidered*, Paradigm Publishers, London, pp. 43–65.

McCulloch, J & Pickering, S (2009), 'Pre-crime and counter-terrorism: Imagining future crime in the war on terror', *British Journal of Criminology*, 49(5): 628–645.

McDonald, M (2002), 'Human security and the construction of security', *Global Society*, 16(3): 277–295.

Menon, M (2021), *Manpower Ministry starts new house visits scheme to check on welfare of maids*, The Straits Times, 26 April, <https://www.straitstimes.com/singapore/manpower-ministry-starts-new-house-visits-scheme-to-check-on-welfare-of-maids>.

Milivojevic, S & Pickering, S (2013), 'Trafficking in people, 20 years on: Sex, migration and crime in the global anti-trafficking discourse and the rise of the 'Global Trafficking Complex', *Current Issues in Criminal Justice*, 25(2): 585–604.

Milivojevic, S & Segrave, M (2012), 'Evaluating responses to human trafficking: A review of international, regional and national counter-trafficking mechanisms', in J Winterdyk, B Perrin & P Reichel (eds.), *Human Trafficking: Exploring the International Nature, Concerns and Complexities* (1st edition), CRC Press, USA, pp. 233–264.

Minaker, JC (2001), 'Evaluating criminal justice responses to intimate abuse through the lens of women's needs', *Canadian Journal of Women and the Law*, 13(2): 74–106.

Mirza, N (2018), 'Reframing agency in abusive contexts: Beyond 'free choice' and 'open resistance', *Journal of Gender-Based Violence*, 2(1): 41–56.

Mullally, S (2015), 'Introduction: Decent work, domestic work: Gendered borders and limits', in S Mullally (eds.), *Care, Migration and Human Rights: Law and Practice*, Routledge, London, pp. 1–10.

Newman, E (2001), 'Human security and constructivism', *International Studies Perspectives*, 2(3): 239–251.

Newman, E (2010), 'Critical human security studies', *Review of International Studies*, 36(1): 77–94.

Nussbaum, MC (2005), 'Women's bodies: Violence, security, capabilities', *Journal of Human Development*, 6(2): 167–183.

Oelz, M (2014), 'The ILO's domestic worker convention and recommendation: A window of opportunity for social justice', *International Labour Review*, 153(1): 143–172.

Palumbo, L & Sciurba, A (2015), 'Vulnerability to forced labour and trafficking: The case of Romanian women in the agricultural sector in Sicily', *Anti-Trafficking Review*, 5: 89–111.

Parreñas, RS & Silvey, R (2017), 'The indentured mobility of migrant domestic workers: The case of Dubai', in P Kotiswaran (ed.), *Revisiting the Law and Governance of Trafficking, Forced Labour and Modern Slavery*, Cambridge University Press, UK, pp. 503–552.

Parreñas, RS & Silvey, AR (2018), 'The precarity of migrant domestic work', *The South Atlantic Quarterly*, 117(2): 430–438.

Parry-Davies, E (2020), 'Modern heroes, modern slaves? Listening to migrant domestic workers' everyday temporalities', *Anti-Trafficking Review*, 15: 63–81.

Paul, AM & Neo, P (2018), 'Am I allowed to be pregnant? Awareness of pregnancy protection laws among migrant domestic workers in Hong Kong', *Journal of Ethnic and Migration Studies*, 44(7): 1195–1213.

Piper, N, Rosewarne, S & Withers, M (2016), 'Redefining a rights-based approach in the context of temporary labour migration in Asia', *UNRISD Working Paper* 11. UNRISD, Switzerland, pp. 1–21.

Pividori, C & Degani, P (2019), 'Reflecting on criminalising male violence against women under human rights and human security discourses: A feminist legal and policy analysis', *Global Jurist*, 19(1): 1–12.

Quirk, J, Robinson, C & Thibos, C (2020), 'Editorial: From exceptional cases to everyday abuses: Labour exploitation in the global economy', *Anti-Trafficking Review*, 15: 1–20.

Raphael, J (2004), 'Rethinking criminal justice responses to intimate partner violence', *Violence Against Women*, 10(11): 1354–1366.

Robinson, F (2011), *The Ethics of Care: A Feminist Approach to Human Security*, Temple University Press, Philadelphia.

Rodgers, L (2016), *Labour Law, Vulnerability and Precarious Work*, Edward Elgar Publishing, Cheltenham.

Romero, M (2018), 'Reflections on globalized care chains and migrant women workers', *Critical Sociology*, 44(7–8): 1179–1189.

Rosewarne, S (2013), 'The ILO's Domestic Worker Convention (C189): Challenging the gendered disadvantage of Asia's foreign domestic workers?', *Global Labour Journal*, 4(1): 1–25.

Schuilenburg, M, van Steden, R & Breuil, BO (2014), 'A critique of security. Towards a positive turn in criminology', in M Schuilenburg, R van Steden & BO Breuil (eds.), *Positive Criminology: Reflections on Care, Belonging and Security*, Eleven International Publishing, The Netherlands, pp. 9–16.

Scott, S (2017), *Labour Exploitation and Work-Based Harm*, Policy Press, Bristol.

Segrave, M (2009), 'Order at the border: The repatriation of victims of trafficking', *Women's Studies International Forum*, 32(4): 251–260.

Segrave, M (2017), '"Exploited and illegal: Unlawful migrant workers in Australia", preliminary findings from the Australian Research Council Discovery Early Career Research Award Research Project', *The Exploitation of Unlawful Migrant Labour: Regulation, Exploitation, Vulnerability*, Monash University, Melbourne.

Segrave, M (2019), 'Theorizing sites and strategies of differential inclusion: Unlawful migrant workers in Australia', *Theoretical Criminology*, 23(2): 194–210.

Segrave M & Powell, R (2015), 'Victimisation, citizenship and gender: Interrogating state responses', in D Wilson & S Ross (eds.), *Crimes, Victims and Policy: International Contexts, Local Experiences*, Palgrave Macmillan, UK, pp. 53–83.

Sharapov, K (2015), 'Traffickers and their victims: Anti-trafficking policy in the United Kingdom', *Critical Sociology*, 43(1): 1–21.

Simeone, L & Piper, N (2021), 'From rights to risk: Labour migration and the securitization of justice', in L Weber & C Tazreiter (eds.), *Handbook of Migration and Global Justice*, Edward Elgar Publishing, Cheltenham & Northampton, pp. 222–240.

Skrivankova, K (2010), 'Between decent work and forced labour: Examining the continuum of exploitation', *Joseph Rowntree Foundation Programme Paper: Forced Labour*, JRF Foundation, York.

Smart, C (1989), *Feminism and the Power of Law*, Routledge, London.

Snider, L (1994), 'Feminism, punishment and the potential of empowerment', *Canadian Journal of Law and Society*, 9(7): 75–104.

Strauss, K & McGrath, S (2017), 'Temporary migration, precarious employment and unfree labour relations: Exploring the 'continuum of exploitation' in Canada's Temporary Foreign Worker Program', *Geoforum*, 78: 199–208.

Stubbs, J (2002), 'Domestic violence and women's safety: Feminist challenges to restorative justice', in H Strang & J Braithwaite (eds.), *Restorative Justice and Family Violence*, Cambridge University Press, Melbourne, pp. 42–61.

Tadjbakhsh, S (2013), 'In defense of the broad view of human security', in M Martin & T Owen (eds.), *Routledge Handbook of Human Security*, Routledge, New York, pp. 43–57.

Tan, EKB (2010), 'Managing female foreign domestic workers in Singapore: Economic, pragmatism, coercive legal regulation or human rights', *Israel Law Journal*, 43: 99–125.

Tazreiter, C, Weber, L, Pickering, S, Segrave, M & McKernan, H (2016), *Fluid Security in the Asia Pacific: Transnational Lives, Human Rights and State Control*, Palgrave Macmillan, London.

Timoshkina, N (2014), 'Human trafficking: Assumption, evidence, responses', *International Journal of Arts & Sciences*, 7(4): 409–421.

Tripp, AM (2013), 'Toward a gender perspective on human security', in AM Tripp, MM Ferree & C Ewig (eds.), *Gender, Violence and Human Security: Critical Feminist Perspectives*, New York University Press, New York, pp. 3–32.

True, J (2012), *The Political Economy of Violence Against Women*, Oxford University Press, New York.

Truong, TD, Gasper, D & Handmaker, J (2014), 'Migration, gender, social justice and human insecurity', in TD Truong, D Gasper, J Handmaker & SI Bergh (eds.), *Migration, Gender and Social Justice: Perspectives on Human Insecurity*, Springer Open, The Hague, pp. 3–26.

Ueno, K (2009), 'Strategies of resistance among Filipina and Indonesian domestic workers in Singapore', *Asian Pacific Migration Journal*, 18(4): 497–517.

Valverde, M (2010), 'Questions of security: A framework for research', *Theoretical Criminology*, 15(1): 3–22.

Velonis, AJ (2016), '"He never did anything you typically think of as abuse": Experiences with violence in controlling and non-controlling relationships in a non-agency sample of women', *Violence Against Women*, 22(9): 1031–1054.

Visel, S (2013), 'Who cares? – The ILO Convention "Decent Work for Decent Workers"', *Transnational Social Review*, 3(2): 229–243.

Walklate, S (2018), 'Reflections on community safety: The ongoing precarity of women's lives', *Crime Prevention and Community Safety*, 20(4): 284–295.

Walklate, S, Fitz-Gibbon, K & McCulloch, J (2018), 'Is more law the answer? Seeking justice for victims of intimate partner violence through the reform of legal categories', *Criminology & Criminal Justice*, 18(1): 115–131.

Walklate, S, McCulloch, J, Fitz-Gibbon, K & Maher, JM (2019), 'Criminology, gender and security in the Australian context: Making women's lives matter', *Theoretical Criminology*, 23(1): 60–77.

Walklate, S & Mythen, G (2016), 'Counterterrorism and the reconstruction of (in)security: Division, dualisms and duplicities', *The British Journal of Criminology*, 56(6): 1107–1124.

Weber, L (2007), 'Policing the virtual border: Punitive pre-emption in Australian offshore migration control', *Social Justice*, 34(2): 77–93.

Weissman, D (2007), 'The personal is political- and economic: Rethinking domestic violence', *Brigham Young University Law Review*, 2(3): 387–450.

Wells, C (2004), 'The impact of feminist thinking on criminal law and justice: Contradiction, complexity, conviction and connection', *Criminal Law Review*, pp. 503–515.

Wonders, N & Jones, L (2021), 'Challenging the borders of difference and inequality: Power in migration as a social movement for global justice', in L Weber & C Tazreiter (eds.), *Handbook of Migration and Global Justice*, Edward Elgar Publishing, Cheltenham & Northampton, pp. 296–313.

Yamanaka, K & Piper, N (2003), 'An introductory overview', *Asian and Pacific Migration Journal*, 12(1-2): 1–19.

Yeoh, BSA, Huang, S & Devasahayam, TW (2004), 'Diasporic subjects in the nation: Foreign domestic workers, the reach of law and civil society in Singapore', *Asian Studies Review*, 28(1): 7–23.

Zedner, L (2009), 'Fixing the future? The pre-emptive turn in criminal justice', in B McSherry, A Norrie & S Bronitt (eds.), *Regulating Deviance: The Redirection of Criminalisation and the Futures of Criminal Law*, Hart Publishing, Portland, pp. 35–58.

Chapter 4

Women Migrant Domestic Workers and the Everyday Home Workplace

Introducing the Woman Migrant Domestic Worker

In this research, a total of 52 women migrant domestic workers were interviewed. These workers represented a diverse range of backgrounds, motivations and experiences. While this research did not set out to have an analytically significant sample from the different countries, efforts were made to contact women from as diverse sources as possible. One methodological limitation to be acknowledged is the lower likelihood of women in breach of their immigration conditions of entry and stay (such as living outside their employer's home, working in more than one household or overstaying of work visas) agreeing to an interview, even with assurances from friends that their disclosures would remain confidential (see Chapter 1 for more details).

The experiences of the workers in this study (and elsewhere) reveal that many women who migrate for domestic labour end up working as live-in migrant domestic workers for years or even decades. As illustrated in Figure 4.1, approximately half of the worker-participants (n = 21) had been working as a migrant domestic worker for at least half a decade at the time of the study. With the exception of two workers, who shared that they would be moving to another employment sector to work in factories (in Taiwan and Malaysia), all of the workers noted that they had no plans to work in a different sector or to return to their country of origin in the near future. The length of time for which some of these women had worked as migrant domestic workers – the longest being 30 years – and the recurrent movement between different countries reflect the long-term temporal and circular nature of migrant domestic labour. Yet, in Singapore and Hong Kong, women migrant domestic workers are classified and regulated as (permanently) *temporary* migrant workers who must renew their visa every two years (Bailey et al. 2002; Boersma 2019). In this regard, the concept of 'permanent temporariness' (Bailey et al. 2002), in contrast to the traditional definition of temporary migrant workers, more accurately captures women's realities, as their migration has taken on a more permanent character but they are still subjected to the disciplinary power that accompanies their temporary status. This power not only shapes their participation

DOI: 10.4324/9781003250364-4

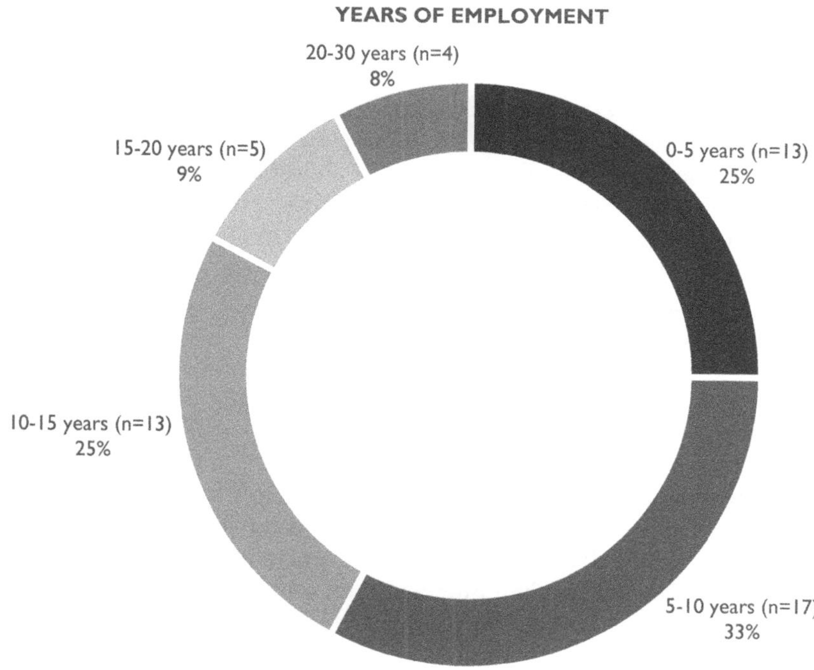

Figure 4.1 Years of employment as a migrant domestic worker.

and inclusion in the host society, but also constrains them in their everyday lives (see also Parreñas 2015; Boersma 2019).

Among the women interviewed, the circumstances that led to their labour migration varied; however, their accounts of why they had decided to find work abroad revealed how economic motivations sat alongside experiences of gender inequality. For example, for some of the women, low educational attainment and labour market segmentation meant that they would be much better remunerated working as a migrant domestic worker than in any job they could secure in their country of origin:

> Because I didn't study high [*laugh*]. But even though [some women] have high degree in Philippines, it is very difficult to get a job. And many high degree [women] they also work as domestic workers. But this [migrant domestic work] is high salary. [*Julia, Filipina, five years in Taiwan, ten years in Singapore*]

While men and women in developing Southeast Asian countries are both affected by the economic displacements arising from global restructuring processes, women are concentrated in 'feminine' sectors, which bear the brunt of funding cuts and have a direct impact on women's economic security (Chang & Ling 2010; Parreñas 2015). For the women interviewed, labour migration into domestic work thus represented a strategy for securing better remuneration, which was particularly attractive as it enabled them to financially support their children and families. Among the 52 workers, close to one-third were married (n = 17), while there were almost as many (n = 14) who were separated from their husbands. For this latter group, separation had meant that they were the sole financial provider for their children, which was a major impetus for their decision to look for work overseas. One such worker was Polly, who had responded to an employment agency's advertisement in the newspaper after the birth of her daughter:

> Why I came to Hong Kong? The reason is my family is broken. I have one daughter and my husband is like a butterfly [promiscuous]. I think ... after I have my daughter and then, in my mind, I am always thinking about my daughter's future and then because when I had my daughter, I didn't have a job because I take care of my husband, like a housewife and then after I had my daughter, I was thinking where I can get the money to support my daughter in the future and then one day I go to the market and I saw the newspaper. They said they have, uh, hire the domestic helper. Then I think, oh, this kind of job [similar to the work I do as a housewife] maybe I can do. [*Polly, Thai, 27 years in Hong Kong*]

Among the workers who identified as single or never married (n = 21), none had children or dependants. However, approximately three-quarters of this group noted that they had familial obligations and allegiances towards their parents, siblings and other relatives. For example, as the only daughter in her family, Jennifer had to fulfil filial responsibilities towards her elderly parents:

> At that time, I just wanted to work in Singapore. The pay in Philippines was too low. I was working as a saleslady. My salary was maybe only 3000 pesos [approximately AUD90] for one month. That's why it is not enough for my family. I have a father and he cannot work already because he is old. And I have a mother, she is sick, she has asthma and if you buy the medicine, the money will lost [be used up]. [*Jennifer, Filipina, two years and eight months in Singapore*]

However, women's migration to sustain and support their families also needs to be understood in the context of traditional gendered ideologies, whereby care responsibilities remain disproportionately imposed on mothers, daughters and wives (Parreñas 2015). For instance, one of the workers, Sascha, confessed that she had not wanted to pursue migration and domestic work but had been pressured by her father to work in Singapore (and later Hong Kong) to support her siblings and their children:

> My father, my family, they asked me to go and work in Singapore and they just asked me to work and work and just keep sending money for them. Actually, I don't want to go and work in Singapore, but then I also thinking I will be free, so I was scared but I was feeling that I can be free to be myself because I get too much pressure inside this family. [*Sascha, Filipina, eight years in Singapore, 18 years in Hong Kong*]

Sascha's situation was complicated in that she was reluctant to undertake labour migration but felt significant pressure to do so, being the sole financial provider for her entire family. Yet doing so had provided her with a measure of freedom and independence from her family. Accessing work to sustain and provide financial support for their families via remittances is recognised as a major reason for women's migration to undertake live-in domestic labour overseas (see Ehrenreich & Hochschild 2002; Parreñas 2015). For the majority of the women in this study, the motivation to support their family was likewise the main motivator. However, many of them also spoke of their complex personal and familial situations (involving family violence and family breakdown, for example) that had motivated them to seek work abroad. For example, Tasha explained that she had initially returned home to Indonesia after working for ten years as a domestic worker in Singapore, and she had not planned to return to Singapore. However, the discovery of her husband's infidelity and the subsequent breakdown of her marriage prompted her to acquiesce to her ex-employer's request to return to her domestic work:

> Because, to be honest, I cannot stay at home because I just divorce with my husband. My husband had an affair with my friend. Sooner or later he will bring back [marry] my friend. Some more, the house is just nearby [to my own house] so how can I stay at home, right? So, I just wanted to run away because I cannot face it. [*Tasha, Indonesian, 17 years in Singapore*]

For another worker, Ellie, the decision to look for employment abroad as a domestic worker was partly motivated by pecuniary gains and also because it represented an opportunity to escape from her abusive ex-husband. Migrating for domestic work allowed her to support herself and her family, while putting some distance between her ex-husband and herself, and thereby securing her safety. Ensuring that her ex-husband would remain far away was her primary motivation in choosing Hong Kong as a destination. Most of her neighbours were working in Singapore, but she perceived this destination as too risky because information of her whereabouts might be disclosed to her ex-husband:

E: The first thing is salary of course, then also because I run away.
S: From your family?
E: No, not from my family. I talked to my family first when I decided to work in Hong Kong. I run away from my ex-husband, that's why. Then I just wanted to go far away from home, far. I wanted to disappear for a while, because I have so many neighbours there [in Singapore], so they [the ex-husband] can maybe contact them or what, so the good choice is Hong Kong because not so many people, not so many friends here. [*Ellie, Indonesian, two years and seven months in Hong Kong*]

The above excerpts reveal that accessing (well-remunerated) work is a major motivation for women's decisions to enter and/or re-enter the domestic labour industry, as it enables them to provide financial support for their children and other family members. However, for some women, the goal and driver of labour migration is not only about work and earning money. It is also seen as an opportunity to overcome gender inequalities, escape gendered violence and ensure their own safety because 'home' is no longer a safe or desirable place to live. Recognising the complex needs and motivations of women migrant domestic workers helps us to understand the concerns and priorities that inform their decision-making processes and responses to unlawful and substandard employment situations.

The Work Destination

Of the 52 workers interviewed in this study, 23 had worked as a migrant domestic worker in more than one country – 14 had worked in both Singapore and Hong Kong, while Taiwan and Malaysia were the next two most common destinations. When asked how they had decided on their destination, given that there are several that prospective workers can choose from, the women talked about the costs of migration, personal security, cultural familiarity and perceived safety of the employment location. For Beatrice, a single mother of three children, Singapore was a more attractive destination than Hong Kong, as the cost of entry is lower and the visa processing time is shorter:

> The process to Singapore is faster than the one to Hong Kong. Singapore can be done in like one or two months. Hong Kong or Taiwan will be like five or seven months. Even though Taiwan and Hong Kong salary is higher, but I am interested to go to Singapore. And I know a bit of English, so I interested to come to Singapore to work. I think maybe easier. [*Beatrice, Indonesian, seven years in Singapore*]

Across the group the key consideration was affordability, including migration costs; however, this was not the only or primary factor determining choice of location. Perceived safety was also very important. For example, even though Malaysia and the Middle East were lower-cost destinations than Hong Kong, Singapore or Taiwan, they were generally considered to be the least desirable destinations for work, as they were too 'scary':

> I don't like to go to these kinds of country because I heard in Malaysia, the law is no protect to the domestic worker. So many domestic workers suffer in Malaysia. Malaysia and Saudi Arabia [domestic workers suffer] the most. [*Kelly, Indonesian, nine years in Singapore, five years in Hong Kong*]

Kelly explained that she eventually decided upon Singapore as her first work destination because her family and friends had told her that 'Singapore is very nice' and so she decided to 'try my luck'. As far as Kelly was concerned, she had sufficient information to support her decision to leave Indonesia, given that other women in her village had spoken highly of the destination. Not all the workers interviewed expressed similar sentiments regarding the safety of Singapore – indeed, it compared poorly against Hong Kong and Taiwan, as employers in Singapore are known to prohibit workers' access to phones and/or external communications. The perception that Hong Kong is a better destination country (that is, where there are more employment benefits and stronger labour protections) was also reflected in the workers' migration trajectories. Specifically, among the women in this study, more had shifted their country of work from Singapore to Hong Kong than vice versa. There were only two workers who had moved from Hong Kong to Singapore, whereas six times as many workers (n = 12) had done the reverse. While this reflects what Paul (2011) terms 'stepwise migration', the majority of women in this research (n = 29) had no plans to relocate to a 'higher-tier' destination, suggesting that their understanding and perceptions of workplace desirability were not just tied to extrinsic or economic rewards.

In the literature, most of the conventional discussion of the causal factors underpinning women's domestic labour migration is focused on economic factors or the changing regimes of care and migration (see also Oishi 2005; Parreñas 2015; Lutz 2016). However, it may be that, in addition to economic considerations, unequal gender relations, experiences of gendered violence, perceptions of safety and legal fairness also influence a worker's decision to migrate and their choice of destination. On the one hand, certain desires were common to all of the workers interviewed; yet on the other hand, the women shared a diverse range of individual aspirations and priorities. These varied contextual realities, which form the backdrop of women's employment and migration trajectories, can have a significant influence on their evaluation of their employment situation (that is, what constitutes good/poor or sustainable/unsustainable conditions) as well as their determination of the most secure option or the response that can best meet their needs and enable their safety. Another significant aspect of a worker's everyday reality and employment experience is their employer. As discussed in Chapter 2, the worker–employer relationship has direct implications for the everyday working and living conditions of women migrant domestic workers. Given that employers' (in)securities *and* practices of security inform the worker–employer relationship as well as the everyday working and living conditions of workers, the following section maps the situation of employers, the circumstances surrounding their employment of a live-in female domestic worker, and their expectations of workers.

Introducing the (Female) Employer

> [At first] it is just to look after my son when he was young, because I need to go to work. In Hong Kong, we don't finish work early, so I need the helper to cook for me as well, to cook for the family. I hired her for six years, everything in my home went well and my son grew up, so I think it is time for a change [of workers] because my mum needed one [a domestic worker]. So, we hired one for her, for eight years. But recently we have another one [a new worker] just hired. Because my mum has the brain degeneration problem and then we need two helpers. Because now you know my mum now, she cannot sleep at night-time. She would not sleep at night-time for one to two days and then one maid could not sleep because she needs to look after her, so they need to share the job. One to look after my mum at night-time and one to look after her in the daytime. So, that is why we hire two. [*Julie, Hong Kong, Employer*]

Julie, a 40-year-old manager living with her husband and two children in Hong Kong, shared her motivations for employing a domestic worker, which were very similar to those of the majority of the ten employers. The motivation to employ a live-in migrant domestic worker revolved around three areas of work: the everyday maintenance and upkeep of the house, caring for children, and eldercare. However, these areas did not appear to be siloed activities. Rather, when I talked to employers and workers, it became apparent that workers very often also clean, cook and wash while they provide care. Motivations can also shift as familial circumstances change. For example, three employers who had decided to keep employing a domestic worker even after their children had grown up, and there were no longer any care responsibilities, explained that they had done so because of the convenience of having another person relieve them of their everyday household responsibilities. As Evelyn described:

> I think it is nice to come home to a clean place and you don't really have to worry about your laundry, your food and everything is clean. It offers us a level of comfort. And you are so used to coming back to a clean place, and one day if we don't hire a [live-in] maid. Then we

> maybe get a part-time maid to come in once a week, but I am very sure it will be very different. You need to get used to different things, and I guess it will bring in a different set of problems. [*Evelyn, Singapore, Employer*]

Notwithstanding this, the interviews with middle- to high-income employers highlighted that the employment of women migrant domestic workers needs to be understood against the institutional design of meeting care needs through the migrant domestic worker program. As discussed in Chapter 1, Singapore and Hong Kong are heavily reliant on the labour of women migrant domestic workers to fill the 'care deficit'; a situation that is exacerbated by a rapidly aging population in both city-states. This delegation of reproductive labour to migrant women from developing economies reflects not just the exploitative transfer of reproductive labour to migrant bodies (Mezzadra & Nielson 2013), but also the persistence of a gender ideology that assigns the responsibilities for the household and the care of dependent relatives to women. As Ava, a 45-year-old civil servant living with her husband and one adult child, told us, she is fully responsible for the governing of the household, including the training of the new worker, organising and delegating of household tasks, and the everyday management and supervision of the worker:

> [When the worker first arrived] I had to teach her. I taught her how to speak Cantonese, how to cook, because she didn't know anything at all. She didn't know anything about cooking Chinese food. I have to teach her how to cook, I have to demonstrate for her because she didn't know at all. Then after demonstrating for the first time, she didn't know, ok, that's fine. But even after teaching her for 10 times, she still didn't know. So, I felt that it was hopeless, no matter how I tried my best, it was useless, so after two months, I told the agent, 'This won't do, I cannot keep her at my place because no matter how I taught her, she couldn't learn'. And some more, my son was very young at that time, and I had to go to work, so she had to bring my son to the kindergarten, right? And she told me she couldn't bring him there because she couldn't recognise the way there. So, I had to take care of her too at that time. [*Ava, Hong Kong, Employer*]

Ava's experience was reflected in the descriptions of many other female employers of their everyday management of their migrant domestic worker. In most households, the absence of the husband in the everyday domestic workplace was marked. Even though it had been a mutual decision to hire a migrant domestic worker, the women were responsible for communicating the household's needs to the worker and instructing them in how to perform various chores. Echoing feminist scholars' observations that waged domestic labour is essentially both a product and a reinforcement of the traditional gender-based division of labour, the findings in this study reaffirm that the domestic sphere continues to be construed as 'women's work', and that women remain primarily responsible for the bulk of housework and childcare responsibilities. The main distinction is that female employers assume an elevated status in 'managing' women migrant domestic workers who complete the menial aspects of domestic labour – a status that Rothman (1989) terms the 'mother-manager'. The situations and factors that lead to the employment of women migrant domestic workers shape employers' requirements and expectations of these workers. For example, most of the female employers (n = 7) expressed their dissatisfaction with their worker's quality of housekeeping, with five employers noting that it was 'not up to their standards'. However, none had terminated a worker's contract because of this issue. Despite their dissatisfaction with the quality of housekeeping, employers were willing to overlook those problems because the main priority was the worker's childcare labour. One such employer is Wendy, a 30-year-old full-time working mother of a two-year-old boy, who shared that:

> I don't have specific rules or timetable for her. I just told her the most important thing is to take care of my child. If you don't have time to do other household chores because you were too busy with my child, I can accept that, it is fine. Because the first thing is taking care of my child, preparing food for him. If there is no time for other housework, just tell me, it is ok. [*Wendy, Hong Kong, Employer*]

Another employer, Julie, echoed the same view – she saw the safety of her son as of foremost importance. Therefore, even though she would have preferred better cooking from the worker, this was not a requirement that she found she had to act upon:

> At that time, he [my son] was about three years old. So, I told her that safety come first. The other things [other household responsibilities], if she did something wrong, I would forgive her, but always put my son's safety first. But other colleagues, they would ask for more. They will ask them to do very well in everything, in cooking. But for me, I would say that I am not that demanding, my family is simple, not too difficult and I did not ask her to cook very well for me. Actually, I would like her to cook much better food for me, but it is okay. [*Julie, Hong Kong, Employer*]

The respective priorities and needs of workers and employers define their attitudes, opinions and actions regarding live-in domestic labour. As the following section details, these contextual circumstances, alongside the overarching structures of migration and labour law, inform the dynamics of worker–employer relationships as well as the working and living conditions of women migrant domestic workers.

Employing a 'Stranger' in the Home: Trust, Surveillance, Control and Respect

Within the feminist scholarship on live-in domestic work, the employment relationship between the employer and the woman migrant is largely characterised as one that is unequivocally exploitative and reflects highly unequal power dynamics (Ibarra 2010; Anderson 2016). As established in the previous chapters, the institutional, legal and policy context is critical in supporting the practices, expectations and attitudes of employers. In particular, the labour migration system in both Singapore and Hong Kong is currently structured so that the everyday responsibility for the care of women migrant domestic workers (that is, providing daily sustenance and medical treatment) is delegated to the employer. Within the context of live-in employment conditions, this produces and reinforces relations of personal dependency whereby workers' bodies become controlled by employers (that is, control over where they are allowed to sleep, how much they are given to eat, what they can wear at work, when they can rest and when they are allowed to go out). This arrangement encourages the misperception that it is acceptable that employers can have full control over workers' bodies and mobilities, including requiring workers to be physically and emotionally available around the clock (Constable 2003; Lan 2006; Paul & Neo 2018). Consequently, feminist scholars have argued that entry into live-in domestic labour comes at significant opportunity costs for women migrant domestic workers as they are expected to be fully available and devoted to the needs of employers, while their personal and emotional relationships are then often neglected or suspended (Blackett 2019; Lim & Paul 2021). In this employment context, employers are often framed as holding absolute authority and power over workers.

Yet this study's findings reveal that it is not accurate to view employers as singular power-holders or assume that they enter the employer–worker relationship with a perception of predetermined control. Inasmuch as individual employers monitor, control and determine the nature of work and the working conditions of women migrant domestic workers, both employers and workers' lived experience of safety and security – specifically, how these are interpreted, managed and enabled – also needs to be understood in relation to the intersection of state structures and relational experiences.

'You Need to Be Able to Trust Her': Building Trust through Surveillance and Control

In Singapore and Hong Kong, the continued reliance on working mothers and wives to perform housework and caregiving duties has produced an environment where it is exceedingly common for middle- to high-income families to purchase domestic and care services from migrant women. However, this does not entail a straightforward purchase of labour services and the delivery of service needs (Anderson 2001; Albin 2012). It also involves the employment (and inclusion) of a relative stranger in the private home to provide intimate and care labour for the family – a job that is predicated on relations of trust (Ruijter, van der Lippe & Raub 2003; Zelizer 2010). Correspondingly, employment expectations are not just based on the worker's competency in completing particular job tasks but are also contingent upon the personal attributes of the worker (Romero 2002; Himmelweit 2007). Indeed, the value of trust, which is often associated with the integrity of the worker, was consistently emphasised by the employers in this study. When asked what they thought was the most important factor in the employment of female migrant domestic workers, all of the employers talked about the need to trust their worker as they cannot monitor her actions or the quality of her work around the clock. As one Hong Kong–based employer, Tammie, explained:

> You need to be able to trust her. If you cannot trust her, you will be thinking that she is lying and then you wouldn't know if that is true or not. Mutual trust is very important. I need to be able to trust her. If you don't trust her, then it is better if you don't use her. If you are suspicious of her all the time, then you have to check on her all the time, it is really very troublesome. [*Tammie, Hong Kong, Employer*]

Yet alongside their focus on trust, the employers in this research had all utilised some measure of surveillance and/or imposed technical control and restrictions on the movement of their workers. As illustrated in Figure 4.2, the

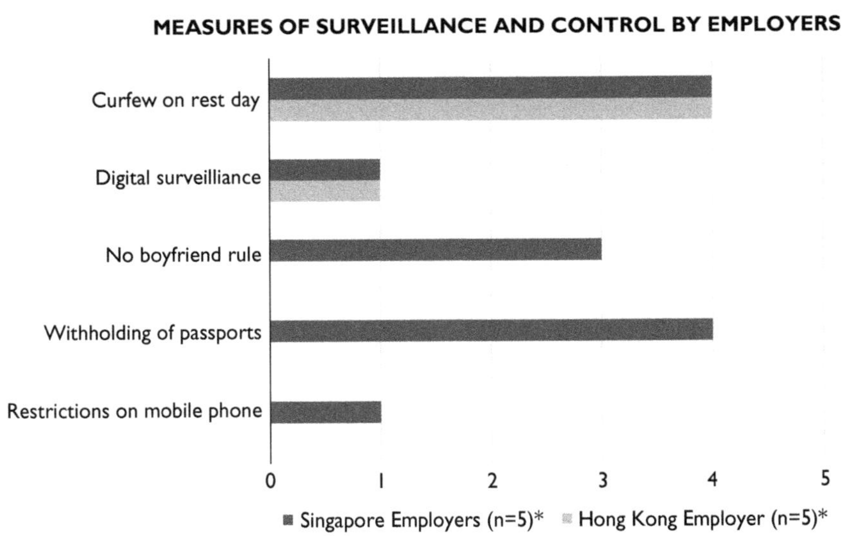

Figure 4.2 Measures of surveillance and control used by employers.

measure most used by employers from both Singapore and Hong Kong was the imposition of a curfew on the worker's rest day (n = 8), and the second-most common was digital surveillance (n = 3). In addition, the Singapore-based employers adopted the practice of holding onto their workers' passports (n = 4), and some had a 'no boyfriend' rule (n = 3).

In explaining their rationale for adopting these practices or rules, employers largely justified their actions in terms of security, specifically, as a necessary measure to safeguard their house and family members. For example, Wendy revealed an acute sense of vulnerability in having to delegate the care of her three-year-old son to a relative stranger:

> I definitely need to install this camera at home because I have no other family members at home. It is only my child and her, so I definitely need to take this safety precaution. I am really scared that ... I don't know what she [the worker] does with my child. My child is still very young, he cannot totally present [articulate] what he has done and his feelings. I just depend on my helper. I have no choice but to trust her. [*Wendy, Hong Kong, Employer*]

In this way, surveillance cameras in the home provided greater confidence to employers such as Wendy, who linked CCTV (closed-circuit television), and the capacity to be made promptly aware of threats, to a general sense of security or peace of mind. In contrast, the two other employers who used surveillance cameras in their homes described it as a mechanism for safeguarding against outsiders, rather than for monitoring or disciplining the everyday behaviour of their workers. One employer, Abigail, explained that she only logs on to the CCTV to look at her dogs when she goes on holiday and has never interfered with what her worker does:

> This house is filled with it [surveillance cameras], and it is to look at the dogs, not at her [the worker]. And she is used to it. In every house that we had, from the car park till the house, there are CCTVs. Honestly, I don't know ... you just have to live with it. These days when you go to the shopping centres and you go to the HDB [public housing] lifts, they have it. As long as you don't install CCTVs in the private spaces like the rooms and all, it is ok. [*Abigail, Singapore, Employer*]

Another employer, Tammie, clarified that she only checked the camera occasionally, when her worker was out of the house:

> All my children are now of school-going age and I am out at work and my helper is out buying groceries, so there is no one at home, so I decided to install the CCTV. Last time I didn't have one. But now, everyone is out of the house, so we are worried that there will be strangers entering. [*Tammie, Hong Kong, Employer*]

Both Abigail and Tammie did not think that the introduction of cameras into the domestic workplace affected or undermined the existing relations of trust they shared with their worker, as they had never confronted their worker over behaviours observed via CCTV. Instead, their everyday approach to and management of the employer–worker relationship remained the same. Yet the workers in this study who were the subjects of surveillance, and were unable to monitor or manage these technologies themselves, expressed feelings of ambivalence that were incongruent with the employers' perceptions.

Of the 52 workers interviewed, six revealed that they were working or had worked in a household where surveillance cameras were used. These six workers had a caring responsibility for the elderly or for young children. Four of these six were told in advance about the use of cameras, while two discovered their employers' use of cameras indirectly, either while cleaning or when the employer asked them about a prior action by the worker observed on the camera. Overall, the majority of the workers said that they preferred employers not to use cameras, as they felt that it conveyed a lack of trust in them:

> That [the use of surveillance cameras in the home] is stressful one. We cannot rest. We need rest also. But if there is CCTV, we never stop. Employers never let us rest. A lot of maids stress because of the CCTV. A lot of maids don't like it, [because it is] like [the employer] never believe us like that. [*Sylvia, Indonesia, 17 years in Singapore*]
>
> I don't like [the use of surveillance cameras in the home]. Because if the camera there means the employer cannot trust you to do anything, right? Like so many eyes look at you. For me, the good employer is she trust me, everything trust me. But bad employer is never trust me. This is a bad thing for me. If you no trust me, you don't take me [don't hire me]. I always say like that. Because we stay in their place and they don't trust us, then we cannot stay, right? You ask me to take care the house, clean and cook, but you put camera in the house inside, for what? Better if you ask the camera to do, right? [*Judy, Indonesian, two years in Singapore, seven years in Hong Kong, one year in Macau, two years in Singapore*[1]]

However, for some of the women, the issue was not only about whether employers trusted them but also about how the cameras had been used to monitor and organise their behaviour. For example, Amanda stated that she was informed that there would be cameras in the home when she signed her employment contract. However, what she did not expect and was dissatisfied with was how her employers used the cameras to monitor and violate her privacy:

> They [the employers] have camera before [I started working for them] already. [During the interview], they told me have one camera but now have a lot more. It [the work] is not so good because have so many

> cameras. Cannot open the telephone, in my room also cannot use because have camera. Even if close the door also employer can see. Even in toilet what I do they can see. [*Amanda, Indonesian, two years in Singapore, seven years in Hong Kong*]

When discussing the use of cameras, Amanda expressed anxiety about the extent of their presence in the domestic workplace and being constantly monitored to the point where she had no private space to which she could retreat and temporarily evade her employer's gaze. She had to be constantly conscious of what she was doing as her employers might be observing her remotely on camera. As a result, for the previous one and a half years, Amanda had been unable to contact her family safely and comfortably on a regular basis. In the case of another worker, Jennifer, her employer did not disclose the use of surveillance cameras and she only realised that she was being watched when her employer confronted her about why she had been resting instead of working on a particular occasion:

> [When I first came here] I didn't know they have CCTV. Then I already in their house, then I know they have CCTV. They didn't tell me. But it doesn't matter to me they have CCTV; I can work, I can work. But then even just sitting down for five minutes because my leg pain, she will see from the CCTV and say, 'What are you doing at the back? You sitting there? Why you not doing work?' 'I am just resting.' 'Why are you resting so long?' [*Jennifer, Filipina, two years and eight months in Singapore*]

This incident made Jennifer feel that she had to work continuously to convey to her employers that she was fully devoted to her duties. In these three cases, surveillance cameras functioned as a disciplinary mechanism that intensified the employers' control over workers' bodies and performance of their labour. This practice of control, which Johnson et al. (2019, p. 8) describe as 'operated through the continuous ambiguity of never knowing when one is being watched, by whom and exactly what one might be called to account for', was regarded by all three workers as a threat to their bodily and social integrity, as they were unable to escape their employer's gaze while in the domestic workplace.

However, the conversation with Jennifer also revealed some of the unintended consequences of the use of surveillance in the domestic space. Specifically, she talked about the cameras as beneficial for her at times, serving as evidence when she was accused of stealing:

> One time, the grandpa's watch was lost. He didn't know where he put because he already old, so he didn't know where he put. They already forget where they put the things, then when I go out on Sunday, she will want to check my bags. But I tell them they can check the CCTV. [*Jennifer, Filipina, two years and eight months in Singapore*]

On the one hand, the use of surveillance cameras can extend the control and power exerted by employers. On the other hand, it can also help to document and evidence workers' employment conditions, which may overcome some of the impediments that women migrant domestic workers encounter when trying to obtain proof of their victimisation in support of labour claims or police reports. Indeed, one of the workers interviewed said that it was she who suggested the use of surveillance cameras to her female employer. Evonne recounted that when her female employer decided to return to work after two years, her employer was concerned about the risks of leaving Evonne with her two-year-old son under no supervision. To prove that she was trustworthy and put her employer's mind at ease, Evonne told her employer that she would be happy with the use of cameras:

> She cannot trust me actually, she worry later like I will bring another guy to the house. I told her, 'If you trust me, just trust me. But if you don't trust me, but you still want me to work with you, you can put camera.' I told her like that. My madam was angry when I said that, but then she put the camera. But I am confident that I won't do it like that [bring a guy to the house], so it is okay. Then I don't know what happened [to the camera] because my madam's brother pulled the wire and it spoilt. But then my madam never put new one. Until now she trusts me because I never do anything. [*Evonne, Indonesian, six years in Singapore*]

Evonne's situation reveals some of the dynamic and fluid aspects of power and security in migrant domestic labour, where a practice traditionally adopted by employers to manage workers and counter perceived risks can in some situations be subverted by women migrant domestic workers to enable, rather than constrain, their everyday safety and security. However, at the same time, it also demonstrates how the burden of soliciting employers' trust and improving workplace relations is primary placed on workers, such that they have to 'make sacrifices' in order to earn their employer's trust, acceptance, respect and recognition. Evonne's situation also highlights the tensions around the concept of 'choice' within the domestic workplace, whereby livelihood security and the corresponding need to earn the employer's trust mean that workers may have to 'choose' to accept conditions they would otherwise consider unacceptable. In the literature, surveillance cameras are largely regarded as a control mechanism that enables employers not only to constantly monitor workers from a distance, but also to interrupt, interfere with and organise the everyday behaviour of workers (Lee, Johnson & McCahill 2018; Johnson et al. 2019; Hierofani 2021). In this respect, the use of digital surveillance is generally viewed as a sign of employers' mistrust, and as a measure that significantly violates workers' rights to privacy and extends existing structures of unequal power relations. Yet the interviews with employers and workers in this research suggest that the camera itself is perhaps not the main issue, but rather the conditions and manner in which it is used.

More broadly, the examination of how employers and workers use and experience surveillance cameras in the everyday workplace points to an important question – how can we reconcile employers' very real and valid perceptions of risk, and at the same time ensure that the measures they adopt to counter their fears do not violate a worker's right to privacy or lead to excessive interference in a worker's behaviour? Addressing this question is especially important since women migrant domestic workers are generally not in a position to influence or stop such household decisions, even though they are directly affected by them. In both Hong Kong and Singapore, the current labour migration framework is still structured in a manner that prioritises employers' interests over workers' rights and fails to account for the power imbalance in employer–worker relations. While Singapore has recommendations regarding the location of CCTVs and employers informing workers of the location of cameras, the general data protection law allows for personal or domestic exemption,[2] and it is not illegal for employers to install surveillance cameras in bedrooms and toilets as there are no privacy laws in the domestic workplace[3] (Kok & Tai 2015; Ng 2018). In Hong Kong, the Office of the Privacy Commissioner for Personal Data (PCPD) has implemented a self-regulatory framework, which emphasises 'best practice' guidelines based upon principles of 'open' and 'fair' monitoring (Office of the Privacy Commissioner for Personal Data 2015). What this means in practice is that the employer has complete authority to decide whether a camera will be installed, where it will be installed and what happens to the images, while the worker has little power to influence such decisions, even if they are impacted or made to feel unsafe or untrustworthy. In the current climate, the only 'real' option for a woman migrant domestic worker is to choose not to work for a household that uses surveillance cameras. However, in situations such as Jennifer's, where the worker realises that she is being subjected to covert surveillance only after the employment contract has been signed, the options for redress are extremely limited. In both city-states, there are formal grievance mechanisms that allow workers to lodge employment complaints, yet the costs and risks associated with accessing these mechanisms make it an untenable option for most women migrant domestic workers. In this regard, much stronger state intervention is required, particularly with respect to recognising women migrant domestic workers as real workers and the home as a workplace where workers' rights to privacy and data protection need to be recognised and respected.

Implications of Labour Migration Policies: Passports, Curfews and Pregnancies

As discussed above, anxieties about familial vulnerabilities arising from having a domestic worker in the home were shared by both the Singapore-based and the Hong Kong–based employers in this study. However, there were clear disparities in the measures taken to mitigate the risks posed by employing women migrant domestic workers *and* in the reasons for such measures as shared by employers from the two city-states. In particular, the biggest disparity relates to the practice of withholding workers' passports and the 'no boyfriend' rule, which in the case of Singapore need to be understood in the context of the security bond requirements to which Singapore-based employers are subjected. Under Singapore's labour regulatory framework, employers are liable to lose their security bond should the following occur:

- Employer or worker violates work permit or security bond conditions.
- Failure to pay worker's salary on time.
- Failure to send worker home when her work permit is expired, revoked or cancelled.
- Failure to account for worker's whereabouts (i.e., worker goes missing).[4]

Employers are discharged from the security bond after the work permit is cancelled and the worker returns to her country of origin. MOM states that the bond is 'between the employer and the Government of Singapore' and is designed 'to ensure that both employers and workers will comply with the conditions of the work permit'. By holding Singapore-based employers legally accountable for the conduct and mobility of their migrant domestic workers, MOM essentially expands the state's locus of migration control by explicitly placing responsibility onto employers to monitor and regulate their workers. This situation aligns with Lan's (2006) description of employers becoming an extension of state power, such that their practices of control over women migrant domestic workers effectively become a mechanism for immigration control. Evident in this research was that, for the employers interviewed, in practice this translated into a range of measures intended to identify and immobilise potential risks via the control of workers both inside and outside the domestic workplace.

Four of the five Singapore-based employers stated that they imposed a curfew during their worker's rest day and held onto their worker's passport, which they justified as a 'safety precaution' for themselves. This was despite the fact that all of the employers were aware that it was unlawful to do so.[5] The following quote from one employer, Sophia, illustrates what many other employers told us – that withholding the worker's passport serves the two functions of deterring workers from running away and safeguarding the employer's interests should the worker run away:

> I would keep the passport, so that they don't run and I don't get fined [under the security bond conditions]. It is just a lot of trouble if they disappear with their passport to another country and you are stuck there, left high and dry. [*Sophia, Singapore, Employer*]

In Singapore, women migrant domestic workers are issued with a work permit card, which is used for identification purposes. Some employers argued that having this form of identification is sufficient for the everyday, which justified the withholding of their workers' passports. While the Singapore-based employers recognised that the act of keeping their worker's passport gave them control over the worker's autonomy and mobility, all four Singaporean employers who engaged in this practice justified it as necessary to protect themselves from workers potentially leaving at any time, which would result in financial and other consequences. The only employer who did not withhold her worker's passport, Evelyn, explained that she did not do so as it would be a breach of labour laws *and* because she had sufficient trust in her worker, who had been with the family for nearly two decades. She did, however, express empathy with employers who keep their worker's passport:

> I understand that, maybe for some [employers], they just needed to be very, very sure that they can fully trust the person, then do that [allow workers to keep their passports]. Because they have to pay the [security] bond money if she [the worker] runs away or becomes pregnant. [*Evelyn, Singapore, Employer*]

The repeated emphasis on 'trust' brings to the fore how women migrant domestic workers negotiate their security in the domestic workplace via relations of trust, rather than through the protections offered by the law. It also highlights the tensions surrounding security in an employment context where employers are made to be responsible for their women migrant domestic workers – an arrangement that entrenches workers' precariousness. Throughout the interviews, most of the Singapore-based employers talked about the risk of having to pay or lose their bond if their worker were to violate work permit or security bond conditions. They claimed that this risk justified their practice of withholding their workers' passports as they have a legal responsibility to monitor and ensure their worker's good behaviour – a situation produced and reinforced by the labour migration system, and which entrenches relations of dependency and employers' paternalistic responsibility (Chin 2019; Constable 2019). For the Singaporean employers, withholding the worker's passport was thus a means to negotiate security and trust in the employer–worker relationship; however, the interviews with the Singapore-based women migrant domestic workers revealed that this practice actually undermined trust and made them feel unsafe. For some of them, not being in possession of their passport was identified as 'not acceptable', as the passport is their personal property and it is against the law for employers to withhold it. Other workers noted the importance of retaining their passport in case they needed help:

> I prefer to keep my own passport. Because I heard that maybe if the passport is with me, I can go back if I don't like. The agency gave my employer my passport, but that time my passport about to expire, then I

> renew and then I didn't give them back my passport because I know the passport is for me. [*Cherry, Filipina, six years in Singapore*]

> For myself, it is better [that I hold onto my passport]. In case I need help, so it is easy for me. [*Molly, Burmese, one year and six months in Singapore*]

Notably, both Cherry and Molly had previously worked for employers who subjected them to a protracted period of exploitative employment. In Molly's case, her employer had been physically abusive; while Cherry's employer had subjected her to unlawful deployment. In this context, for both Molly and Cherry, having possession of their passports and other personal documents represented a security measure to moderate their employers' control over them and maintain a degree of autonomy over their own mobility. However, for Evonne, an Indonesian worker who had a history of taking out loans from illegal moneylenders, her employer's action was appreciated:

> For me, I prefer that my madam hold [my passport]. Because sometimes I am worried about myself because … I can't control myself, I know I cannot do this or that, but it is human nature, cannot tolerate. So, for me it is better like this. Everything I can talk with my madam so I am not worried [that my madam will stop me from going home or use my passport to control me]. I saw in the news a lot also, like employers worried they will run away or use the passport to [borrow money from a] loan shark. I have problem about money, a lot of problems like that so, [for me it is] safer to keep with employer. [*Evonne, Indonesian, six years in Singapore*]

So, for Evonne, having her employers hold onto her passport was not identified as a cause for concern as she enjoyed a good relationship with them. Moreover, she perceived their actions as *helping* her to manage her problem with money, rather than as a means to control her. This perspective was shared by some other workers, who noted that they had no problem with their employers keeping their passports, not because a passport is not an important document but because they felt that this withholding was not used as a form of control:

> I am ok with that because whether me or my employer keep, if I need, I can ask. Because my employers keep all their passports together, so when we go holiday, can all take together. Like last week I wanted to go Batam, I just said [to my employer] I wanted to go Batam, can I take my passport? [And she was given her passport.] So, it doesn't matter for me [who holds my passport]. [*Tasha, Indonesian, 17 years in Singapore*]

The above findings suggest that not all of the workers perceived their employers' practice of withholding their passport as a threat to their safety and security. But, just as clearly, this sense of security seemed to result from the fact that they shared a good relationship with their employers and saw the objectives of their employers as consistent with their own security concerns and needs. Yet the employer–worker relationship, which is mediated and influenced by relations of trust (and predicated on workers' willingness to sacrifice), can be fraught, as it produces a degree of dependence and a lack of control for workers. For some workers, such as Cherry and Molly, past experiences and the relative absence of trust in employment relationships meant that the withholding of passports was identified as a threat to their self-interest and safety as it undermined their control over exit options. The disparities between how different workers perceived the same employment practice highlight the subjective and siloed nature of workers' experiences of risk and security in the domestic workplace. More broadly, they also point to the centrality of the affective dimensions of this workplace context in shaping how workers perceive risks and carry out their own security practices (Crawford & Hutchinson 2016). Acknowledging the emotional dimensions of the processes surrounding the production of (in)security in this work context at the everyday level provides a more nuanced insight into what security and insecurity feel like for women migrant domestic workers, and the factors that shape these perceptions, including the meanings these workers attach to the informal obligations and dependencies between employers and workers. It also helps to explain workers' actions (or inaction) in response to particular employment practices.

However, exploring the experiences of workers who had asked their employer to return their passport revealed that even if these workers disagreed with their employer holding onto their passport, there was little they could do about it. The authority to determine who keeps the worker's passport remains with the employer, despite the legal protections in place:

> Actually, I tried asking [for my passport] already, but the employer not allow. They said, 'Passport and work permit I keep. If you need you ask from me.' So, if I want to send money, I ask from them and they let me. But I can understand because they [the employers] scared the helpers make problem like that. If [the worker] have passport and work permit, can do anything, right? Can go to different places, like Malaysia. But then if [the worker] have problems, the employer also must take care of the helper. If we have the problem, the first call is the employer. The employer also must go if something happens. So, for me, I don't mind, it is ok. They give me [my passport and work permit] is ok, they don't give me, is ok. [*Susie, Indonesian, 15 years in Singapore*]

Critically, this highlights that, in many cases, women migrant domestic workers acquiesce to the demands of their employers. The power imbalance in the domestic workplace translates into workers having limited, if any, leverage to push back or assert their rights because of the potential risks to their employment security. This means that workers may be aware of their rights but may not be able to articulate their demands, even when they disagree with their employer (Anderson 2016; Paul & Neo 2018). While a worker's decision to go along with their employer's demands (and assuage their employer's anxieties) can be understood as a means to negotiate longer-term workplace and employment security, it also reveals how in spite of their inclusion in legal and regulatory frameworks, workers' security is not guaranteed or protected by law. Instead, it is strongly tied to and mediated by workplace relations and employers' sense of security, which are in turn shaped by labour migration regulations. For the Singapore-based employers in this study, relations of trust were not just dependent on the quality of care provided by the worker or the absence of a direct threat to their family's well-being, but were also mediated by the risks produced by the labour migration system. The state-produced threat of financial penalty significantly extends employer (and state) power and control over workers' conditions of stay in the country. The Singapore Government has established a legal and regulatory system governing the domestic workplace that technically guarantees some employment rights and legal security for women migrant domestic workers. However, other features of that system – in particular, those that make employers accountable for workers, such as the tied-visa scheme and security bond – directly undermine those legal protections and contribute to everyday insecurities for these workers.

The intersections between worker security, state regulatory practices and employer practices become even more apparent when we examine the labour migration system in Hong Kong and the responses of the Hong Kong–based employers interviewed in this study. In Hong Kong, the legal responsibilities of an employer for the presence and conduct of their migrant domestic worker are significantly less onerous than those in Singapore.[6] Employers may be punished if they violate their obligations as stated in the Standard Employment Contract, the Employment Ordinance or the Immigration Ordinance; however, there are no legal penalties for employers should the worker breach labour or immigration laws. As Constable (2019, p. 11) explains, 'Hong Kong workers are held responsible for their own actions and government publications mention employers' responsibilities with regard to their own behaviour and treatment of workers, not *for* the worker's behaviour'. Therefore, under Hong Kong's regulatory framework, women migrant domestic workers and employers are regarded as solely responsible and liable for their own actions. In practice, this has translated into some differences in how Hong Kong–based employers treat their domestic workers, particularly in terms of technical control over their mobility and access to external communications.

Unlike the Singaporean employers, all of the Hong Kong–based employers in this study shared that they did not withhold their workers' passports, monitor or restrict their workers' access to mobile phones, or limit their workers' personal relations, and that they considered such practices to be ethically and legally inappropriate (see Figure 4.2):

> I have a friend who keeps her worker's passport, but I didn't do that. I did ask some of my friends and they told me that in Hong Kong, we don't have the right to keep her passport or her personal belongings because in Hong Kong everything is about human rights and freedom. So, if in the contract, if it doesn't specify that we can do this or do that, then I don't want to leave any loose ends for them to use or have risks that allow them to sue us. I am worried about breaking the law like that. [*Wendy, Hong Kong, Employer*]

Echoing Constable's (2019) findings, it was clear in this research that in a labour migration system where there are no security bond liabilities, like Hong Kong, employers do not hold anxieties like those felt by Singapore-based employers about the risk of workers running away, and the withholding of passports (or communication devices) is not seen as enabling financial security. On the contrary, in Hong Kong such measures are considered risky strategies that may increase the possibility of legal repercussions for the employer should the relationship with their worker sour.

Notwithstanding their aversion to some practices of surveillance and control, the Hong Kong–based employers shared similar critical attitudes to those held by Singapore-based employers towards migrant domestic worker pregnancies. In both contexts, employers considered pregnancy to be wholly incompatible with live-in domestic labour as they would have to bear the 'burden' of caring for a worker who is 'unfit' to work:

> During her pregnancy, if she has any problems or feeling unwell or even, miscarriage, then you still have to pay for her medical fees. So, you will be very worried and not sure what will happen during this period. So, of course I will not want her to have boyfriend in case she becomes pregnant. [*Ava, Hong Kong, Employer*]

> If she is pregnant, how can she do my housework for me? She won't be able to do that for me. Because when we go to work, it is a desk job, it is in an office. But in her case, it is different. Physically, she has to mop floors, clean the house. It will affect her ability to work, that is for sure. [*Tammie, Hong Kong, Employer*]

The common view among the employer participants was that the domestic worker 'takes care of my family, not a family of her own and definitely I don't take care of her'. This reflects the implied obligations within this type of employment relationship where the worker is expected to subordinate her needs to those of her employer (Blackett 2019; Lim & Paul 2021). In a 2015 study on female migrant domestic workers who become mothers while working in Hong Kong, Constable (2015, p. 96) observed that employers sought domestic workers who are 'unencumbered by daily responsibilities to their own family members and who can devote themselves to the needs of their employers'. The employers I spoke to hold the same view. This reveals how women migrant domestic workers in Singapore and Hong Kong are reduced to a commodity or unit of labour: they are seen as critical to sustaining (their employer's) family life but are not entitled to have an autonomous life with their own children or family while working. This disregard for the human needs and rights of women migrant domestic workers is largely due to employers' perceived entitlement to workers' bodies and mobilities. Yet this attitude also needs to be understood against existing state priorities and regimes of migration control. In particular, the live-in conditions, which make a clear demarcation between work and private time difficult, also problematically suggest that women migrant domestic workers can and should be available to employers whenever they are needed (Anderson 2016; Blackett 2019; Lim & Paul 2021).

Despite an overall negative attitude towards worker pregnancy, the practices used by employers to discipline and limit the movements and social lives of workers were vastly different in the two city-states. Among some of the Singapore-based employers, the approach was to establish clear rules to manage undesirable behaviour. Abigail described how she would explain to her worker the rules of employment in relation to pregnancy and the consequences for the worker should these rules be violated. She noted that as long as her worker did not breach the rules, the worker could avoid employer interference in her private life:

> I would just remind her about the pregnancy part. Whatever it is that you want to do outside, it is fine, just don't bring it home. That is one [rule]. So, even if you want a day out and you want to do what you want to do, I am fine. But just know that if you get pregnant, I am sorry, I will send you back. You are bearing the consequences of your actions. [*Abigail, Singapore, Employer*]

For Abigail and the majority of the Singapore-based employers, maternity rights were not a matter of importance because the worker would be returned to her country of origin should she fall pregnant. For Zoe, the only employer who maintained a strict 'no boyfriend' rule, this approach was grounded in her personal convictions about premarital sex and dating, which she used to justify and rationalise her intrusion into her worker's privacy, thus viewing herself as a moral guardian: 'There is nobody to watch her. Her family is not here to keep the boundary.' Such moral control and discipline of female migrant domestic workers is, as Lan (2006, p. 166) notes, 'similar to the surveillance from a patriarchal family over the behaviour of a virtuous daughter'. However, in seeking to 'protect' the virtue of the woman migrant domestic worker, the 'no dating' policy blurs the boundaries between the worker's private and professional lives and reinforces the subordinate status of workers in the domestic workplace. Anderson (2016, p. 65) suggests that such an attitude 'overrides any thought of the social and emotional needs of workers'. Thus, even though Zoe euphemised her rules as a form of 'protection', in fact they operated as a form of control to discipline her worker's conduct, even outside work time, especially as the rules were supplemented by threats of termination and repatriation.

Employers imposing their attitudes regarding romantic relationships and pregnancy onto their workers reflects how the livelihood and economic security of women migrant domestic workers are dependent on the gendered performance of the 'respectable woman' who is self-disciplined enough to contain her sexuality and sacrifice her interests for those of her employer's family. Such expectations of respectability and feminine virtue were echoed by the Hong Kong–based employers, although none of them reported prohibiting their workers from forming romantic attachments as this was perceived as either irrelevant (as the worker was married) or 'overly controlling':

> Because employers *can* do that in Singapore. In Hong Kong, we have no right to tell them to do that … even my daughter, I can't tell her to not have a boyfriend, right? You cannot control her. When she goes out, can you control who she goes out with and who she hangs out with? I don't think you can. [*Tammie, Hong Kong, Employer*]

The only Hong Kong–based employer who said that she imposed a curfew for the explicit purpose of minimising the risk of worker pregnancy was Wendy. She explained that she prohibited her worker from staying outside overnight for this reason:

> It is quite risky to allow her [the worker] to stay outside overnight. I don't know who she is going out with and where she is going. Because I am just very worried that she will come back pregnant. If she comes back pregnant, what should we do? [*Wendy, Hong Kong, Employer*]

Wendy's concerns and anxieties were directly related to the legal protections offered under the Maternity Provision of Hong Kong's Employment Ordinance. Under the Maternity Provision, women migrant domestic workers in Hong Kong are afforded the same maternity rights and entitlements as local workers, including the right to legal contestation against wrongful termination (Hong Kong Labour Department 2022). According to the Labour Department (2022, p. 17), an employer who contravenes this provision 'is liable for prosecution and, on conviction, a fine of HKD100,000'. However, these legal protections for women migrant domestic workers were perceived by the majority of the Hong Kong–based employers in this study to be unfair and a source of insecurity for employers. In particular, they complained that the structure of the current law places them in a vulnerable position where their options are very limited:

> The best is if I can just give her compensation because then it gives us both a choice. But then the law now, the employer doesn't have a choice. I cannot fire you because I have no choice. If there is a choice, I can give you compensation, you can go. It is difficult … If she becomes pregnant and you fire her, she is also very poor thing. She is also in a difficult situation if you fire her. So, like myself, I am also an employee, then I also feel that we should have protection, but then should we have more choices for employers? If I have the ability to give her compensation, then I would like to have the choice to give her compensation. I really don't want her to become pregnant because how can she work if she becomes pregnant? She can't do any work. [*Tammie, Hong Kong, Employer*]

> To be fair, others [regulations and laws] I can accept, but for the point about pregnancy I think it can be better. It can be changed to better protect the employer. Why do I want to hire a domestic worker? If she cannot perform her duties, I think this is a breach of contract, so I think I should have the right to terminate. Because I need her to do housework and take care of the house. So, why should I have to turn around to take care of you when you become pregnant? Who is going to help me then? I mean, in this case, I feel that it completely doesn't fulfil my objective of hiring a domestic worker. But then I cannot fire you. I feel that this is an issue in Hong Kong … I just don't understand why is the government unable to protect the rights of employers? [*Wendy, Hong Kong, Employer*]

As Wendy describes, for the Hong Kong–based employers worker pregnancies were not simply an issue of individual reproductive rights. As a result of the labour law, such pregnancies were seen by employers as representing an extremely undesirable financial imposition for them, especially as the employment and upkeep of a migrant domestic worker can be costly, in terms of both money and time. Breaking down the expenditure involved in employing a female migrant domestic worker, Ava explained:

> Some employers will feel that the expenses are too much, because like the air ticket, food, accommodation, everything. It would be like HKD5000 to HKD6000. And agency fees now are too expensive, almost HKD9000. For us, because all three of us are working and have salaries, so it is ok. But maybe not for other families. And if the maid suddenly terminates her contract, then you have to look for a new maid and buy a new insurance, right? Then you need to give new round of agency fees. It is actually quite stressful financially. And under the regulations, if you don't provide food, you need to give them like HKD1000+ of food allowance, which is quite

> a lot I think. Some of the employers I think they really don't have enough money, or their salary is too tight to employ a maid, but then they cannot not employ a maid because it will cost even more to find someone to take care of their child. [*Ava, Hong Kong, Employer*]

Thus, even though the Hong Kong–based employers were not subjected to security bond liabilities, they did face other associated financial and legal burdens, not least because of (1) the lack of clear operational guidelines and systems to support the law (for example, related to how employers should navigate caring for a heavily pregnant domestic worker) and (2) the structural dependency on women migrant domestic workers for everyday domestic labour, which is created by the absence of quality childcare and eldercare options.

Significantly, the Maternity Provision does not necessarily translate into security for women migrant domestic workers. The experiences of the two Hong Kong–based workers interviewed in this study who had become pregnant during the course of their employment reveal that women migrant domestic workers who carry to term are rendered equally if not more insecure by Hong Kong's labour law. In one of these cases, the worker, Sascha, recounted that when she became pregnant during her last employment contract, her employer did not terminate her contract. However, her employer was very unhappy with her and 'in revenge' made her complete physically demanding tasks, such as 'moving the fridge, [and] moving the cupboard', and even prohibited her from leaving the house to attend her pregnancy check-up appointments:

> *S:* At first, she [the employer] is not happy, but then at the end, she offered me that if I want, I can deliver the baby here [in Hong Kong]. But I get so stressful because she made me very hard to work while I am pregnant. She asked me to put the chair to climb up, clean the toilet. And the doctor asked me to go for the check-up, but she didn't allow me to go.
>
> *Siru:* Do you know why she offered to let you deliver in Hong Kong?
>
> *S:* Because even though I am pregnant, I still do my job. I continued to work and before I also have bleeding [during the pregnancy]. But I just tried to tolerate because I want to save up for my baby and I need also to finish the contract [to ensure I would get a good reference]. So I only just ask her to release me ten days before the contract finish. [*Sascha, Filipina, eight years in Singapore, 18 years in Hong Kong*]

Sascha eventually quit of her own accord five months into the pregnancy because she was worried about the risk of miscarriage. Because she had terminated her employment contract ten days before it was due to finish, her employer deducted ten days' worth of wages. Sascha explained that she later found out from her friends that it was unlawful for her employer to have done so:

> [After I asked her to release me] she deducted the 10 days salary. After that I found out from my friends that actually she cannot deduct because I also have the maternity leave and the payment [maternity leave benefits]. But I did not get anything because my employer tricked me. She tricked me because she said she asked in the Hong Kong Labour Department that she is not entitled to pay me for maternity leave. It is just like I believed more to my employer, she is saying that and I trust her so I signed the agreement with her to say that they were not responsible and they will not pay anything. [*Sascha, Filipina, eight years in Singapore, 18 years in Hong Kong*]

Upon learning that she had been entitled to maternity benefits, Sascha, once back in the Philippines, went to the Labour Department to ask whether she could file for financial compensation from her employer. However, she was told that in signing the agreement she had waived her legal right to claim compensation: 'They get angry and they said, it is all your fault, it is your mistake. Why you sign [the agreement]?' Sascha's situation highlights how the labour regulations and processes in Hong Kong do not necessarily translate into genuine physical, legal or financial security for workers. Instead, structural factors such as state regulations that reinforce worker dependency on employers, the limitations of the law and the absence of social security protections combine to produce insecurities for both workers and employers. The above examples also demonstrate how the normative expectations of domestic workers and state apparatuses converge to produce anxieties for employers as well as influence how employers navigate and enable their own security. At the same time, how employers negotiate their security has implications for workers' everyday working and living conditions and can leave workers in a highly insecure position.

Yet the interviews with women migrant domestic workers revealed a diversity of views about employers' practices of control and surveillance. In particular, the range of reactions and interpretations with respect to the routine practices of surveillance and employers withholding workers' passports points to the complex positionalities that determine how workers characterise and understand security. This suggests that for women migrant domestic workers, the meaning and pursuit of safety and security in the domestic workplace is not solely associated with the presence or absence of particular employment practices. Instead, the complex and messy interplay of labour migration law, social relations and norms, and individual employment experiences challenges the binary understanding of power and control that constructs women migrant domestic workers as either actively resisting or being passively victimised by employers.

Conclusion

In both Singapore and Hong Kong, the system of laws and regulations is designed to maintain the temporality of women migrant domestic workers, and employers in the two city-states differentially perceive these labour and migration laws as having a negative impact on their legal and financial security. In turn, the potential risks of employing a woman migrant domestic worker whom employers see as unreliable and/or dishonest are intensified by the legal and regulatory framework, with implications for how employers manage the private/public boundary in their relationship with workers. The interviews with employers revealed that their perspectives and fears of such risks served as justification for their imposition of practices of surveillance and control. Seen in this light, the practices of surveillance and control used by employers can be understood as an extension of state power. What was also apparent is that for employers of live-in migrant domestic workers, there is no clear division between the personal, the private and work. Workers' problems and subjectivities are largely constructed as a threat that might undermine their focus on and commitment to the employer's family and their performance of 'motherly' or 'wifely' duties. Therefore, employers in both city-states adopted subtly different routine practices of security, all of which were premised upon the perceived need to curtail workers' mobilities and employment rights.

Expressing a self-interested need to protect their family members and house, the employers in this study enabled their own security at the expense of domestic workers' employment entitlements, human rights and everyday security. Nonetheless, the everyday lives, experiences and decision-making of employers and workers alike were influenced not only by systemic factors (laws and policies) but also by the relational aspects of domestic and care work. In particular, the emotional aspects of domestic labour are critical in shaping women migrant domestic workers' experiences. And this needs to be recognised and responded to at the institutional level, alongside reform of the laws and regulations that underpin workers' temporariness, disposability and legal precariousness. Notwithstanding the importance of the relational and emotional aspects of waged domestic labour, it is evident that workers have little capacity to demand that their rights be upheld in the face of certain employment practices, as there are significant disincentives for them to do so. This raises questions about the labour protections, rights and equity of access to assistance and support available to women migrant domestic workers. The next chapter examines how women migrant domestic workers enable safe working and living conditions for themselves; and the individual, market and systemic factors that enable or constrain their choices and negotiations, in particular, the labour and migration regulatory framework.

Notes

1 The sequence reflects Judy's migratory movements. She had worked in Singapore for two years before relocating to Hong Kong, and then Macau before deciding to relocate back to Singapore.
2 Anything the home-owner does in terms of the collection of personal data such as CCTV images in a personal or domestic context does not need to comply with the general data protection law (Ng 2018).
3 If surveillance cameras are in areas where the workers undress, it could constitute an outrage of modesty, and employers will be referred to the police. However, this is dependent on workers coming forward to file a complaint of intrusion of privacy, which is 'very rare' according to MOM (Kok & Tai 2015).
4 Employers are required to file a missing person police report and cancel their worker's work permit within one week if the worker goes missing. Failure to find the worker within one month from the cancellation of their work permit will result in forfeiture of half of the security bond (i.e., SGD2500) to cover repatriation and other related costs.
5 On the MOM website (last updated 2021), employers are reminded that under the Passports Act, 'it is an offence to keep or withhold any passport which does not belong to you'. Under labour regulations, women migrant domestic workers in Singapore *must* also 'have unrestricted access to the[ir] passport and belongings'.
6 Hong Kong–based employers are only legally required to ensure that migrant domestic workers do not enter into live-out arrangements (unless with official permission from the Immigration Department) and do not undertake part-time employment.

References

Albin, E (2012), 'From "domestic servant" to "domestic worker"', in J Fudge, S McCrystal & K Sankaran (eds.), *Challenging the Legal Boundaries of Work Regulation*, Hart Publishing, Oxford, pp. 231–250.

Anderson, B (2001), 'Just another job? Paying for domestic work', *Gender and Development*, 9(1): 25–33.

Anderson, B (2016), *Worker, Helper, Auntie, Maid?: Working Conditions and Attitudes Experienced by Migrant Domestic Workers in Thailand and Malaysia*, International Labour Organization, Asia Pacific, https://www.ilo.org/wcmsp5/groups/public/---asia/---ro-bangkok/---sro-bangkok/documents/publication/wcms_537808.pdf

Bailey, AJ, Wright, RA, Mountz, A & Miyares, IM (2002), '(Re)producing Salvadoran transnational geographies', *Annals of the Association of American Geographers*, 92(1): 125–144.

Blackett, A (2019), *Everyday Transgressions: Domestic Workers' Transnational Challenge to International Labor Law*, Cornell University Press, Ithaca.

Boersma, M (2019), 'Filipina domestic workers in Hong Kong: Between permanence and temporariness in everyday life', *Current Sociology Monograph*, 67(2): 273–293.

Chang, KA & Ling, LHM (2010), 'Globalization and its intimate other: Filipina domestic workers in Hong Kong', in MH Marchand & AS Runyan (eds.), *Gender and Global Restructuring* (2nd edition), Routledge, London.

Chin, C (2019), 'Precarious work and its complicit network: Migrant labour in Singapore', *Journal of Contemporary Asia*, 49(4): 528–551.

Constable, N (2003), 'A transnational perspective on divorce and marriage: Filipina wives and workers', *Identities: Global Studies in Culture and Power*, 10(2): 163–180.

Constable, N (2015), 'Migrant motherhood, "failed migration" and the gendered risks of precarious labour', *TRaNS: Trans-Regional and -National Studies of Southeast Asia*, 3(1): 135–151.

Constable, N (2019), 'Tales of two cities: Legislating pregnancy and marriage among foreign domestic workers in Singapore and Hong Kong', *Journal of Ethnic and Migration Studies*, 10.1080/1369183X.2019.1592403

Crawford, A & Hutchinson, S (2016), 'Mapping the contours of "everyday security": Time, space and emotion', *British Journal of Criminology*, 56(6): 1184–1202.

Ehrenreich, B & Hochschild, AR (2002), *Global Woman: Nannies, Maids and Sex Workers in the New Economy*, Metropolitan Books, New York.

Hierofani, PY (2021), 'Productive and deferential bodies: The experiences of Indonesian domestic workers in Malaysia', *Gender, Place and Culture: A Journal of Feminist Geography*, 28(12): 1738–1754.

Himmelweit, S (2007), 'The prospects of caring: Economic theory and policy analysis', *Cambridge Journal of Economics*, 31(4): 581–599.

Hong Kong Labour Department (2022), *A Concise Guide to the Employment Ordinance*, viewed 1 Feb, https://www.labour.gov.hk/eng/public/ConciseGuide.htm

Ibarra, ML (2010), 'My reward is not money: Deep alliances and end-of-life care among Mexicana workers and their wards', in E Boris & RS Parreñas (eds.), *Intimate Labours: Culture, Technologies and the Politics of Care*, Stanford University Press, California, pp. 117–131.

Johnson, M, Lee, M, McCahill, M & Mesina MR (2019), 'Beyond the "all seeing eye": Filipino migrant domestic workers' contestation of care and control in Hong Kong', *Ethnos: Journal of Anthropology*, 10.1080/00141844.2018.1545794

Kok, XH & Tai, J (2015), 'Do maid cameras cross the line?', *The Straits Times*, 1 Nov, viewed 12 Dec, https://www.straitstimes.com/singapore/manpower/do-maid-cameras-cross-the-line

Lan, PC (2006), *Global Cinderellas: Migrant Domestics and Newly Rich Employers in Taiwan*, Duke University Press, Durham.

Lee, M, Johnson, M & McCahill, M (2018), 'Race, gender and surveillance of migrant domestic workers in Asia', in M Bosworth, A Parmar & Y Vázquez (eds.), *Race, Criminal Justice, and Migration Control: Enforcing Boundaries of Belonging*, Oxford University Press, Oxford, pp. 13–28.

Lim, N & Paul, AM (2021), 'Stigma on a spectrum: Differentiated stigmatization of migrant domestic workers' romantic relationships in Singapore', *Gender, Place & Culture*, 28(1): 22–44.

Lutz, H (2016), *Migration and Domestic Work: A European Perspective on a Global Theme*, Routledge, London.

Mezzadra, S & Neilson B (2013), *Border as Method, or, the Multiplication of Labor*, Duke University Press, Durham.

Ministry of Manpower (MOM) (last updated 2021), 'Can an employer keep a worker's passport?', viewed 1 Feb, https://www.mom.gov.sg/faq/work-pass-general/can-an-employer-keep-a-workers-passport#:~:text=According%20to%20the%20Passports%20Act,to%20the%20passport%20and%20belongings

Ng, D (2018), 'Spying on maids with CCTV: Where do we draw the line?', Channel NewsAsia, 6 Oct, viewed 12 Dec, https://www.channelnewsasia.com/cnainsider/maids-domestic-workers-cctv-cameras-abuse-employer-789361

Office of the Privacy Commissioner for Personal Data (2015), *Monitoring and personal data privacy at work: Points to note for employers of domestic helpers*, viewed 1 Feb, https://www.pcpd.org.hk/english/data_privacy_law/code_of_practices/files/points_to_note_15102015_e.pdf

Oishi, N (2005), *Women in Motion: Globalization, State Policies and Labor Migration in Asia*, Stanford University Press, California.

Parreñas, RS (2015), *Servants of Globalization: Migration and Domestic Work* (2nd edition), Stanford University Press, California.

Paul, AM (2011), 'Stepwise international migration: A multistage migration pattern for the aspiring migrant', *American Journal of Sociology*, 116(6): 1842–1886.

Paul, AM & Neo, P (2018), 'Am I allowed to be pregnant? Awareness of pregnancy protection laws among migrant domestic workers in Hong Kong', *Journal of Ethnic and Migration Studies*, 44(7): 1195–1213.

Romero, M (2002), 'Global woman: Nannies, maids and sex workers in the new economy', *British Journal of Industrial Relations*, 42(4): 747–755.

Rothman, BK (1989), *Recreating Motherhood: Ideology and Technology in a Patriarchal Society*, Norton Publishing, New York.

Ruijter, E, van der Lippe, T & Raub, W (2003), 'Trust problems in household outsourcing', *Rationality and Society*, 15(4): 473–507.

Zelizer, VA (2010), *Economic Lives: How Culture Shapes the Economy*, Princeton University Press, New Jersey.

Chapter 5

Negotiating Everyday Work and Help-Seeking

Resolving Work-Related Problems: External Institutions

The majority of the women migrant domestic workers in this research (n = 48) reported that they had at some point during their employment in domestic work experienced either unlawful working and living conditions (that is, conditions that contravened labour legislation in Singapore and Hong Kong) and/or conditions that were not unlawful but have been identified in state labour guidelines as substandard employment. Of this group, more than three-quarters (n = 39) had experienced multiple forms of unlawful and/or substandard employment practices. Only four of the 52 workers did not recount experiences of unlawful and/or substandard employment conditions, as illustrated in Figure 5.1.

Despite nearly half of the workers identifying that their employers or ex-employers had subjected them to unlawful employment practices, only a minority (n = 7) had decided to contact state authorities about this, and even fewer (n = 4) ended up lodging labour complaints or police reports. For the other workers, including those who had experienced substandard labour conditions, their perceptions of and responses to their employment situations varied. Workers' definitions and understandings of their employment conditions have critical implications for their negotiation of everyday work situations and strategies to keep themselves safe. Notably, not all of the workers in this research who had experienced unlawful working conditions identified their situation as bad or unsustainable. Their evaluation of their employment conditions was not always based on objective legal or regulatory standards. Rather, their determination of 'good' or 'bad' employment was based on a myriad of personal assessments, including their relationship with their employer (as further discussed in Chapter 7). For the workers who did identify their employment situation as bad or unsustainable (n = 31), there were three key outcomes that they sought: (1) securing better employment conditions without having to change employer or request an early contract termination, (2) completing the two-year contract and then finding a new employer and (3)

DOI: 10.4324/9781003250364-5

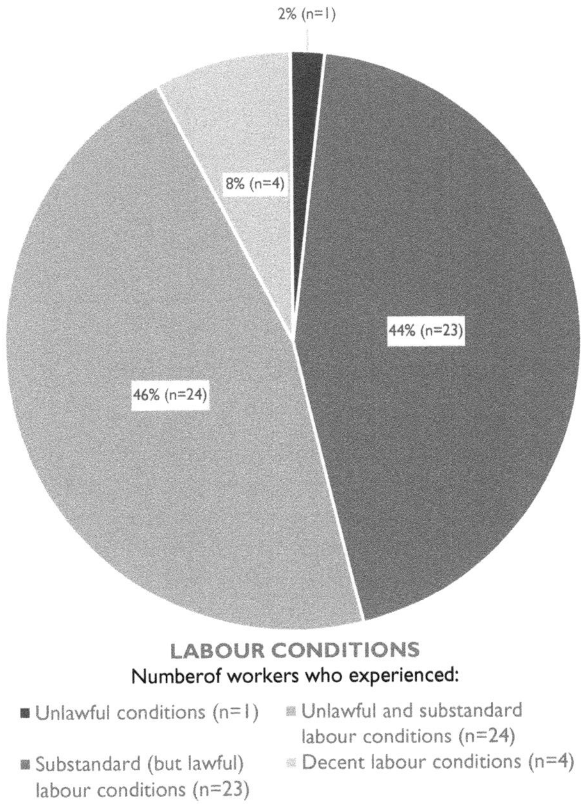

Figure 5.1 **Distribution of labour conditions experienced by women migrant domestic workers.**

negotiating an early contract termination and transferring to a new employer. Each of these will be discussed in turn.

Of particular significance is the value that workers placed on responses and strategies that would not antagonise their employers or trigger employment termination. Being able to work and live safely is a key objective for women migrant domestic workers. As such, the two strategies commonly employed by workers are, the performance of emotional labour to negotiate safe work and/or approaching third-party intermediaries to secure desired outcomes. For example, when explaining how they managed conflict with their employers and dealt with various work-related problems, many of the workers spoke of the importance of tact, knowing when and how to talk to employers and also knowing whether employers are open to communication (that is, negotiation or explanation):

> Sometimes madam suddenly angry, I will explain and tell her. With my previous employers, I will see. If they have black face [bad mood] like that, I will keep quiet and go away. But if they talk nicely, then I can explain. Depends on the mood [of the employer]. [*Beatrice, Indonesian, seven years in Singapore*]

> With my employer now, I will talk back and tell her if I want something. They are easy going. My employer last time was not so nice, when I just a little talking, they are not happy so after that I don't care. If the employer no good, I just keep quiet. [*Rowena, Indonesian, 13 years in Hong Kong*]

A Hong Kong–based NGO staff member, Nora, also commented on the challenges of conflict resolution and the negotiation of safe work in the domestic workplace, not least because of the nature of the employment relationship, which is highly intimate due to the type of labour involved and the proximity of employers and workers:

> The negotiations between the female domestic worker and the female employer, and then that negotiation between that female domestic worker with the multiple members of the household, maybe even children, quite often other adults, it is a very fine balancing act for everybody. [*Nora, Hong Kong, NGO staff member*]

The above issues speak to how the intimacy of domestic labour can affect how workers manage the employment relationship when problems arise. However, as discussed in Chapter 4, the labour and migration regulations and policies in Singapore and Hong Kong have produced a context where, in most cases, workers have little direct power to negotiate improvements or changes to their working and living conditions. For instance, when talking about her employment experience in Hong Kong, Bella explained that she had tried to tell her employers that she did not like their verbal abuse, but after a few futile attempts, she gave up:

> [If the employer is angry with me], I will ask why, I will explain. I tell them, if they are not happy to [with] me, let me know. Give and take. If I do wrong, I just say sorry and if they do wrong, they also say sorry. But this employer, I don't try to explain because they don't listen to me. Before I tried to explain but they don't understand, so no point to tell. So, until I quit, I just keep it [my unhappiness] to myself. [*Bella, Filipina, six years in Singapore, three years in Hong Kong, ten years in Singapore*]

Another worker, Jessie, shared that in her first overseas employment contract, her ex-employer, who worked as a flight attendant, paid her below Hong Kong's minimum allowable wage, and only provided her with aeroplane food, insufficient to sustain her throughout the day. Over a three-month period, Jessie lost nearly 10 kg. When I asked her whether she had tried to tell her ex-employer that she needed more food, Jessie explained that she was not able to do so because:

> She [the employer] was so strict and I wasn't able to speak like this [in fluent English]. The other thing was, I had culture shock. Because I just came from Nepal, nothing was the same, everything is so different and so culture shock. I cried and just stayed there. [*Jessie, Nepalese, 18 years in Hong Kong*]

Many of the other workers faced similar difficulties in communicating with their employers, either due to language barriers or their employers' attitudes. Some of them shared that, instead of talking directly to their employers, they preferred to contact third-party intermediaries – namely, placement agencies and NGOs – for assistance in conveying their requests or concerns.

Placement Agencies as Negotiators and Mediators

> When they [the employers] made me work in two places, I complained in the agency and also about the work hours. 5 o'clock wake up, 12 o'clock sleep. I don't want like this. I complained already [to my employers], but they don't care. [*Fannie, Indonesian, one year in Singapore, five years in Hong Kong*]

> Agent [is who I would contact if I needed assistance]. For me, I must contact my agent. When I have problem with my employer, must contact my agent. I tell to them the whole story and the problem and because I cannot manage [the employer's demands] already, I tell them I want to transfer. I tell the situation to the agent. [*Lina, Filipina, six years in Singapore*]

Within popular discourse, employment intermediaries tend to be positioned as exploitative figures that profit from vulnerable migrants (McKeown 2012; Yeoh, Goh & Wee 2020). Yet both Fannie and Lina identified their placement agencies as the first point of contact for support and assistance when they had a work-related problem. This was also the case for over half of the 43 workers who had paid employment intermediaries (recruitment and placement agencies) to help them organise and manage the migration and employment process. When I asked these women why they identified placement agencies as their first source of support, three-quarters reported that prior to their departure from their home country and/or upon arrival in the destination country, they were told by the employment agents that their first point of contact for all work-related issues should be the placement agency, as they would help them talk to their employer and resolve any problems. A smaller group of worker participants (n = 6) shared their expectation that, as they were fee-paying users of the agency service, the agency had a responsibility to them to help improve their work situation, either by addressing job insecurities and/or providing support by helping workers to negotiate a better outcome: 'Because we paid the agency fees, so we think that the agency has responsibility over the employment conditions and it is easier to go to agency than directly to the employer' [*Susie, Indonesian, 15 years in Singapore*].

Describing the support and assistance they were seeking from placement agencies, women migrant domestic workers primarily talked about two aspects of the role of agencies: (1) negotiating better working and living conditions and (2) mediating a transfer of contract to a new employer when the employment situation became intolerable. These outcomes potentially allowed women migrant domestic workers to secure safe employment; something that was particularly imperative for these women who had migrated to support their families.

Agencies' familiarity with employers – and therefore being better positioned to communicate with and advise employers – was the other reason why women migrant domestic workers preferred going to placement agencies for assistance. For example, Nelly explained that, for her, community networks and placement agencies were both essential, but that they play different roles and serve different purposes:

> I will go to find some community [organisations] to help but I will also go to the agency first because they know about us, they can connect with my employer. Because whenever we go to the community, they don't know about my employer also, so whenever I talk bad thing about my employer, they will say, 'Ok, ok' only, but my agency will be the first one to know about my employer. [*Nelly, Indonesian, three years in Singapore, one year in Taiwan, five years in Hong Kong*]

Nelly, like many other workers in my research, identified the agency as the most effective and best-equipped organisation to reach out to employers, and to bring about immediate improvements to workers' working and living conditions. This sentiment was also reflected by Jasmine, who shared that she advises other Nepalese women who are planning to work in Hong Kong to use an employment agency:

> We [domestic workers] don't know the situation, how will the employer be, if the employer will treat them very bad. Even if I recommend my sister or my friend to come here, if the employer will be so bad, if they will treat them badly, we cannot help them. We just have to recommend them and introduce them, but we cannot help them. We are still workers. If they will come through the agency, the agency can save them. [*Jasmine, Nepalese, eight years in Hong Kong*]

For Jessie, a Nepalese worker who volunteers with the domestic worker union, the value of placement agencies lies in their capacity to provide immediate and practical assistance when workers have a work-related problem. She explained that while there is a strong and growing union presence among Nepalese domestic workers in Hong Kong, it remains the agencies, not the union, that are best placed to provide immediate and effective responses for women migrant domestic workers:

> Just in case they lose the job or the employer is too rude to them, so they can run to agents [who have shelters] and they can settle for a few days and the agent can help [by giving them food and temporary shelter]. We don't guarantee that they will do 100% but just easy to run to them. Like we don't say it is a 100% but just in some way can access help and contact them. And if they [agencies] are good, they will go and pick them [up]. And agencies will be 24 hours available, but we [union members] are not. If we are in employer's house, we cannot just run and help them. [*Jessie, Nepalese, 18 years in Hong Kong*]

However, the discussions with workers about their agency experiences also revealed a degree of ambivalence among the workers. On the one hand, there was dependency and an expectation that agencies would provide frontline assistance and support, in particular, around negotiating with employers to help secure better employment conditions. On the other hand, at least half of the workers expressed scepticism and dissatisfaction with the actual assistance they received. They felt that agencies were more invested in ensuring that workers complete their employment contracts and facilitating a smooth loan repayment process than in supporting workers' welfare:

> They [the agency] not much take care about us. Because they want us to return the money back first. So, they are crazy when the maids go back again and again. That's why they are so strict to the workers. If no finish [salary] deduction, then maid got problem, then of course the agency will become crazy because they cannot take the money. Most important for them is the money. [*Maya, Indonesian, 15 years in Singapore*]

> I am curious why the contract say I only take care of three kids, but after a few months, I am going to the company and I did painting also. I asked my agency why I have to do like this [going to work at the employer's company]. It is illegal I said. Then they said, 'Never mind, more people is more harder work than you.' Because money, money, money. It is all about the money. They take already our money so they don't care. [*Amy, Filipina, 24 years in Hong Kong*]

Amy's and Maya's experiences echoes the findings of Goh, Wee and Yeoh's (2016) study on the gendered debt finance regime in Singapore, which showed that placement agencies are primarily concerned with the management and reduction of financial risk associated with workers defaulting on their placement loans. To mitigate this risk, placement agents are invested in mediating the employment relationship so that the worker completes her loan repayment; however, this process is not always about securing a satisfactory compromise for both parties. Instead, the workers interviewed in my research talked about how agencies were more likely to encourage them to 'bear with it' and/or dismiss their concerns:

> I went to my agency's office, then I told that my employer sent me to the friend. Then the agency said, 'That thing no need to talk about.' She said, 'Just understand your employer' like that. But when I tried to seek help from agency, they don't listen. They listen to employer, like, 'There is no need to complain, no need to talk about it, no need to tell us. Just do whatever the employer says.' [*Rina, Singapore, 1.5 years in Macau, 10 months in Malaysia, 11 months in Singapore*]

Rina's experience echoes Sally's observations (below) that agencies in Hong Kong rarely provide substantive support to help improve or change a workplace situation, and they more often leave workers in a tenuous position to 'choose' between enduring the exploitative work conditions for two years or risking their financial security by trying to change employer:

> Filipino workers are more on unions or NGOs or the consulates, not the agencies because we already experienced like, we ask the agency [for help] and the agency just tell us, 'You come here to work. You don't complain.' We always encounter that from agencies. So, just sacrifice like this. And 'if you don't like to sacrifice, they will say, 'then you have to terminate your contract and then I will give you another employer. But if I were to give you another one, then you have to pay another amount.' All is our choice. [*Sally, Filipina, one year in Singapore, 30 years in Hong Kong*]

Although placement agencies have significant scope to intervene and shape the everyday working and living conditions of women migrant domestic workers, the comments by workers suggest that it can still be challenging to rely on agencies to enable safe and sustainable work. Yet in both Singapore and Hong Kong, the governments have identified placement agencies as one of the main institutions that women migrant domestic workers can approach for assistance, especially for first-time arrivals. In Singapore's case, workers are explicitly encouraged and advised to approach agencies when they encounter work-related problems.[1] While there are licensing and accreditation schemes alongside other measures to incentivise ethical behaviour by migration intermediaries,[2] the regulations in both city-states have been largely silent on the legal obligations of agencies to the worker following their placement. In addition to leaving workers' access to assistance and support dependent on the goodwill of individual placement agents, this also creates, as Goh (2018, p. 102) notes, a situation where placement agents have little right to mediate or negotiate better living and working conditions on behalf of the worker if the employer is unwilling to allow third-party involvement. This suggests that even though employment intermediaries can and do have the capacity to improve employment conditions for some women migrant domestic workers (see also Yeoh, Goh & Wee 2020), there are limits to their capacity to reform the system and guarantee better employment conditions for all.

Civil Society Organisations (CSOs): NGOs and Labour Unions as Secondary Sources of Support

Alongside placement agencies, faith-based organisations and civil society organisations (CSOs) – namely, NGOs and labour unions – comprise the other major source of support for migrant domestic workers in Singapore and Hong Kong. While only six workers I spoke to had sought help from CSOs, the interviews with staff members of CSOs indicated that the nature of the support and advice they provide to workers on a day-to-day basis, in relation to employment issues, is not substantially different from that of placement agencies.[3] This assistance included, for example, recommendations on how to negotiate with employers and manage conflict, advice and support in relation to approaching employers for contract movement, as well as legal advice and assistance with accessing formal grievance and justice mechanisms to obtain compensation. The six workers who had approached CSOs for help noted that they had done so only *after* they had first sought the assistance of their placement agencies. NGOs were seen as a secondary institution that could help to negotiate safer working and living conditions. One such worker was Tina, who had sought support and advice from a frontline NGO after her requests to the placement agency to help her younger sister were ignored. Tina's younger sister had gone to Tina for advice when her employer started to reduce her food portions as punishment; and since she was familiar with the placement agency, Tina took it upon herself to approach the agency about her sister's situation:

> First time for her case, I actually talked to the agency but then she [the employment agent] never respond to me. So I went to the Singapore NGO because it is for domestic workers who are abused, right? So, that's why I choose the NGO because they can advise better. Then I go back to the agency and talked to the agent again. I said, 'If no action again, I will go to the house of the employer and take my sister.' [*Tina, Filipina, two years in Lebanon, four years in Singapore*]

Tina had approached the NGO primarily for advice, in particular to understand the agency's responsibilities. After consulting with the NGO, Tina went back to the agency and was able to successfully pressure it into talking to her sister's employer. For Tina, the NGO functioned as a reliable alternative resource when the placement agency had not been helpful. Margaret, who worked at the helpdesk of an NGO in Singapore, similarly explained that the women migrant domestic workers who call her NGO are most often those who have tried to engage the assistance of their agencies in resolving work-related problems, but who have failed to bring about any change in their employment situation:

> It is months of trying to get people like agencies to help and employers to understand, but nothing comes out of it and I think that is the pushing point [to call us] and they also happen to know that there are people out there who can help them. [*Margaret, Singapore, NGO staff member*]

Margaret further noted that, during the two years for which she had worked at the helpdesk, only a small minority of workers had actually lodged a complaint against their employer with the labour department in Singapore. Instead, most calls from workers were likely to result in mediation sessions between workers and their employers:

M: Because they [the workers] are afraid that if authorities are involved, then what if they get banned [from working in Singapore] forever? 'What if I complain and I get charged or blacklisted?'

S: Would they get blacklisted or banned for making a complaint? Does that happen?

M: They won't unless they gave false statements. It is just their feeling that 'What if I complain and something happens?' And most of them will ask, 'If I go to MOM or I go to the police, can I work again in Singapore?' So it is mostly about being able to find employment again in Singapore after their case has concluded. [*Margaret, Singapore, NGO staff member*]

Being able to work is a key priority for many domestic workers. Therefore, when contacted by distressed workers seeking help, NGOs would try, as much as possible, to prioritise suggestions and strategies that would ensure the worker's employment security. What also emerged from the interviews with other Singapore-based NGOs was that mediation sessions can include efforts towards resolving worker–employer disputes and addressing the concerns of both parties, or negotiating with the employer to allow a contract transfer for their worker. However, these mediation sessions are not legally mandated and are therefore dependent upon the employer's voluntary participation. When I asked the NGO staff members about what happens when employers refuse to participate, they provided differing accounts of the actions that their organisations would take in response and the implications for workers:

J: When we get a call from [a distressed worker], we will activate our support service and find out what is happening and how do we help this person. After we receive a call, we try to analyse what the issue is about and then, if we need to, we will go and recommend employers to do a mediation.

S: So, when would you recommend a mediation session?

J: You will find that after talking to them [the workers] and advising them and after that [if] the employer is still not cooperative and doesn't want to do anything [to improve the situation], then this poor girl is still stuck, then we will recommend the employer to come for a mediation. For us, we do not encourage them to run away [from the employer's house] because most of the time they will lose their job and they still have loans to pay off. We would like to find out what the problem is and try to solve. Sometimes we give them advice and then through the advice they are able to overcome the difficulties and challenges.

S: Ok, but in those cases where the employers are already not very cooperative, would they be willing to go through mediation?

J: By and large, we will tell them that if you can't resolve this, we will just have to refer the case to the MOM, we will have to escalate it. Usually they will say yes after that because they don't want to get into trouble with the government. And most of the time we find that actually we can solve it if mediation is done correctly, the concerns of both parties can be addressed instead of just escalating. [*Javier, Singapore, NGO staff member*]

There was no clarification by Javier as to whether cases have indeed been reported to MOM, or what happens to a worker when MOM becomes involved in their case. However, Joel, who heads another NGO in Singapore, explained that the threat of authorities' involvement cannot always be utilised as leverage against employers. One of the biggest issues is that not every worker will qualify for MOM intervention:

> Chronic non-salary payment or having to work in two houses, three houses, or help out in the employer's business, or you have to do dangerous work like clean the outside of the window unsupervised. These are offences that MOM will investigate. But MOM will not investigate things like have to work till midnight, or have to sleep in a storeroom, or I don't have enough privacy. MOM doesn't investigate these things. [*Joel, Singapore, NGO staff member*]

Where workers are subjected to substandard but not unlawful working conditions, Joel explained that they face a real and high risk of contract termination *and* repatriation:

> When the workers come, we will look at the case and what she wants. If she wants to transfer and we find that she doesn't have a case that MOM

> will want to investigate, then we will try to persuade the employer, we will negotiate. If you don't have a case that MOM will investigate, you can only think or hope that you can get a transfer through mediation. Nine out of ten times the mediation doesn't work.

When I asked about the significance or benefit of having MOM or other state authorities involved, Joel explained that

> when the police or MOM takes it up, they [the worker] will be eligible to transfer to an employer of their choice and they can choose their agency of choice. So, for those who want to transfer, that is actually the best-case scenario'.

Joel's observations, which were mirrored by the comments of other frontline NGO staff, speak to the gendered dimensions of unwaged domestic labour that underpin normative employment standards for waged domestic workers, as discussed in Chapter 2. While certain problems such as unpaid salaries, illegal confinement and deployment are formally recognised in Singapore as employment law breaches, others – namely, long working hours, inadequate sleeping space and working on rest days – are considered to be beyond the remit of formal legislation. This formal distinction between criminal or labour law offences and 'everyday' but potentially substandard domestic labour conditions reveals labour standards to be strongly entwined with heteronormative conceptualisations and expectations of women's labour. Specifically, the entrenched gendered expectations surrounding domestic and care responsibilities (for example, that mothers must be available 24/7), which inform the need for total flexibility and perpetual availability in waged domestic labour, have in turn led to certain aspects of waged domestic labour being wilfully unregulated.

Exiting Employment: Contract Movement and 'Transfers'

Being able to work and doing so via a path that costs the least was identified as of primary importance to the workers in this study, as this has direct implications for their capacity to send remittances home and support their families. Indeed, when talking about their experiences in negotiating and responding to exploitative employment situations, nearly two-thirds of the workers stated that they would either complete their two-year work contract before looking for a new employer or terminate an existing contract and find a new employer. In this context, the facilitation of a contract movement (that is, negotiating an early contract termination and transferring to a new employer) can be understood as one of the most important strategies for workers to secure protection and better employment conditions. And placement agencies were perceived to be the main service provider who can help them achieve that, especially among the Singapore-based workers. However, early contract termination comes at a cost[4] that is borne by workers, especially if they engage a placement agency to assist with the process. Avoiding another round of debt was part of the reason why some workers decided to complete their two-year contract before looking for a new employer:

> Because I was thinking, if break contract, it will waste the money because I have to pay the agency fees and waste the time because must exit from Hong Kong when we break the contract and have to get a new visa. So, better to just finish contract. If finish the contract, we are easy to find new employer and we will also have good contract in the future. [*Kelly, Indonesian, nine years in Singapore, five years in Hong Kong*]

The desire to avoid additional debt was shared by women migrant domestic workers in Singapore and Hong Kong, and all 11 workers who had requested a 'transfer' had done so only after multiple failed attempts at conflict resolution. However, there was a notable difference between the two locations in terms of workers' concerns and willingness to consider contract termination or transfer as a viable option for escaping 'bad' employment situations. Each group is discussed in turn below.

For the Hong Kong–based workers, early contract termination and transfer of employment is considered to be a very risky strategy because of the two-week rule and employers' requirement of a reference letter. These workers consistently stated that the priority is to complete their two-year contract whenever possible:

> Before I wanted to break contract, but I talked to my friend, then she said, 'No need, if you break contract, very difficult to find another employer. You still very young, you need to earn more money for your future.' [*Wada, Indonesian, five years in Singapore, 2.5 years in Hong Kong*]

The difficulty in finding a new employer in Hong Kong comes from having to find a new employer *and* obtain a new visa within two weeks. In addition to the problems created by the two-week rule, many of the Hong Kong–based migrant domestic workers expressed their concern that by terminating their contracts they would be negatively perceived by prospective employers, which motivated them to remain in their current role until the end of the two-year period, despite difficult working conditions. For example, when asked about the ease of finding a new employer in Hong Kong, Mila explained that:

> It depends on if you break the contract. If you finish contract, then it is ok, it is easy. And if you finish contract, the employer will trust you because if you break, then they will think that you are not good, cannot trust like that. [*Mila, Filipina, 17 years in Hong Kong*]

In a labour market context where employers value the completion of a contract and perceive it as an indicator of worker dependability, there is tremendous pressure on women migrant domestic workers to endure their employment situations until the end of the contract. However, the pressure to complete a contract did not only come from employers. The immigration authorities in Hong Kong also had a part to play. Queenie explained that, aside from employability concerns, her reluctance to break a contract was also in part due to the belief that the immigration authorities would take a harsher attitude during the application and interview process for a new visa:

> Sometimes difficult because employers will ask, 'Why you didn't finish two years?' We must explain. If we finish, then easy. And the immigration official will make a lot of noise and ask a lot of questions, like, 'Why you don't finish?' [*Queenie, Indonesian, two years in Singapore, four years in Hong Kong*]

The belief that the Hong Kong immigration authorities would 'punish' workers for not finishing a contract was a key factor shaping workers' decision-making, and these anxieties are not unfounded as the Hong Kong Immigration Department has consistently affirmed its commitment to proactively tackle job-hopping.[5] Given the potentially negative implications of contract termination, the Hong Kong–based women migrant domestic workers did not consider early termination and transfer a safe option.

Conversely, the Singapore-based women migrant domestic workers were less impacted by such labour market factors and consequently had a more relaxed attitude towards seeking a transfer, with most identifying it as an achievable solution to employment problems. Their main concern around contract termination related to MOM's precondition of a release letter from their current employer. They noted that there was a very real risk that employers would refuse to sign the release letter – a situation that three workers reported experiencing. However, more than half of the workers explained that if the placement agency is 'good' it will help to convince the employer to allow a transfer. One such worker was Julia, who stated that her prioritisation of placement agencies as a source of support over other service providers or state organisations was primarily because these agencies are better able to ensure that workers can keep working in Singapore, even when the current employment relationship breaks down. For Julia, the primary goal of retaining ongoing employment and earning an income meant that she prioritised seeking help from placement agencies over state authorities (the police and the labour department), or indeed the Philippines embassy, unless the worker had been 'hurt' (physically harmed) by their employer:

> Because if agency can settle [the problem] first, then no problem. If you go to the police or something like that, it is very difficult you know

> because they have to bring out [investigate] everything. Once they go to the MOM or police or they go to the Philippine Embassy, then after that my friends were sent back to the Philippines. So, it is very bad, it won't help. Especially if they still want to work in Singapore. If you have problem with your employer like you cannot get salary, talk about it you know, or call the agency. If can settle through agency, why not? There is no problem, no need to go there to police. [*Julia, Filipina, five years in Taiwan, ten years in Singapore*]

Filing a formal complaint with a state organisation or reporting a problem to the police was seen by workers from both city-states as a less-than-ideal option, because of the risk to one's employment and financial security. In comparison, placement agencies were perceived to be more 'helpful' as they have the capacity to mediate a contract transfer and ensure that workers can continue to work. Women's priorities to maintain secure work and earn a steady income meant that it was often placement agencies that they would go to when they encountered work-related problems. However, this was not necessarily because these employment intermediaries were considered to be an ally or a reliable, satisfactory resource. Instead, what is evident are the profound ramifications for workers of the current labour migration regime in both Singapore and Hong Kong, and the limitations of the welfare protections offered by countries of origin. Specifically, in seeking to contain and manage the presence of women migrant domestic workers, policies are instituted to restrict their labour mobilities, so that approaching placement agencies for assistance becomes the most strategic and 'safest' option for Singapore-based workers who need to ensure secure employment, as it poses the lowest risk of jeopardising these workers' livelihood security. This has troubling ramifications for women migrant domestic workers who encounter unlawful and/or substandard employment conditions, as the justice and labour protections offered through formal mechanisms are likely to be 'traded off' by these workers in situations where the use of these mechanisms threatens their security. As the next section discusses, despite the protections and entitlements offered to migrant domestic workers under the existing infrastructure of labour and criminal law, the potential negative consequences of accessing formal justice mechanisms mean that only a small minority of workers choose to come forward.

Negotiating Protection and Security through Formal Mechanisms

> It [referring to the labour legislation] is like [seen by the employer as] very rude. Actually, it depends on the relationship between the employer and the worker. If your employer is ok, then no need to complain anymore, it is ok. You only say like that if your employer is not good. Then you tell

> them, 'You have to follow the law, the contract'. But if your employer is good, you have nothing to complain. [*Delia, Filipina, five years in Egypt, one year and eight months in Jordan, three years in Hong Kong*]

In my conversations with workers, many of them expressed that they would like certain employment conditions (such as no curfew on rest days, uninterrupted rest time and private sleeping quarters) improved. However, like Delia, most of them also explained that they would not appeal to labour (or criminal) law unless necessary, as it could damage the worker–employer relationship. Similarly, in the interviews with staff members from frontline NGOs, all of them stated that pursuing labour claims and/or litigation against employers is not the primary focus for most workers; rather, workers preferred advice on how to navigate difficult employment relationships and how to communicate their needs to employers. For example, Jasmine noted that, while there are many Nepalese domestic workers who approach the Union of Nepalese Domestic Workers in Hong Kong with complaints about their employers and work conditions, since the union's official establishment in 2005, only three workers had filed a formal complaint with it:

> They don't want to go [file a claim at the Labour Department] because they say that if they are going to the Labour Court, they immediately will break contract and when they will finish the case? It will take like six months, four months or even one year. So, it takes more months and [during] that period, she will have to spend her own money. Even if they finish the case, even if they will win the case, if the new employer will know about that, the new employer will not be happy. So, they are scared that if they file a case, even if they win, they may not get a new employer because the employer will be scared that if they do something wrong, the girl will go to the Labour Department to complain them. So, most of the girls, they won't be willing to go Labour Court. They will just discuss with us how they are surviving there, we will teach them how to handle it and manage their employers. They have to concentrate on their housework and talk to their employers. [*Jasmine, Nepalese, eight years in Hong Kong*]

The accounts provided by staff of the NGOs in both Singapore and Hong Kong made clear that there are a number of significant potential consequences that a worker needs to consider when deciding whether to file a formal complaint or approach state authorities (police, embassy staff or labour officials) for support in navigating work-related problems. These consequences can include an immediate loss of accommodation and/or contract termination. Therefore, even though some union members argued for the symbolic value of law (for example, in providing a warning to employers), all of the NGO staff noted that their foremost priority is to ensure that workers are fully aware of the possible consequences of different courses of action and of the options available to them. Specifically, the worker must decide whether she should pursue formal interventions or instead negotiate her work problems via alternative pathways or mechanisms that do not jeopardise her (and her family's) livelihood. In this context, the entitlements and remedies offered by legal and regulatory frameworks in Singapore and Hong Kong are not perceived to be a fundamental right that can be substantively accessed by all. Instead, the majority of the stakeholders in Singapore and Hong Kong observed that accessing formal dispute resolution mechanisms comes at a cost that many workers consider prohibitive. This is exemplified in Scarlett's account of a client who had been physically abused by her employer:

> As a social worker, I informed her [that she should file a police report and leave her employer] because your safety should be the top concern regarding your situation. Of course, I would suggest that you protect yourself. I suggest you maybe call the police or you have to run away from your employer. But I remember the next week, she came to me and said, '姐姐 [sister], after I think and consider about your opinion, I decide not to break my contract or call the police, I decide to finish my contract. I think I can tolerate for the mild physical abuse because this is my first time to come to Hong Kong to work. Because my agency already informed me, if I cannot finish one contract, the Indonesian consulate will blacklist me, and so I have to accept until I finish my contract. [*Scarlett, Hong Kong, Social worker*]

Scarlett's description above raises concerns about employer accountability and worker protection, especially when workers are choosing to complete their two-year contracts and find a new employer before filing a labour complaint, to ensure their secure employment status. Notably, four of the seven workers in this study who had accessed formal labour grievance or criminal justice mechanisms had done so *after* the conclusion of their employment contract. On the one hand, this reinforces the weight that migrant domestic workers accord to having a job. On the other, it offers an insight into how existing labour migration regulations in Singapore and Hong Kong are inherently limited, and raises questions about the extent to which this infrastructure can be considered responsive to the needs of women migrant domestic workers and effective in addressing exploitation and abuse in domestic work.

Seeking Help from Authorities: Workers' Reflections

Cherry, a Filipina woman, is one of the seven workers who had engaged with formal mechanisms (that is, by filing a labour complaint or lodging a police report) after experiencing unlawful and/or substandard employment conditions. She had three employers throughout the six years spent working in Singapore. Her duties included general cleaning, cooking and washing. With the exception of the first, her employers had subjected her to conditions that contravened the labour standards set out in Singapore's EFMA. The main problem with her second employer was 'not enough food':

> Not enough food. From the beginning there was no food. For lunch, they give me instant noodles, they ask me to eat twice. Half for today and half for tomorrow. And then for dinner, three persons [shared] for one order, instead of one person for one order.

After enduring this situation for two months, Cherry made multiple complaints to the placement agency, which eventually led to the employer's termination of her contract. Cherry was then sent back to the placement agency, which arranged a third employer for her. Although both the working conditions and the employment relationship in this third placement were good initially, the situation deteriorated after a year when her employers ran into financial difficulties and outsourced Cherry's labour to their friend and tenant. This outsourcing was in breach of her work visa conditions, which stipulated that the worker can only work at the home address of the employer as shown on her work permit. In addition, Cherry's duties in the employer's home were not reduced to reflect this additional workload and neither was she paid any money for these additional duties. Cherry eventually decided to request a transfer because she was physically exhausted. However, her employers refused to permit the change of employment and attempted to send her back to the Philippines, which then drove Cherry to the police:

> One day I collapsed and then I decided to transfer [employers]. Then I asked them [the employer] I want to transfer because I am not happy and then I am so tired. I said I want to transfer and then they buy me a ticket instead of release papers. They bought my plane ticket back to the Philippines. So I run away to the police station and report to police about this case.

However, no police case was filed against her employers as the police concluded that Cherry's case was an employment dispute, which fell under the purview of MOM; and no assistance was provided by the police to transfer the case to MOM. Instead, at the request of her employers (who had filed a missing person's report at another police station on the same day that Cherry ran away), the police dropped her off at her employment agency in Singapore, where she attempted to negotiate with her employers for the release papers that would allow her to transfer to another employer. This attempt at mediation was unsuccessful and on request of the employers, the agency sent her to the airport and attempted to repatriate her. Cherry's friend had to help her contact a local NGO, which managed to prevent her repatriation by explaining her case to an immigration officer, who then referred them to the

MOM officer stationed at the airport.[6] In doing so, the NGO managed to ensure that Cherry would not be forcibly repatriated, after which it provided her with accommodation at one of its temporary shelter services and assisted her to file a formal complaint with MOM. At the time of the interview, Cherry was awaiting the conclusion of the investigation into her case.

Cherry's story provides a glimpse into women migrant domestic workers' experiences of employment disputes and attempts to secure safe work conditions. Including Cherry, there were four workers who had filed a labour claim or police report. Table 5.1 details the situations that led to these workers approaching the authorities and the progression of their engagement with the various formal mechanisms. In addition to these four workers, three others – Judy, Gina and Amy – had sought information and advice from the respective labour ministries in Singapore and Hong Kong: two women contacted MOM and one woman contacted the Hong Kong Labour Department.

At the time of the research, Molly and Cherry were still waiting for their investigations to conclude, and while both Jessie and Wada had been successful in obtaining pecuniary remedies, Jessie did not receive the full amount owed to her. When asked whether she felt that it was unfair that the Labour Tribunal had not awarded her the full amount of compensation despite documented evidence of underpayment, Jessie said that it was not unfair: 'even the judge was from the top, he didn't point me out [make things difficult for me], and he didn't side with my boss'. This perception of impartiality, confidence in the rule of law and due process, and conviction that the legal and regulatory system will protect workers was shared by nearly all the workers interviewed in this study:

> It is very fair. It protects us because if the employer abuses us, we can report them to Immigration and police and they will give us action. For example, if our employer abuse us, we can sue the employer for abusing us. [*Rita, Filipina, 15 years in Hong Kong*]

> I heard some friends that the employer treats her bad and beats her like this, and if you complain to the police or the Immigration, then they will know the employer is really bad and the employer is then put to the jail, so it is fair, right? No like, 'Oh she is only a domestic helper, the employer is rich, so we cannot put to the jail'. So, the law in Hong Kong is very good and fair. [*Christie, Filipina, five years in Taiwan, eight years in Hong Kong*]

Workers' confidence in the procedural fairness and integrity of the legal and regulatory systems was primarily reflected in their very straightforward conceptualisations of how things would proceed should they decide to pursue a formal employment-related or criminal complaint. They articulated a firm belief that they would then get the justice they deserve. Yet, when asked whether they would ever lodge a labour claim or file a police report to secure

Table 5.1 Female migrant domestic workers' experiences with accessing formal mechanisms

Name/nationality	*Current work location*	*Nature and location of report filed*	*Reasons for, process of and outcome of filing a formal complaint*
Cherry, Filipina	Singapore	Labour complaint, Singapore, MOM	• Unlawfully deployed to clean for employer's tenant and friend. • Requested a transfer after collapsing from exhaustion, employers attempted to repatriate her and she went to the police to make a report. • The police report was not accepted, as her complaint was considered to be an employment dispute, which fell under the purview of MOM. • She is awaiting conclusion of her case.
Molly, Burmese	Not working	Criminal report, Singapore, police	• Made to work in conditions that were both against her human dignity[i] (i.e., restricted water and food intake, limited use of toilets, verbal abuse and excessive working hours) and unlawful (physical abuse) by her first employer in Singapore. • Repatriated back to Myanmar after a suicide attempt and the employment agent in Myanmar helped to bring her back to Singapore to file a criminal case against her ex-employers for abuse. • She is awaiting conclusion of her trial.
Jessie, Nepalese	Hong Kong	Labour complaint, Hong Kong, Labour Department	• First employer in Hong Kong paid her less than the mandatory minimum wage, did not provide her with sufficient food and was verbally abusive. • After deciding to terminate Jessie's contract, the employer refused to write a good recommendation letter, which would have negatively impacted upon Jessie's future employment prospects. • Jessie then went to the Labour Department to file a case against her employer for underpayment of wages. • She was eventually awarded half of the salary that was owed to her.

(Continued)

Table 5.1 (Continued)

Name/nationality	*Current work location*	*Nature and location of report filed*	*Reasons for, process of and outcome of filing a formal complaint*
Wada, Indonesian	Hong Kong	Labour complaint, Hong Kong, Labour Department	• First employer in Hong Kong unlawfully deducted her wages whenever she broke something in the house. • Wada kept a monthly record of the deductions and when her contract ended, she went to the Labour Department to file a claim for the illegal deduction of wages. • She was reimbursed nearly one month's worth of salary.

i These conditions are technically not criminalised under Singapore's labour laws; however, the term 'victim's right to human dignity' was used in a 2017 court judgement against employers who had starved their domestic worker and caused her physical injury.

compensation, many said no. Workers' confidence in the capacity of the legal and regulatory systems to provide justice did not necessarily translate into confidence that accessing these formal mechanisms would be in their best interests or ensure their security. Instead, the experiences of the workers who had direct contact with the state authorities indicated that the government authorities lacked a serious commitment to recognising and responding to women migrant domestic workers' risks to exploitation. For example, Gina, who was on her first employment contract, had wanted to apply for a transfer two months into the job as her workload was much more demanding than had been disclosed to her before she signed the contract:

> I told them [the employer] that I can't do it anymore because too much work. I wake up sometimes before 5 am because the kids have school and must prepare everything like breakfast and I need to clean everything before she [the employer] comes down [from her room]. Sometimes I sleep at 10 pm? Or if too much work in the kitchen, I sleep at 11 pm. It is too much. Then we talked at the agency, but they don't want [to agree to the transfer]. [*Gina, Filipina, two years in Taiwan, one year in Malaysia, one year in Singapore*]

Before contacting MOM to see whether it could help her to negotiate a transfer, Gina had tried to communicate and negotiate with her employer through the placement agency, but to no avail. She had hoped that MOM would be able to help with the transfer process by stopping her employers from forcibly repatriating her. However, the advice that MOM officials provided left her very frustrated and feeling that there was no viable alternative but to '*tahan*' (endure) and wait for her contract to finish:

> I tried to call MOM also, but just the same advice, 'Talk to your employer first, then go to the agency'. And they [MOM] said, 'We cannot do anything if your employer wants to send you to Indonesia'. That's why I decided to *tahan* and finish.

In this case, the intersecting factors of Gina's personal aspirations, her unequal worker–employer relationship and inadequate immigration policies and implementation, which reinforced this inequality, left Gina in an insecure and dependent state, despite her proactive attempts to negotiate safe work and seek protection. Amy had a similar experience when she contacted Hong Kong's Labour Department for advice because her employers were making her work at another address (which is unlawful under Hong Kong's labour laws). This interaction resulted in the Hong Kong Immigration Department mailing her a pamphlet outlining the labour laws. No further action was taken by the authorities to investigate her case, nor did they provide any assurance that Amy would not be incriminated should additional problems arise.[7] The risk of being prosecuted and held accountable for her employers' actions left Amy in an even more precarious position.

In both Amy's and Gina's cases, the absence of any follow-up measures to address their complaints suggests that their problems were interpreted not as forms of exploitative employment, which require state intervention, but as minor work disputes that can and should be resolved between workers and employers. This 'hands-off approach' reflects a tolerance of the risk of exploitation, placing the burden of protection on workers themselves, and thereby further diminishing workers' security. Although both Singapore and Hong Kong have instituted a range of legal and regulatory measures aimed at the protection of female migrant domestic workers and the prevention of their exploitation, it appears that such measures only come into effect *after* a formal complaint or report has been made. This means that workers are essentially left unsupported by the state if they do not access formal dispute resolution mechanisms. Yet, as the following section discusses, the current labour migration regime in Singapore and Hong Kong is not designed or implemented in a manner that substantively supports workers' access to formal mechanisms, as there is little to no certainty of employment security.

The Consequences of Seeking Justice: Implications for Employment and Financial Security

> Sometimes the police will say [to the domestic worker], 'If you pursue a case, you wouldn't be able to work'. And it is true, if they actually call the police and the contract is terminated, they will have to wait for a long time for the case to be solved and in the meantime they are not allowed to work. And if she is pursuing a case, the domestic worker has to keep paying for visa extensions, which is a barrier to access to justice. [*Chloe, Hong Kong, NGO staff member*]

> If we ask them, 'You want to make a case and then we can help? If we don't have time, we can still assist you'. But they [the workers] don't like because it will affect them. Losing their jobs and their experience is no good if they complain employers. Because if you have experience like you complain the employer, even if you win or lose, the [employment] record is no good. [*Polly, Thai, 27 years in Hong Kong*]

The above quotes illustrate a significant consequence of accessing formal justice and dispute resolution mechanisms for women migrant domestic workers – the negative implications for their employment and financial security. For a worker who decides to file a formal complaint, she needs to grapple with the very real possibility that her employer may decide to terminate her contact. Yet the labour migration rules around 'employer-tied visa' requirements and finding new employment in the case of premature contract termination place considerable restrictions on workers' flexibility to leave employers. For women migrant domestic workers, the risk is not simply losing one's job but also potentially losing the right to remain in Singapore and Hong Kong, which can have significant financial repercussions for the worker and her family. In addition to the threat of immediate termination, there is also a high likelihood that the worker will not be allowed to work for the period of time during which her case is being processed and investigated. Although Singapore and Hong Kong have in recent years revised their labour migration policies to include provisions that allow workers to find a new employer onshore while their case proceeds, the protections are still very limited. One reason for this is that they are only permitted on a discretionary basis. Of the four workers who had accessed formal justice mechanisms, two, Cherry and Molly, had applied for permission to work but only Molly had received approval. Cherry was unsure why she was not granted the permission to work.

Further, even in cases where a worker is permitted to seek new employment, her ability to secure work is contingent upon whether she can find an employer willing to hire someone who has an ongoing case. As Victoria, an employee of an NGO that supports victims of sexual assault, explained:

> [For the workers who come to us], generally, they would get the permission to work. But the problem here is that they need to interview with a new employer, who needs someone to start now or quite soon. But by the time you apply to the Immigration Department and they grant you permission to work, it could be anything up to two months, by which time the employer who probably needs someone urgently no longer wants to employ that person. And also, there are other things they may need to take time off work for, such as medical appointments, follow-up appointments, attend lawyers, legal appointment and then the actual court trial, which employers may not be so happy to let them take time off work to do. So, in that sense, it is not just on the authorities, but also on the general public and whether we are a supportive community towards victims. [*Victoria, Hong Kong, NGO staff member*]

Women migrant domestic workers were also concerned that lodging a formal complaint or filing a claim might be seen as 'making trouble' and could dissuade prospective employers from hiring them. Julia, whose employers had been making her complete chores outside her contractual obligations, explained that she had not considered reporting her employers to Singapore's labour department because:

> I don't want to get into trouble and I don't want to create trouble for them [her employers] too. I just want a good record to come out and finish my contract. I don't want to make trouble. Because like if complain

> to MOM, like something not good for the relationship [with her employers]. [*Julia, Filipina, five years in Taiwan, ten years in Singapore*]

Although the extent to which having a 'bad record' impacts upon workers' chances of securing a new employer is uncertain, this perception that filing a formal complaint may lead to a 'bad record' nonetheless influences workers' decision-making processes. Given the punitively high costs and risks associated with formal justice and dispute resolution mechanisms, it is not surprising that women migrant domestic workers do not perceive such mechanisms as resources that can be substantively accessed. Employment and maintaining a steady income represent the immediate priority for workers; the risk of not being able to work for an extended period threatens their ability to fulfil their needs. Uncertainties around the length of time required to complete case investigations, especially for criminal cases, and the issue of compensation (or lack of) further compounds the problem. While workers are likely to be awarded some compensation for labour claims in relation to salary disputes, especially if they have documented evidence, compensation is not assured for either labour or criminal complaints. In both Singapore and Hong Kong, the court can issue an award order for payment or compensation, which is legally binding; however, the *enforcement* of a judgement to recover restitution remains extremely limited. In Singapore, this is considered to be a 'civil claim' and a 'matter between the worker and employer' (Toh 2017). In Hong Kong, the Minor Employment Claims Adjudication Board and the Labour Tribunal both do not have executory powers, so even in cases where the worker is awarded compensation, there is a possibility[8] that she might have to spend more time in the district court in order to collect the awarded sum (Constable 1997). Although the performative element of legal justice is important for some survivors (to be further discussed below), these challenges in operationalising legal and criminal justice responses reflect a prioritisation of legal justice outcomes that do not necessarily begin from or engage with the context of the lives or needs of women migrant domestic workers. While the laws and regulations outlined in the various legislative instruments make it clear that women migrant domestic workers are entitled to support and protection from law enforcement, there remained a strong sense among the workers interviewed in this study that the legal and criminal justice system was of limited value to workers, given the time, effort and costs required.

Motivation to Report

It is clear from the analysis thus far that, as a consequence of the labour migration regimes in Singapore and Hong Kong, there are significant costs and risks that women migrant domestic workers must shoulder should they decide to access legal and regulatory interventions. Given this broader context, a question that emerges is: why did the four workers who lodged an employment or police complaint choose to do so? For three of them, anger towards their employer for treating them unfairly was the major driving force. Jessie shared that one of the main reasons why she filed a claim for under-payment of wages was that she was furious with her employer for attempting to repatriate her and refusing to write her a recommendation letter, despite her silence and sacrifice over the course of her employment:

> The thing is that they are so rude to me. They don't treat me well. So it made me furious every time. I was so angry and upset. She is bad and then I am bad like that. Revenge mind like that. Because if she is so kind to me, of course I will consider her [be considerate to her]. That is our tradition, like our Nepalese blood I think. For us, I will be very angry if you behave rude with me. But for a few hours if you are nice to me, I will forget everything. I will not be angry again. Our case is like that. [*Jessie, Nepalese, 18 years in Hong Kong*]

Likewise, Rina shared that once she was settled in with her new employer, she planned to lodge a formal complaint against her ex-employer with MOM because she felt that she had been unfairly treated *and* that her ex-employer needed to be held accountable for their actions:

> It is unfair for me, right? They sent me back to agency after I reject [their demands to work for their business]. So, for her, it is like as a maid, you don't have a right to complain. Just do whatever I ask you to do. But I know I have the right to reject. So I want to complain because, before me, she said all the maids not complaining. She said I am the first maid that I love to complain, so calculative because I don't want to work in the office. So I want to complain because I want her to stop sending the maid to the office like that. [*Rina, Filipina, 1.5 years in Macau, 10 months in Malaysia, 11 months in Singapore*]

While only indicative, given the small number of women who had proceeded to file a formal complaint or report against their employers, these examples suggest that a domestic worker's decision to access formal grievance mechanisms is driven by an underlying need for reciprocity, which, as the following chapter discusses, is a significant factor shaping how women migrant domestic workers understand and define their working and living conditions. Specifically, the findings reveal that, instead of assessing employer and work standards via objective indicators of exploitative employment practices, workers' perceptions of and responses to their employment situations are strongly associated with whether their employer is appreciative of their sacrifices and is able to reciprocate with a reasonable degree of compassion and sympathy.

Conclusion

Very few of the workers interviewed in this study had accessed formal dispute resolution mechanisms and these findings are not exceptional. Indeed, the data in the literature generally indicates that very few women migrant domestic workers seek legal and regulatory interventions. Indisputably, women migrant domestic workers are not simply victims to the machinations of their employers and many of them do adopt various help-seeking strategies to change their situations. However, the analysis in this chapter illustrates how their responses to poor working conditions and their negotiation of safe work are structured and constrained by the intersections between immigration policies, regulatory practices and the business model used by placement agencies, in both Singapore and Hong Kong. For example, workers' prioritisation of placement agencies over other service providers when seeking help or advice is inextricably linked to the labour migration regime in both city-states. Specifically, in a context in which workers' right to freely change employers is restricted by state law or regulation, either via the requirement for a release letter (as in Singapore) or the two-week rule (as in Hong Kong), placement agents become the 'safest' source of assistance for workers who experience difficult employment conditions and want to find a new employer. While I had not set out to focus on placement agents, the pivotal role that they play in women migrant domestic workers' everyday navigation of safe work emerged from the analysis. In particular, the findings show that in spite of the risks and costs associated with approaching placement agents for help, many workers are dependent on them to mediate employer–worker relations or facilitate contract transfer when the employment relationship breaks down. The workers in this study expressed much frustration and dissatisfaction over the quality of services they received from their placement agents. Yet, because of the gendered labour migration laws and policies in Singapore and Hong Kong, workers' power to independently negotiate improvements to their working conditions or exit an unsustainable employment situation without compromising their livelihood security is significantly constrained. Thus, the combination of these factors has produced a need for placement agents.

In summary, the practical utility of laws and regulations is limited, as is the current approach of introducing insular reforms to penalties or new policies for protection or as a response to exploitation, especially when the current system is still structured primarily to protect the integrity of the border instead of prioritising and responding to workers' needs, security and concerns. This problem is further compounded by a range of other issues such as discrimination, the absence of an adequate welfare system to support women through the process of lodging a claim or complaint, and a general lack of assistance with navigating the system (for example, around filing a claim, processing paperwork or language barriers). In making this assertion, I do not mean to argue that legal and criminal justice protections are irrelevant to safe and sustainable working conditions for women migrant domestic workers. Improving labour standards remains an important goal for the migrant domestic workers' rights movement. However, there is a need to foreground workers' voices and experiences, and to consider their responses within the broader systemic and employment context in which *they* determine what constitutes safety and security and how best to enable both. In particular, workers' experiences and perspectives point to the significance of emotional labour in their everyday negotiation of safe work – an aspect that remains largely unacknowledged by formal systems of protection and justice. The links between laws and regulations, the employment context and workers' perceptions of safe and secure work in the domestic workplace are examined more closely in the next chapter.

Notes

1 In MOM's guidebook for newly arrived women migrant domestic workers, placement agencies are listed as one of the main parties that workers can contact if they have labour-related problems.
2 Singapore has implemented a demerit point system that can lead to licence revocation if placement agencies fail to comply with regulations set out in Employment Agencies Act 1958. In Hong Kong, under the Code of Practice for Employment Agencies (CoP), section 62A of Employment Ordinance, overcharging of fees for workers by placement agencies, if guilty and convicted, can lead to license revocation and other penalties.
3 This comparison with placement agencies is in specific reference to the type and nature of frontline assistance provided for distressed women migrant domestic workers. It is acknowledged that CSOs in Singapore and Hong Kong have contributed in various capacities beyond everyday support and assistance.
4 In Singapore, placement agencies are legally allowed to charge migrant domestic workers one month's salary per year of contract of employment, while placement agencies in Hong Kong are allowed to charge workers 10% of their first month's salary.
5 Hong Kong Immigration Department had set up a special duties team in June 2013 specifically to combat job-hopping. Since then, they have consistently released annual data on number of visas revoked for job-hopping, and in 2021, announced that they will be undertaking a joint operation with the Labour Department to educate and conduct inspections of placement agencies to combat job-hopping (The Standard 2021).
6 As noted in Section 3.1, to prevent the forcible repatriation of female migrant domestic workers (and other low-wage migrant workers), Singapore has implemented a provision where a worker can stop the repatriation if she approaches an immigration officer and informs the officer that she has an outstanding dispute with her employer and is being forced to return to her country of origin. The immigration officer has a responsibility to then refer her case to the MOM officer stationed at the airport.
7 Under Clause 4(c) of the SEC, it is stated that 'any breach of Clause 4(a) and 4(b) of the contract which forms part of the conditions of stay to be imposed on the Helper will render the Helper and/or the aider and abettor liable to criminal prosecution' Hong Kong Immigration Department 2019).
8 Under the 'A Concise Guide to the Employment Ordinance' (Hong Kong Labour Department 2022, p. 9), it is stated that an employer who 'wilfully and without reasonable excuse' fails to pay the award is liable to prosecution. However, there is no

further information as to whether the state will proactively ensure that employers pay the settlement or whether it is dependent upon the worker to file a complaint.

References

Constable, N (1997), 'Sexuality and discipline among Filipina domestic workers in Hong Kong', *American Ethnologist*, 24(3): 539–558.

Goh, JMC (2018), Agents as migration infrastructure: Circulating debt and channelling Indonesian domestic workers in Singapore, Master's Thesis, National University of Singapore, Singapore.

Goh, JMC, Wee, K & Yeoh, BSA (2016), 'Who's holding the bomb? Debt-financed migration in Singapore's domestic work industry', *Migrating out of Poverty Research Programme*, Consortium Working Paper 38, University of Sussex, Brighton, pp. 1–34.

Hong Kong Immigration Department (2019), 'Standard employment contract and terms of employment for helpers', viewed 1 Feb.

Hong Kong Labour Department (2022), 'A concise guide to the Employment Ordinance', viewed 1 Feb, https://www.labour.gov.hk/eng/public/ConciseGuide.htm

McKeown, A (2012), 'How the box became black: Brokers and the creation of the free migrant', *Pacific Affairs*, 85(1): 21–45.

The Standard (2021), 'More than 4,400 job-hopping foreign domestic helpers recorded until October this year: Immigration Department', viewed 1 Feb, https://www.thestandard.com.hk/breaking-news/section/4/183122/More-than-4,400-job-hopping-foreign-domestic-helpers-recorded-until-October-this-year:-Immigration-Department

Toh, YC (2017), 'MOM: Salary recovery matters are civil claims', *The Straits Times*, 19 Jan, viewed 10 Sep, https://www.straitstimes.com/singapore/mom-salary-recovery-matters-are-civil-claims

Yeoh, BSA, Goh, C & Wee, K (2020), 'Social protection for migrant domestic workers in Singapore: International conventions, the law and civil society action', *American Behavioural Scientist*, 64(6): 841–858.

Chapter 6

Rethinking Gendered Labour Exploitation and Safe Work

'Exploitation' as Identified by Industry Stakeholders

Within academic, policy and public debates on the extent and practices of labour exploitation, the line between acceptable and unacceptable employment conditions dominates the discussion (Anderson & Rogaly 2005; Coghlan & Wylie 2011). As discussed in Chapter 3, critical research on human trafficking and modern slavery has identified that exploitation as defined in legal frameworks emphasises only the most extreme and physically visible forms of exploitation and harm and has been unable to capture the multitude of ways in which migrant workers experience exploitation (O'Connell Davidson & Anderson 2006; Skrivankova 2010). Indeed, it is well established that the majority of migrant workers are subjected to a range of exploitative practices (Anderson & Rogaly 2005; Coghlan & Wylie 2011). In view of the complexities of worker experiences, a number of scholars have argued in favour of a continuum of exploitation, to better capture the diversity of employment experiences, from criminal practices to decent work (see O'Connell Davidson & Anderson 2006; Andrees 2008; Skrivankova 2010; Coghlan & Wylie 2011; Huckerby 2015). These developments in research have been critical in advancing our understanding of labour exploitation and supporting the identification of operational indicators that provide guidance for frontline respondents such as state actors and NGO staff members (Skrivankova 2010). However, previous research in this area has largely been based on the analysis of responses to labour trafficking and forced labour in the Global North, with comparatively little attention given to how such responses are mapping out among industry stakeholders in relation to female migrant domestic labour in the Global South. Identifying how the concept of exploitation is interpreted by frontline respondents matters, not least because their assumptions of what is a 'genuine' work-related problem and who is a victim determine intervention and response efforts (Ham, Segrave & Pickering 2013; Pickering 2014; Segrave & Powell 2015). In this case, even though frontline NGO staff members have limited capacity to affect workers' access to formal victim support provisions (that is, the right to work and remain in the destination

DOI: 10.4324/9781003250364-6

city-state), they form a key part of the broader support infrastructure for women migrant domestic workers, particularly in helping workers to reach out to employers and assisting them to access legal and regulatory interventions.

From the interviews with frontline NGO staff members, it was evident that there are inconsistencies in their perceptions of what constitutes exploitative employment. For some NGOs whose objective is to secure pecuniary compensation for ex-women migrant domestic workers, the definition of 'exploitation' is intentionally narrower to focus on 'people who are owed compensation'. Others referred to the state's main labour legislation as the benchmark for exploitative employment:

> [Employment Act], that is a benchmark because that follows international labour standards. In fact, 12 hours [length of workday] is the norm [for women migrant domestic workers]. Most domestic workers work that much, even those with 'nice employers' work about 12 hours. But if you work for 12 hours, under our labour law, it is exploitation, it is not allowed. Then there are public holidays, which they are denied. There is no such thing as paid annual leave for them. Things like overtime pay, all of these [they] don't have. But when we tell MOM that, they are like, 'Oh, no wonder you say all [women migrant domestic workers] are exploited, because you have these kinds of impossible standards'. Because the Employment Act [which covers those entitlements] is not what they recognise [for women migrant domestic workers]. [*Joel, Singapore, NGO staff member*]

Another NGO staff member, Noah, argued that when it comes to live-in domestic labour performed by women migrants, it is not appropriate to determine the presence or absence of exploitation solely on the basis of formal labour standards. Instead, Noah claimed that there is a need for a more 'discerning' approach to account for what he considers to be workers' unrealistic or mismatched expectations of everyday working and living conditions in the domestic workplace:

> There was this case where she [the domestic worker] was promised she would definitely have a room to sleep in and three meals etcetera and definitely give her eight hours of sleep. But when she comes and she has to sleep with the grandfather who wakes up three times in the night and because of that she has to wake up three times at night, so she calculates and doesn't get exactly eight hours of sleep [and contacts us]. Then we just have to tell her, 'You come here with your eyes open. If you tell people that you have experience in working in eldercare and you didn't take this into consideration, that an older person has to wake up many times in the night?'. So these are the things that we have to be very discerning on this, because we cannot be looking at the generalised statement that 'all maids

> must be entitled to this, this, this'. You have to look at the kind of job she is doing. There are girls who come here eagerly for a job, but the reality of it … they didn't realise that, 'Eh, this is not what I envisioned it to be'. Some of them are … most of them looking for a job will say, 'I can take a little bit more, doesn't matter, right'. But it is when they really get on the job that they realise it is too much for them to ask. There are many like that. [*Noah, Singapore, NGO staff member*]

The assumption that certain responsibilities, such as waking up in the middle of the night to care for an elderly household member, are a normal and expected part of the job for women migrant domestic workers reveals the gendered expectations surrounding women's labour. Specifically, underpinning the idea that these workers should not expect well-defined working hours despite being waged employees are gendered assumptions about women as 'selfless' carers, who are obligated to subordinate their interests and well-being to the personal needs of others, in this case, the elderly or children they are paid to care for.

'Mismatched expectations' were also invoked by Tom. He talked about the type of cases where his organisation can help – those involving abuse, wage disputes or lack of food, and those that his organisation is unable to provide support for (where there is depression, homesickness or a mismatch between workers' and employers' expectations), which he classified as 'problems from the workers':

> The top two are actually problems that the employees face, that we need to help. So, I think one is about abuse, one is about salary. So, physical abuse cases are actually about 10% of the total cases that we handle. Sometimes, they [workers] don't have enough food. Because you work and you don't eat, that is abuse. There is another about 10% to 15% is salary dispute. So, these work out to about 30%. The other two is actually very much problems from the workers. We have about 10% that they actually can't adapt, so they want to ask for transfer. There is a mismatch of the expectations of the employer. For example, they [the worker] said that 'This house so big, you want me to clean?'. Then we have [some workers] maybe missing home, like wants to go home, homesickness. Some mental depression, for instance, again because of homesickness. Very minor, minor issues. Those unfortunately won't form a trend or cannot be a category that we think that we can address. It is more very individual. It is very emotional or sometimes quite minute. [*Tom, Singapore, NGO staff member*]

According to Tom, there is a clear division between problems that are classified as the employer's fault and problems that are the worker's responsibility. This distinction largely aligns with the legal and regulatory frameworks in

Singapore, which establish that issues categorised as the responsibility of workers are those that fall outside legal and regulatory remits. Some NGO staff members also expressed little sympathy for 'unhappy' domestic workers, who were considered not to be exploited or subjected to poor working conditions but simply to have 'mismatched expectations' (that is, who were dissatisfied with the work they had to do or unable to adapt to working life abroad). This reflects a clear prioritisation of workers' physical well-being, with little regard for the gendered, relational and interactive aspects of live-in waged domestic labour, in particular, how it involves emotions and affect. Of the 20 CSO staff members interviewed in this study, only one specifically addressed the need to recognise the relational aspects of the employment relationship in domestic labour:

> [Many workers] value that harmony and peace [in the home], you shouldn't underestimate that because they are at complete mercy in a way of their employer's mood. So, harmony and peace might hold greater value for them, as long as they are not being grossly underpaid or physically or emotionally abused, harmony and peace might have greater value for them than we think. [*Nora, Hong Kong, NGO staff member*]

Nonetheless, Nora noted that her organisation's focus remains on monitoring and estimating labour exploitation based on the prevalence of particular employment conditions as reported by workers (such as inadequate rest, wage manipulation, inadequate remuneration and physical abuse). In examining how and what frontline NGO staff members define as exploitation, it is clear that they are simultaneously drawing upon 'ungendered' labour regulatory frameworks *and* gendered expectations of domestic labour to identify actual harm and exploitation. Yet the interviews with women migrant domestic workers revealed that the prominence accorded to legal and regulatory categories of harm and exploitation poorly reflects the meanings and assessments adopted by workers themselves.

'Exploitation' as Identified by Women Migrant Domestic Workers

Forty-eight (92%) of the 52 workers interviewed had experienced unlawful and/or substandard employment conditions. This data was obtained by comparing workers' descriptions of their experiences against the labour regulatory frameworks in Singapore and Hong Kong. 'Substandard' employment in this context refers to employment conditions that are included under employment guidelines for employers but are not legally regulated. As detailed in Chapter 2, compliance with conditions related to, for example, daily working hours, accommodation, curfew on rest days and restrictions on communications is left up to the discretion of individual employers. In presenting this data, I wanted to illustrate the prevalence of such substandard employment conditions in both city-states based upon the official indicators. However, this classification *does not* represent how the women migrant domestic workers in this study defined and understood their employment experiences.

Notably, none of the workers used the term 'labour exploitation' when talking about various employment conditions and work experiences. Instead, when describing their experiences they used terms such as 'can or cannot accept (or unacceptable)' and 'can or cannot tolerate (or intolerable)'. To foreground workers' voices, I will be using the terms that they have used to refer to employment conditions, rather than 'exploitation'. However, this terminology fails to capture precisely the complexities and ambiguities reflected in the workers' descriptions and assessments of their experiences. Specifically, the language they used obscures the interplay of fluid (and shifting) boundaries between the employment practices that workers term as unacceptable or intolerable and their accounts or descriptions of what they consider to be the problem. This reflects an issue that Devault (1990, p. 98) refers to as 'linguistic incongruence' – that is, a situation where the language used does not accurately represent individual experiences, in this case women's experiences. Instead, the social and academic constructs that we rely upon to translate women's experiences do not always correspond to what is meaningful in women's lives, as there are many parts of female consciousness that have been left out of the dominant interpretative frames, which structure how women learn to speak and hear. Consequently, to elicit and thereby better understand the incompletely articulated aspects of women domestic workers' experiences, there is a need to go beyond the 'standard vocabulary' and listen to the talk that occurs in interviews, to the accounts that are not always simple or straightforward (Devault 1990). I return to this issue of labelling workers' experiences at the end of this chapter, to argue that a different terminology is perhaps necessary to capture the fluidity of workers' experiences in negotiating safe employment in the gendered domestic workplace. For the purposes of this chapter, the terms 'unacceptable' or 'intolerable' are used to indicate employment practices that are negatively perceived by workers.

In the conversations with workers around their understanding and evaluation of the domestic workplace, four key employment practices were most identified by workers as unacceptable or intolerable: (1) restricted freedom to socialise or communicate with non-household members (including speaking to neighbours and access to mobile phones), (2) working excessive hours, (3) working on rest days and (4) verbal abuse. With the exception of working on rest days, which seems to be a regulatory grey zone[1] in Hong Kong and Singapore, the other employment practices are not classified as unlawful in both city-states. By comparison, even though the workers in this study had experienced unlawful employment conditions, they focused less on those practices. Instead, they spoke at length about employment practices that are considered by some stakeholders and legal structures to be 'unregulatable' – and to this the discussion now turns.

Restricted Freedom to Socialise: Social Isolation and Limitations on Communication Devices

> Employer no let us talk to our friends [from] Indonesia. Sometimes, we meet downstairs or even at the playground, we cannot talk because we have to work. Even if we go outside, we go to work, not for holiday. And in Singapore very boring because [I] don't have holidays, that's why I think maybe Hong Kong better. And no telephone also in Singapore. I tried to ask [my employer if I can use the phone] also. I asked, 'Can I bring this one [mobile phone]?'. Then [they said] no, everything no. [*Queenie, Indonesian, two years in Singapore, four years in Hong Kong*]

Queenie's story of being prohibited from contacting other women migrant domestic workers is a common experience, especially among Singapore-based workers. More than half of the 52 workers (n = 27) shared that they had worked for employers who controlled their access to mobile phones and/or required them to obtain permission before they could leave the house. In addition, out of this group of 27 workers, four reported that they were even expressly prohibited from talking to people who were not part of the family (such as other domestic workers and neighbours). Forced isolation was also one of the main reasons why some of the Singapore-based workers had relocated to Hong Kong, where there is a mandatory day off. For women migrant domestic workers, the weekly rest day does not simply represent time off work. For Amanda, who has worked in both Singapore and Hong Kong, the once-a-week rest day was a time when she could contact her friends and family. Not being able to maintain regular contact with their families was identified as a particular issue by the 27 workers. Of these workers, 11 noted that for the duration of their two-year contract, they were not able to contact their families, while four other workers said that their employers gradually permitted them access to telephones, after a few months into the contract. However, their usage was restricted to their rest time at night or their rest days. In two cases, the employers had retained the letters that the workers had written to their families instead of sending them out, as promised. Recalling that it was the only time when she had directly 'confronted' her first employer, Nelly shared:

N: When I clean my employer's cupboard, I found so many of my letters never sent to Indonesia. Then I feel so bad … because no contact with my mother. I wanted to complain to my employer.

S: So, did you ask your employer why she didn't send the letters?

N: Yah, then she said, 'I am busy.' Then I said, 'You every time busy, you don't have time to send, you can tell me, I can give to my friend instead'. Then she became angry like that, so ok Yah. [*Nelly, Indonesian, three years in Singapore, one year in Taiwan, eight years in Hong Kong*]

Another worker, Tasha, was also very angry when she found out that her ex-employer had not sent any of her letters to her family in Indonesia, as was promised:

> I didn't have the phone, so I can only call [my family] when they [the family] went holiday. Some more it is the 婆婆 [grandmother] was the one who helped me, give me money to buy phone card so I can call home. Then I wrote letter to my family, they also didn't send because my mother never received. Of course, my parents will worry right because there was no news from me. But they [the employer] don't care. So, maybe out of 100%, I think that they are only nice to me 20%. Because I am human being, even though we are your maid no doubt but we got the heart also, so why can't you treat us like a better person, so we can work for you better also. [*Tasha, Indonesian, 17 years in Singapore*]

In all of the above examples, the workers faced multiple unlawful and/or sub-standard employment practices. For example, in Tasha's case, she was unlawfully deployed to clean for her employer's friend and subjected to illegal salary deductions. Yet it was their employers' restrictions on socialisation or communication with non-household members that triggered strong feelings of resentment and frustration among the workers interviewed. For these workers, there was a clear association between accessing communication devices (such as mobile phones and letters), maintaining contact with family and being respected as a human being. It is not just about the prohibition or control over their right to socialisation and communication, but also the feeling that their employers were not treating them as an equal; a human who has a family and needs a social network independent of her job. As one of the workers, Maya, stated:

> I definitely cannot tolerate if I cannot talk with each other [other people]. Because we are human, right? We must talk also. Like my neighbour, she cannot talk with other people. She had to write letter and put in front of my house to tell me about her problems. [*Maya, Indonesian, 15 years in Singapore*]

Such restrictions on contact and communication with non-household members had a significant impact on workers' capacity to form meaningful social networks of support, which limited their capacity to access help. This was exemplified in the case of Nelly, an Indonesian woman, who shared that she had been very frustrated with her work conditions at her first workplace. However, she did not manage to reach out to anyone because:

> That time is first time [working overseas]. I don't have any experience that's why. I was very scared also and maybe because I still young, I was scared to do something, to have trouble. And because in Singapore,

> I cannot connect to everyone because no off day and no phone, so I cannot do anything. So, I just follow the employer's rule. I don't want the employer to get angry with me. I am so scared that if I do something, my employer will do something to me like bad things, so I just keep quiet. [*Nelly, Indonesian, three years in Singapore, one year in Taiwan, eight years in Hong Kong*]

Many of the workers had experienced similar feelings of social isolation and the associated vulnerability. In some cases, restrictions on workers' access to communication and socialisation, exacerbated by their limited English language skills, resulted in a situation where they felt completely isolated and could see no feasible means of seeking redress and protection. It is worth noting that for nearly all of the workers who had experienced such restrictions (n = 26), this occurred in their first ever overseas employment contract, which, as identified in Paul's (2017) study, further compounds the problem of social isolation because they have yet to form social networks and connections with other migrant domestic workers. As discussed in Chapter 4, work permit conditions that hold employers legally responsible for the control and supervision of workers may be a key reason why Singaporean employers are more likely to adopt controlling measures to restrict and monitor workers' movements and communications (see also Huang & Yeoh 1996; Human Rights Watch 2005; Poon 2009; Tan 2010; Wessels, Ong & Daniel 2017; HOME & Liberty Shared 2019).

Overworking and Excessive Working Hours

Excessive working hours and being overworked comprised the second most identified problematic employment practice. Similar to restrictions on workers' communications, specific hours of work are not enshrined in employment or criminal law in Singapore and Hong Kong. Although one of the clauses in Singapore's SEC requires the employer to specify the hours of continuous rest that they will be providing to the worker, the contract is not legally binding. In Hong Kong, there are no legal stipulations with regard to maximum working hours. Of the 52 workers interviewed, 18 reported that they had to work excessively long hours on a regular basis.[2] These 18 workers said that they felt overworked because they had too many chores to complete and were physically exhausted as they regularly had fewer than five hours sleep at night. A common theme in their narratives was the number of chores they had to complete, which were often a lot more than stated in their employment contract and amounted to an excessive volume of work. For example, Abby, who had lost more than 15 kg over the three years of working for her first employer, shared that while her employer did not specify a fixed time when she had to wake up, the number of housekeeping chores and childcaring responsibilities she had to complete each day meant that she could only go to sleep at 1 am and had to wake by 5 am:

A: Every day I sleep at 1 am because I am ironing at night because I cannot iron in the morning. I am taking care of the baby. She will make me finish everything, but I also don't want to leave my job if I am not yet finished with ironing, because the next day will have more and more ironing. Sometimes, she will tell me to rest first, but I cannot rest because I am thinking my work is too much.
S: But why do you have to wake up so early at 5 am?
A: Because I wake up when everyone is sleeping so I can clean the house. I must vacuum every day and she [the employer] will check if I wake up or not. She [the employer] will listen to the doorbell [a bell pull that connects with a bell, and which rings a bell when pulled] because she have the bell in the kitchen. [*Abby, Filipina, nine years in Singapore*]

Echoing Moras's (2008) study, which examined the tensions arising from waged domestic labour in the private workplace, the above example demonstrates that the problem of overworking is not simply about the number of working hours per se, but also about the lack of clarity around working hours, the absence of well-defined tasks and working under surveillance. While the authorities in both Singapore and Hong Kong have consistently argued that due to the private nature of the workplace it is unfeasible to have standardised working hours or ensure that employment contracts reflect well-defined job tasks, as per the public workplace (as detailed in Chapter 2), the absence of such regulatory protections can create a situation where workers end up working excessive hours and having long standby hours.[3]

The requirement to be on call 24/7 was very common among the workers in this research, especially those who had caregiving responsibilities for young children and the elderly. Of the nine women who talked about the need to be present and available 24/7 to meet the needs of household members, all except one complained that they had to sleep in the same room as a child or elderly ward, which meant that if the child or grandparent woke up at night, their sleep would also be disturbed. It also meant that they had little to no privacy for the duration of their employment contract. One such worker, Julia, had been employed to care for a grandmother who had Alzheimer's disease. She explained that, even though her employers were nice to her, it was very difficult working for that family because:

> This grandmother ... she make the night-time, daytime [time disorientation]. Too long the working hours and night-time, I cannot sleep. When I tell the family, they tell me always, 'Once she sleeps, you sleep, quickly go and sleep too'. But the grandmother is really always awake, you know. She stays awake all the night and last time I almost give up, but I said I think of my daughter. [*Julia, Filipina, five years in Taiwan, ten years in Singapore*]

The lack of clearly defined working and resting hours, and the difficulty of negotiating hours of work while living and working in the same space as employers, was why Amy had jumped at the chance to reside in a separate location from her employers' house when the opportunity arose. Notwithstanding the risk of repatriation if she was reported to the authorities,[4] Amy shared that:

> For me is because … we have tried already live in, right? Because even you finish the work at 9 pm and you try to sleep, but even then, they will knock on your door to tell you to do something. But that is our privacy, right? Just like finish the job, we still have tomorrow to work, right? Why are you still knocking the door of the helper? And in the stay out, if you finish the work, then you can go home and take a rest. You can relax. No need to think about the employer. [*Amy, Filipina, 24 years in Hong Kong*]

The only worker who expressed positive sentiments about this type of sleeping arrangement was Ruby, who stated that, while it was 'not very good to sleep because I have to look after her [the grandma]', she was 'ok' with it because she 'liked the grandmother a lot' and could rest in the afternoons. Ruby's comments reveal that, while this sleeping arrangement is not ideal, her perception of her employment situation (that is, whether it was acceptable or exploitative) was contingent upon and embedded in social relations formed through her day-to-day interaction with the grandmother.

Working on Rest Days

The third most identified employment practice by workers as a problem was working on rest days. Although in Hong Kong employers are legally required to provide workers with a continuous rest period of not less than 24 hours, this law is rarely, if ever, enforced. In Singapore, even though the government's guidelines indicate that employers should not compel workers to work on their rest days, this is not enshrined in law and is a discretionary decision for employers. Seventeen of the workers interviewed mentioned that they worked on their rest day (generally completing light housekeeping chores) before going out, reflecting the findings of other studies that have reported high levels of this occurring (see Moras 2008; Parreñas 2015; Anderson 2016; Barua, Haukanes & Waldrop 2016). Nonetheless, whereas the abovementioned practices (restrictions on communication, excessive working hours and being on call 24/7) were identified by most workers as unacceptable, attitudes towards working on rest days were much more ambivalent.

While there was a general sense shared by the workers of not wanting their employers to ask too much of them on their rest days, many expressed that they were not unwilling to do *some* housekeeping chores on those days. When asked why they were willing to do so, the workers gave a range of explanations, including that such work is a part of normal employment expectations and that it can be used as leverage in future. For example, to Queenie, who had been with her current employer for nearly two years at the time of the interview and was planning to renew her contract, carrying out additional work on her rest day was acceptable because her employer was 'very nice to me' and the duties were 'just simple things that take a short time, like preparing breakfast or cleaning'. This was a sentiment shared by Molly, who had been subjected to severe exploitation by her previous employers but at the time of the interview was employed by a family that she described as 'very good to me'. Molly stated that she would not hesitate to return home immediately, even if she was out on her rest day, to help her employer clean up after her father-in-law had urinated or defecated in his bed or clothes. She insisted that she was 'ok with it' and strongly disagreed with the suggestion that she was being taken advantage of:

> [About the working conditions] I am not working only for the money. Because I know I am a domestic helper, and the helper is family, so that's why if she needs help, I am ok to help. I am not only here to earn money. That's why it is not only just 'this is my off day, you don't have to call me, you don't have to ask for help, you can do it yourself'. I am not like that. [*Molly, Burmese, one year and ten months in Singapore*]

For Molly, having her rest day prematurely cut short was articulated as part of the 'give and take' that demonstrates her appreciation of her current employer's kindness towards her, as well as a 'sacrifice' that helps her to build and sustain a positive employment relationship. Although Molly's preparedness to do 'extra jobs' was not shared by all workers, the workers who talked about sacrificing part of their rest days to complete basic chores had explained that this was in accordance with their internalised standards of what constitutes a 'good' domestic worker. For example, Julia, who had a part-time job as a recruiter of migrant domestic workers and regularly advised her new recruits on what they should and should not do in order to be a 'good' domestic worker, commented:

> They [my employers] told me, when they eat breakfast, no need to keep [the dishes] or anything. I can just leave it for them to do it. But I am very what you know … uneasy for me to see the mess there. So, I said, 'Anyway it is my day off, I can go out later on'. So, I kept and washed everything first. The previous maid was like … once it is her day off, she just took a bath, never did anything and just left them alone. But I don't want myself to become like that. [*Julia, Filipina, five years in Taiwan, ten years in Singapore*]

In both of these cases, the women made a decision to accept work conditions that they perceived to be a normal component of domestic work: not least because these conditions *are* a regular and unquestioned component of a domestic worker's day-to-day experience of employment. The pertinent issue here is not simply to consider worker consent and the acceptability of exploitative practices but, more significantly, to understand how the informal rules governing domestic work and the expectations of domestic workers (such as their constant availability and provision of quality service) affect the perceptions of workers, particularly of employment conditions and standards in the domestic workplace. In turn, what is objectively identified as exploitative and harmful in regulatory frameworks may be accepted by some workers as a legitimate or normal employment practice. The relational context of live-in domestic work contributes to this situation as it can be difficult for workers to articulate their demands or enforce boundaries around work hours (Duffy 2005; Blackett 2019). However, workers do not indiscriminately accept exploitative work conditions; rather, their acceptance is premised upon expectations of reciprocity in other areas of their working and/or living experience.

For Molly and Julia, their willingness to disregard a poor employment practice was future orientated. It was associated with the conviction that, by doing so – by having patience, working hard and making 'sacrifices' – they would be able to attain their goals. 'Sacrifice' in this context can very much resemble exploitation; however, for workers, it may not necessarily be perceived as such. Instead, as noted in Chuang's (2017) analysis of exploited Chinese workers in Italy's garment industry, the (temporary) acceptance of substandard working conditions is perceived as a means to an end, an avenue that they might leverage to 'prove themselves' in order to further other goals, including a better relationship with employers who trust them, higher job security or more material benefits. Correspondingly, the willingness to take on additional responsibilities and overlook certain exploitative practices is closely correlated to workers' perceptions of whether their employer is 'worth it'. This means whether the employer is able to recognise and appreciate the worker's sacrifice and reciprocate with a requisite degree of compassion and sympathy when the worker makes a mistake. For instance, after explaining that she was willing to complete housekeeping and caregiving chores even on her rest days, Julia noted that she had recently had a big fight with her employers and had now changed her mind about working on rest days. When I asked what it was about the fight that caused her to change her mind, Julia explained:

> Because I have a curfew, one day only I am late by one hour. Every time I give way [give in] to them you know, every time I finish my work before I go out, then I every time by 8:30 pm or 8:45 pm, I come back even though my curfew is 9 pm. Then last Sunday only I was late for 20 minutes and my boss was very angry. Then I said, 'Sorry madam for coming back late', but they still keep on saying, 'You know what time you need to come back by?'. I was quite angry that they had scolded me just for being 20 minutes late and they just waited for me to make the child sleep. But they shouldn't do that because it is my day off. They are

> taking advantage of me already, but I keep quiet because I love their kids. But this is not the right way to do to me. [*Julia, Filipina, five years in Taiwan, ten years in Singapore*]

While explaining the situation, Julia repeated the phrase 'please give and take' and stated that she was most angry when her employers compared her curfew time to that of other workers: 'She said like this, "You know most maids have to come back earlier than you?". Then I told her, "Please madam, don't compare. If you want to say everything about my friends, I am the worst off because I have to clean before I go out"'. After her fight with her employer, Julia no longer felt that it was acceptable for her to work on her rest day and was eagerly waiting for her contract to end so that she could change employer. Again, this reveals how informal obligations and expectations play an important role in shaping a worker's sense of what is acceptable and unacceptable employer behaviour. Julia's case illustrates that when informal or non-contractual expectations are not met, which in this case occurred when the employer failed to appreciate Julia's efforts, workers' evaluation of their employment conditions will also change. Accordingly, labour exploitation should not be conceptualised solely as something that happens to a worker, but rather as something that is *experienced* by a worker and is situated within the broader work context, which is not just compliance with labour legislation and workers' rights, but includes the employer's capacity to respect the worker, recognise their efforts and reciprocate appropriately. A perceived lack of respect was a reason cited by many of the workers in this study for their unwillingness to work for a verbally abusive employer, as discussed in the following section.

Verbal Abuse and Lack of Respect

> [When she verbally abused me in public] that is a very unforgettable moment and after that she made me embarrassed and hurt my feelings. And after that I talked to her that, 'Actually you need me and I need you, so I am not a slut that you treat me like this. I have feelings. I get hurt'. But at that moment, she don't want to listen, of course, she is the employer. 'I am the boss' she is shouting at me like that. So, what can I do? She is the boss. [*Kate, Filipina, four years and six months in Hong Kong*]

> I think first is for the culture. The culture of the employer. Because they think that they are the employer, so they should have … they already pay you money for salary, so you have to work for them, so you have to follow their instructions and what they want. Even if there is no rest time, they don't care. Not enough food, they don't care. But you have to work. They not care like whether you are tired or you are homesick, they don't care about the workers. They just care about 'what I need'. [*Polly, Thai, 27 years in Hong Kong*]

For the women migrant domestic workers interviewed in this study, employers' attitudes represented a key measure of their employment conditions. Nearly half of the workers (n = 24) mentioned that employers who are verbally abusive have a very negative impact on their everyday employment experience. Yet, as evident from Kate's and Polly's experiences, employers have a great deal of power to determine the worker's everyday working and living conditions. If the employer is verbally abusive, there is very little that a woman can do, apart from terminating her contract, which, as established in Chapter 5, is rarely an affordable option. On the other hand, as Kate pointed out, employer reciprocity is not perceived by workers as something that can be offered arbitrarily, dependent on the employer's goodwill. Instead, it was identified by the workers as a central aspect of employment relations, and equally as important as other tangible employment conditions such as wages, food, accommodation, job responsibilities and working hours. One of the workers, Sally, recounted that in her previous employment she had requested an early contract termination after half a year into the contract. Even though there was 'not a lot of work', Sally was having a 'really hard time' because her employer used a lot of profanities:

> I find it really hard to work with the old lady, because of too much verbal abuse. Keep on saying so many bad words. And so, that time I always trying to cut my contract, to terminate my contract with her. But she doesn't want to. She tried giving me a higher wage, higher than the minimum allowable wage. Then if she say sorry [after using bad words], I just say, ok, forget about it, but don't do it again. But then, she still keeps on doing it. Like until I already have full [the situation was too much to bear]. So, I just make a letter, like five pages in the paper. I put in her room, that she need to read that [letter]. But after I make the letter, she said, 'I am going to Canada, visit my relative'. She stayed there for like three weeks and until when she came back, she said to me, 'Can we have a talk?'. And then, we went out and have a talk in Times Square and she told me, 'I learned my lesson when you tell me everything, point by point. And now can you help me change. I want to change because I have been like that for how long since I am a kid'. Because the [employer's] experience is like, they have always like one kid [who is taken care of by], one domestic worker [amah]. So, she comes from a rich family. She is used to this kind of like shouting and saying, 'You don't have any sense, use your common sense'. Something like this. 'You stupid. You never think'. [*Sally, Filipina, one year in Singapore, 30 years in Hong Kong*]

The verbal abuse had a significant impact on Sally and she 'really wanted to break my contract'. However, after talking with her employer, she decided to give her another chance and continue the contract. She went on to work with the employer until the employer returned to Canada. Explaining why she had decided to stay on, Sally stated:

> So, [at that time] I cannot take it anymore, so, I really wanted to break my contract. But then when she told me this [that she wants to change], I find that she is so sincere. And so, it became a challenge for me. To help her change. And because it is not for me but for the coming future domestic worker. So, ok, I try [to help her], and it is good. Because [when she said bad words again] I only say, 'Oh, come on', I just said like this and she will just keep quiet. And then later on, we become friends.

The rapport Sally developed with her employer was not an experience commonly shared by other women migrant domestic workers in this study. Yet it reveals the relational and interactive nature of employment relations in the domestic workplace, which require employers to engage with their worker beyond mere compliance with labour standards. And it is vital that employers acknowledge and respect women migrant domestic workers. Indeed, the need for employers to be appreciative and *care for* their workers is a point that some of the employers interviewed in this study raised. Tammie said that she tries to include the domestic worker in the family life as it is important to her that the worker is 'happy' working in her home:

> From my personal perspective, if you are not good to the worker, why would the worker be good to your family? Why would the worker work for you with her heart? For example, some of my friends, when they go out to eat, they would not bring the worker along. They said, 'There is a lot of food at home, why do we need to bring her along?'. But this is not like that in my house. We will go out together to eat, unless she is the one who said that she doesn't want to go. Because I feel that if you just leave her in the house by herself, she can become very lonely and like she is not part of the family. Of course, there is an employer–employee relationship and there are times when I do scold her, like, 'Why did you do it like this? Clean it quickly'. But then when we go out to eat or when it is her birthday, we will eat with her. So, for me, I think a bad employer is one who does not treat her like she is part of the family. Just treat her like an outsider. [*Tammie, Hong Kong, Employer*]

The emphasis on workers' emotional well-being and recognising that domestic workers are human beings who require 'freedom' and cannot be expected to be available around the clock was also reflected in Evelyn's account:

> [It is important that] you kind of do need to realise that your helper is still human at the end of the day. And just like you experience, you know, tiredness and bad days at work, you must realise that happens to your

> helper too. For my helper, sometimes when she is really in a bad mood, it would be because she had received bad news from home. Like in Philippines when they have typhoon and the roof collapses. These kinds of things weigh on her mind. I don't expect her to be cheerful and happy all the time. It is not fair. [*Evelyn, Singapore, Employer*]

What is apparent across these examples is that the development of positive employment relations is a generative and interactive process in which workers and employers alike need to engage. Even though the employment relationship is hierarchal, it is still essential that the employer (and other family members) recognise the humanity and sociality of the worker and include them in the family to an extent. More broadly, the above cases align with Parreñas and Silvey's (2018) assertion that migrant domestic workers, like other workers, do not necessarily measure 'good' employers and 'good' employment conditions according to extrinsic material rewards. Instead, workers value employers who treat them with dignity, which includes being sensitive to their eating preferences; who do not verbally abuse them; and who recognise them as persons, for example, by acknowledging their birthdays or other significant life events. Although the notions of respect and trust cannot be captured within labour regulations, criminal legislation or contractual obligations, workers' perceptions of respect, trust and understanding are closely associated with employers' capacity to abide by fair labour standards, as exploitative employment practices are viewed as an indication that employers do not respect and/or empathise with workers (Anderson 2016; Parreñas & Silvey 2018).

Fictive Kinship and Relations of Reciprocity, Respect, Trust and Empathy

As discussed in Chapter 2, the focus within the extant scholarship on employment relations in migrant domestic labour has largely favoured contractual employment relations over fictive kin relations. For example, research by Miles (1999) and Akalin (2015) describes how, by including the worker as 'one of the family', employers felt justified in increasing their workload and providing them with lower wages or delaying wage payments, as they believed that the worker's affective links to the family mean that she will tolerate such conditions and empathise with the needs and limitations of the family. Other scholars have similarly suggested that the unequal distribution of power and authority in the domestic workplace means that any changes to employment conditions and social relationships are entirely dependent on the cooperation of the employer (Romero 1992; Anderson 2016). Within this frame of understanding, the embrace of familial belonging conceals myriad exploitative employment practices and invisibilises workers' status as workers. Yet this sense of 'belonging to the family' was something that many of the workers I spoke to actively sought and perceived as a strategy to enable their everyday security. Specifically, when asked about how they regarded their current employment and what they considered to be a 'good' employer, 45 of the 52 female migrant domestic workers interviewed talked about being treated like part of the family, and this was used by workers as a positive descriptor of employment relationships. This association between a 'good employer', 'good' working conditions and familial membership suggests that fictive kinship, while not recognised in formal contractual arrangements, is not necessarily incompatible with 'good' employment conditions. In making this assertion, I am not arguing that the presence of fictive kinship necessarily leads to safe and sustainable working conditions for women migrant domestic workers. However, the findings do suggest that the current dimensions of transactional labour law, which are premised upon labour performed in a waged economy, do not fully account for the gendered and relational dimensions of live-in domestic labour as performed by migrant women.

What constitutes 'being part of the family' was described in different ways by the workers in this research. For example, for Sascha, 'being part of the family' was associated with a more egalitarian work relationship in that, even when there was conflict or she had made a mistake, she felt able to voice her disagreement or share her problems without fear of reprisal: 'A good employer is just like a family also, that sometimes you have arguments, then later, is ok' [*Sascha, Filipina, eight years in Singapore, 18 years in Hong Kong*].

Another worker, Bella, who had been with her current employer for six years at the time of the interview, echoed this sentiment:

> If I don't like the way they talk to me, I will ask why. Because they treat us like family like that. Now, if I don't like [the way they treat me], I will tell them straightaway, no need to keep [it in] for so long. Respect is the word. [*Bella, Filipina, six years in Singapore, three years in Hong Kong, ten years in Singapore*]

For Nelly, who specialises in providing care for children and the elderly, 'being part of the family' was associated with increased respect and understanding from employers:

N: The good employer is who can understand about us … treat us very good like family. But not good family, they not treat us like family, they just treat us like helper.

S: What is the difference between helper and family?

N: Like family, we can feel comfortable, how they talk to us and then also whenever the kid is rude to us, the mother will say, 'Don't rude to auntie'. This is comfortable to us, so it is important. [*Nelly, Indonesian, three years in Singapore, one year in Taiwan, eight years in Hong Kong*]

Based on the above descriptions, it is clear that for these workers 'being part of the family' safeguards against intolerable employment practices and/or abusive behaviours – practices and behaviours that are often not recognised within legal and regulatory frameworks anyway (such as verbal abuse or a lack of respect). This illustrates how the protections provided by labour law are limited within the domestic workplace, and that workers perceive emotional ties as potentially offering more protection and security than the law. Further, there is no capacity within labour and criminal legislation to recognise or police the non-physical forms of abuse arising from those relations, even though such abuse has significant implications for workers' everyday negotiation of safe work and well-being.

Some workers talked about 'being part of the family' as being treated with empathy and recognised as humans who can feel lonely and who need communication and understanding:

> [I think they are good] because they treat me like a family. Before I came in the house, I just frankly with them, 'You just treat me like a human, like your family because I also treat you like my family'. The number one is communication. If you don't like me, don't shove me at the outside, you can talk to me. [*Rachel, Filipina, seven years in Hong Kong*]

> Most of the domestic helpers here suffer from so many problems, but my employers are good and they understand. They really understand what my situation is [with my family at home]. Some employers cannot understand their employees, that they are very far from their families, then sometimes they have family problems. But I was very lucky because they treat me as a family member also. So, if I have a problem, I can tell them and they can understand and give me freedom to decide. [*Rita, Filipina, 15 years in Hong Kong*]

> It is work and sometimes I do wrong, she [my employer] will also be angry with me. But this doesn't worry me because even if my employer is angry with me, they treat me like family also. So, I think my employer is very good with me. Like birthday give me present, eating also ... because a lot of employers never give the maid ... cannot eat this, cannot eat that. And sometimes when I need money for my family, I can ask her [for salary in advance] and she said ok, so she is understanding. [*Evonne, Indonesian, six years in Singapore*]

In addition to better treatment and attitudes from employers, for some workers, the concept of familial belonging was also associated with more tangible benefits such as an improvement in one's status within the household and being in a better position to negotiate the scope of one's job, including in relation to level of responsibility, remuneration and employment security.

Strategic Deployment of Fictive Kinship

A: Nowadays the agency will ask them [the employers] to terminate [our contract] because if they terminate [the contract], then [employers] can get free replacement.[5]

S: So, in a way, if you have a good relationship with your employer, even if the agency asked them to change, they also won't.

A: Yeah, that is very important. Because if you get the trust in the relationship with the employer, you can sign the contract with them again and they don't want to let you go. [*Amy, Filipina, 24 years in Hong Kong*]

For Amy, building a relationship with the employer's family can foster relations of intimacy, respect and trust, which gives rise to familial attachment that in turn helps the worker to secure contract renewals. In this regard, Amy saw the maintenance of a close relationship as a means of gaining longer-term employment security and a leverage against the disposability of women migrant domestic workers. This was also reflected in the conversations with some of the other workers, who suggested that their performance of intimate and care labour can support their everyday negotiation of security and well-being. In particular, the formation and maintenance of emotional attachments with the person they are caring for can make it difficult for employers (that is, the person paying their salary) to arbitrarily terminate their contract:

> Even if I do something bad or wrong or I didn't listen to her, she will never terminate me. Maybe she really needs the helper to take care of the child. Even when she said, 'Don't play your hand phone when you working' but I still use and then that time she was really mad at me. Then I said, 'If you don't want me, you can send me back. If I can't do my work, you can send me back to the agency'. But she didn't say anything because she knows I can take good care of her child. [*Kelly, Indonesian, nine years in Singapore, five years in Hong Kong*]

> Because the two boys they love me, that's why if my madam will scold me, the younger one will go, 'You angry with 姐姐 [elder sister]?'. He will scold my madam. So, I am so lucky that the two boys love me. If not, my madam will fire me already. Without them, my madam fire me so many times already. [*Rita, Filipina, 15 years in Hong Kong*]

The above examples suggest that some women migrant domestic workers do have more power and control over their situation and workplace relations than is imagined in the extant literature. The current consensus in academic scholarship on intimate and affective labour is that domestic work is premised upon the maintenance of a dynamic of servitude and subordination, which is reinforced by the worker's perception of 'being one of the family' (Romero 1992; Barker 2012; Shahvisi 2018). However, my findings reveal that the relations of interdependency that develop between domestic workers, their wards and their employers are multi-directional. As much as women migrant domestic workers are dependent on employers as a result of the labour migration regime, the attachments and relationships with employers can be used by workers to negotiate better employment conditions, challenge the authority of employers and enable safe work. Thus, the affective and emotional nature of domestic work, carried out within the familial context, can and does destabilise power relations in the domestic workplace. This was also identified by some of the employers, who noted the importance of building a personal relationship with the worker to ensure reliability and quality of care. Wendy hoped that including her worker as part of the family would enhance the worker's commitment to the welfare and well-being of her three-year-old son:

> I don't want to have a bad relationship with this worker. So I won't set any harsh requirements or rules. I prefer to treat her like a family member. I don't want to be too controlling and have a very strict relationship. I also feel that if we can maintain a good relationship, you will also be good to my family and my child. That is my approach. I think it is better for us and also for the worker. I think she will be happier and more willing to work for this household. Because you are taking care of my child, if you have 黑面 [gloomy face] every day, it is not good for my child as well. I don't want to keep changing my worker because I don't want my child to keep having to adapt to a new worker. I also don't have any other family members at home. [So] I don't know what you are doing to my child when I am not there. [*Wendy, Hong Kong, Employer*]

For Wendy, such strategic emotional engagement with the worker is primarily for the benefit of her child and thus can be understood as another form of security practice aimed at ensuring her child's safety and well-being, not unlike the installation of CCTV. By including migrant domestic workers in the family, employers can have greater confidence in the quality of care provided by the worker and in the worker's commitment to the welfare of the family, and thereby secure better care. More broadly, employers' power is not absolute because, within the familial setting, how the domestic worker feels and behaves can have a direct impact on the well-being of all members of the household. Power relations between employers and workers in the domestic workplace are subtle, complex and go beyond contractual agreements. Nonetheless, as detailed throughout this research and reflected in the literature, the institutional and policy context has created a situation whereby employers still have significant power to define the nature of the employment relationship and the extent to which workers feel a sense of belonging to the employer's family (Lan 2006; Anderson 2016).

Fictive Kinship, Affective Relations and Sustainable Work

Throughout the interviews, workers often spoke about 'going crazy' working for employers who were overly controlling or acted in ways that made their employment experience very stressful. Some workers highlighted the importance of having an 'understanding' employer who recognises and values their labour and contributions. Notably, nearly one-third of the workers articulated their preference for a sympathetic or understanding employer:

> Because whole month we have to bear with that [nagging and scolding], it is mentally torture. If they are nice then we can do nice work. [*Jasmine, Nepalese, eight years in Hong Kong*]

> Because I want to work with heart. Because if we are not comfortable, what use to have so much money? It can be sick also and headache every time. So, salary can be HKD4000[6] but we can be happy in the family, we can work with heart, we can feel like comfortable. That is most important. The money is not enough to cover the happiness. [*Nelly, Indonesian, three years in Singapore, one year in Taiwan, five years in Hong Kong*]

> If every day they are complaining and scolding, it is not good as well. Not comfortable, right? If the employer is nagging, nagging when you are already working so hard. When your employer is not good, it is not comfortable. I prefer going with a good person. If it is not a good employer, even if the salary is very high, I also don't want to work for them. [*Cat, Nepalese, 23 years in Hong Kong*]

Polly believed that when employers treat workers as part of the family, this demonstrates that they see the worker as a 'human' who has emotions and who may 'sometimes be tired or homesick', rather than merely an employee who 'they already pay you money for salary, so you have to work for them, you have to follow their instructions and what they want' [*Polly, Thai, 27 years in Hong Kong*]. For another worker, Judy, 'being part of the family' was important to her simply because it demonstrated her employer's care for her, which made her feel like a valued individual and reduced her sense of loneliness:

> My employer will ask like, 'How? You have new idea? You have new creation?'. It is like they want to know about new things from me. Just interested but she never control. She just said, 'If you have the organisation, don't let your friends hate you because you are more clever

> than them. Just ignore those type of people'. She always tells me like that and supports me. [*Judy, Indonesian, two years in Singapore, seven years in Hong Kong, one year in Macau, two years in Singapore*]

Judy had previously relocated to Hong Kong and Macau, from Singapore, because she wanted a more 'liberal lifestyle', where it is 'very free and very liberal. Everything I can do'. However, after a few years, Judy decided to return to Singapore as she felt that 'it was too freedom, like nobody care about me like that'.

The weight that workers gave to factors like respect, understanding and dignity in explaining acceptable or good employer behaviour suggests that their conceptualisations of safe work were not only linked to physical security or laws and regulations but also grounded in their day-to-day experience and psychological well-being. The workers' desire to be seen as a 'full' human (as opposed to a unit of labour or commodity) raise important considerations about how we understand the concerns and needs of domestic workers. In particular, the findings reveal that employment as a migrant domestic worker, which necessarily entails the formation of emotional relationships with the employer's family, involves workers looking beyond formal equality in contractual principles. As Anderson (2016, p. 44) aptly points out, 'homes are spaces of emotion, they are not where jobs get done, and these emotions are not simply extras but go to the heart of the employment relation'. Consequently, for employment in domestic work to be satisfying and sustainable, it is not sufficient to only ask what laws and regulations are needed to protect the labour rights of women migrant domestic workers. More broadly, it requires thinking about how to structure domestic labour in a manner that can be mutually satisfying for both employers and workers.

Unlawful or Substandard Employment Conditions When the 'Employer Is Family'

Notwithstanding the positive accounts of 'being part of the family', it needs to be recognised that familial belonging and the associated emotional attachment that workers feel towards their employers can blur the boundaries between a professional paid labour relationship and a personal, emotional one (Lan 2003; Anderson 2016; Chiu 2018). Even though it is defined by a formal contractual agreement, the relationship between the employer and worker in this context is inevitably much more personal than that between a supervisor and a worker in a public workplace. Familial belonging and intimacy transform the relationship between employer and worker, which has implications for both the employer's and worker's behaviour and expectations of the work. For example, Jasmine, who discovered only after her arrival in Hong Kong that she was being underpaid by her first employer, shared that she was unwilling to report that employer to the Labour

Department, even though there was a chance she could get her wages back, because:

> I am saying that because they were so good to me. Even though I was a domestic worker for them, but it is still like they were treating me like a family member, a sister. They were so good, even though they give me low salary, they used to buy me clothes, food and even I go out, they will give me travel fare. They were so good, so I never complained. [*Jasmine, Nepalese, eight years in Hong Kong*]

While Jasmine's unwillingness to seek formal recourse may also be associated with concerns for her economic security and/or her lack of familiarity with the labour system (as discussed in Chapter 5), it nonetheless reflects the complications arising from fictive kinship. Domestic work exchanges that become too 'familial' can impact how workers perceive employment practices and/or their response to a legal breach of contract or working conditions. This was exemplified in a conversation about unlawful deployment. One of the workers, Evonne, shared that she knew of other workers who were unlawfully deployed to work in other households with 'no extra money'. When I asked the workers whether they would be happy to undertake such extra work if their employers gave them extra money, another worker, Sylvia, stated that she would be reluctant to agree to this because 'that is not our job. I don't do [cleaning for another person's house] because it is not our job. We do only our job'. Yet Evonne expressed a different opinion:

Evonne: Sometimes for us, don't want to talk anything [disagree with the employer]. So, yes, we do [the additional cleaning], but the heart is like … I will just try to do first, then see what is the reaction of my employer. Give me maybe extra money, or if no extra money, then maybe be nice for us, like extra red packet [a monetary gift given on special occasions] or extra food.

Sylvia: Because they also take care of us, so it is ok.

Evonne: But sometimes, some employers just ask [command the worker] to do only, never respect for you.

This exchange demonstrates the centrality of the employer–worker relationship in shaping how workers evaluate their employment situations: even though Sylvia was initially adamant that she would not perform any duties that fell outside her contract, her position shifted when Evonne talked about the importance of reciprocal relations. From Evonne's response, it is evident that she did not perceive refusing her employer's request to be an option; thus, what mattered most to her was that her acquiescence be acknowledged and duly reciprocated. Echoing the findings of Chiu's (2018) study, which examined familial belonging among Indonesian domestic workers in Singapore, this research found that fictive kinship is strongly associated with workers' reluctance to be overly calculating in relation to both their response to their employers' requests to take on extra tasks and to their willingness to sacrifice certain rights and entitlements. In many situations, this reluctance can impact workers' well-being in that they may choose to undertake, accept or tolerate unreasonable demands from employers in order to earn their trust and 'become part of the family', or simply for fear of jeopardising their status within the family. It is within this context that concerns around employers' extraction of additional labour from domestic workers have emerged (Romero 1992; Parreñas 2015). Nonetheless, the findings from this study demonstrated that fictive kinship is a dynamic process that is constantly in negotiation and is appraised by workers based on daily interactions. And reciprocity is a critical part of this process. In Cherry's case, even though she had initially felt that her employers, whom she was with for three years, had treated her 'like a daughter', she became increasingly ambivalent about being part of the family over time as she felt that her sacrifices (such as undertaking additional unpaid housekeeping duties for her employers' friends and tenants) were not being adequately appreciated or reciprocated:

> They treat me like their family, like ok, for example, during Christmas and my birthday, they treat me. I have a room, I have toilet. Because some other helpers, they sleep in the kitchen, they sleep anywhere. So I am lucky. Because they are good to me, I repay only. I don't want to put them in trouble, that's why. I only wanted the release papers because I am tired. But they wanted me to go back and it is not fair because I didn't complain anything. [*Cherry, Filipina, six years in Singapore*]

This conflicted space, in which the worker feels resentment at being taken advantage of while also feeling appreciative of the positive past experiences with their employer and/or other good aspects of their work, was described by other workers. Sally explained that she had enjoyed a very good working relationship with her employer for two years until he married. At this point, the addition of another adult and a baby to the household led to the workload becoming unbearable:

> Because we have a big house and she wants me to wake up every two hours to check on the baby. And then, of course my male employer will go to work early like 8 am, so I have to wake up early to prepare for breakfast and everything. And she wants me to do all the housework while taking care of the baby. And then I go to the market and I said, I am going to die because one time I already experienced feeling dizzy in the market. So I said I cannot do this anymore. [*Sally, Filipina, one year in Singapore, 30 years in Hong Kong*]

However, in spite of the deterioration of her employment conditions, which are indicative of unlawful and/or substandard employment practices (including her employer not complying with the original employment contract, revoking her food allowance and using most of her sleeping space for storage), Sally eventually left her employer on amicable terms after completing her contract. She was reluctant to lodge any complaint against her employer, as he had been 'good to her'.

Based on the above narratives, establishing how and where workers draw the line between acceptable and unacceptable employment practices is clearly complicated and unlikely to be based solely on overarching laws and regulations. Instead, the formation and development of fictive kin relationships complicates our understanding of exploitation in migrant domestic work as domestic workers are forced to negotiate a completely different type of employment relationship and set of dynamics from that experienced by workers in the public sphere. Workers' judgements are influenced by factors such as subjective calculations of longer-term material and immaterial benefits, perceptions of how they have been treated by their employers and the need to reciprocate their employer's kindness. Thus, these various intersecting considerations help to explain why some workers decide to overlook certain unlawful or substandard employment practices and, more broadly, the choices they make about how to negotiate and contest their exploitation.

Conclusion

The legislative and regulatory frameworks in Singapore and Hong Kong capture a snapshot of the various exploitative practices that occur within the private workplace. However, there is also a range of substandard employment practices that are not systematically recognised as exploitative and for which there are no institutional remedies within the two national labour law frameworks. In particular, the preoccupation in public and policy discourse with exploitative employment practices as defined by the law contrasts sharply with the interview narratives that emerged from this study about 'mundane' employment practices and relational factors that negatively impact workers' quality of work and daily life, not just as a unit of labour but as a human being. My interviews with women migrant domestic workers elicited discussion of various 'unacceptable' employment practices that have been normalised as conventional expectations of domestic workers. While some of these practices are informally discouraged by the Singaporean and Hong Kong authorities, both city-states have refused to introduce formal rules to regulate these practices on the basis that the nature of domestic work is 'quite different from normal work' and therefore that such work conditions are too difficult to regulate (HOME & Liberty Shared 2019). Yet these are the very practices that workers have identified as a key part of their everyday struggles and as negatively impacting their well-being. Importantly, this forces us to consider the extent to which existing labour laws and regulations that were designed to protect predominantly male workers in the productive economy can adequately capture and respond to female workers' experiences of exploitation in migrant domestic labour. For researchers, policymakers and other stakeholders concerned about the experiences of women migrant domestic workers, it may be more productive to consider how gendered and social norms in relation to domestic labour have come to produce certain rules, specific work circumstances and a particular culture that female migrant domestic workers must negotiate. A *sectoral focus* on domestic labour, grounded in workers' lived experiences, can help to identify the norms and expectations that are structurally embedded in the domestic workplace culture, and the extent to which they inform workers' perceptions and interpretations of their work conditions.

The second key observation that emerged from this analysis is that, workers' determinations of what constitutes exploitation and what employment practices are acceptable or unacceptable are not exclusively based on laws and regulations but also on other factors such as workplace culture and the employment relationship. This is not to say that workers are not concerned with labour standards or not aware of the guidelines instituted within legal and regulatory frameworks. In fact, all of the workers interviewed possessed some basic awareness of their rights and entitlements. The amount of information and awareness that workers had varied and was dependent on factors such as length of time in the industry, strength of personal networks and quality of training received in the training centre, but all of the women recognised certain elements of domestic work as unlawful and/or substandard. However, what is also evident is that, despite their awareness, the workers' evaluation of their labour conditions and acceptable or unacceptable practices was not based purely on formal benchmarks but was subjective and varied depending on the circumstances and context surrounding their experiences, the dynamics of the employer–worker relationship on their motivations and, finally, on their expectations of domestic work. For workers, 'exploitation' is not simply a singular employment practice or standard, but rather a state of work. Correspondingly, 'safe work' is not just the absence of exploitation. By adopting a simplistic or normative conceptualisation of exploitation based on legislative and regulatory frameworks, we risk missing out on a much more complex and multifaceted understanding of live-in migrant domestic labour, specifically, one that accounts for the emotional and relational factors that form the core of this work. While 'objective' legal and regulatory frameworks are essential for setting minimum labour standards and have tangible benefits for workers' rights and access to entitlements, it is also necessary to look into how certain employment practices are interpreted by workers, because their negotiation of and response to work conditions are more likely to be based on this interpretation. If the discussion is only centred on exploitation and what laws or regulations are needed to address it, the focus then remains on what employers should not do, rather than on what is needed to ensure that employment is safe and sustainable for women migrant domestic workers. The latter requires us to move beyond criminalisation or accounts of narrowly defined victimisation to critically analyse the broader social and structural context of waged domestic labour and identify the systemic gendered factors that produce and entrench insecurities in the everyday domestic workplace.

By calling attention to these issues, the aim is not to deny the urgent need to ensure that more comprehensive regulatory frameworks are put in place to capture the complexity of harm and exploitation (that is, to fill the gap between institutionally recognised offences and less noticeable harms) in order to reduce workers' precariousness. Instead, my intention is to complicate our understanding of how workers perceive and define labour exploitation and safe work. In particular, we need to explore the various macro and micro factors that shape their individual assessments and subsequently how this affects their negotiation of everyday work.

Notes

1 Under Hong Kong's Employment Ordinance, a migrant domestic worker is entitled to a weekly rest day, which is defined as 'not less than 24 hours' (Hong Kong Labour Department 2022); however, there is little indication that this rule is being strictly enforced. In Singapore, MOM has introduced a mandatory rest day policy, which stipulates that employers are required to provide women migrant domestic workers with a minimum of one rest day a month that cannot be compensated. This will take effect at the end of 2022 and supersedes the current law which allows for the weekly rest day to be exchanged for additional compensation, upon agreement from both employer and worker.
2 For this study, I included workers under the category of 'excessive working hours' when they shared that they had been working more than 12 hours daily.
3 Under Convention No. 189 (Article 10(3)), standby hours are defined as 'periods during which domestic workers are not free to dispose of their time as they please and remain at the disposal of the household in order to respond to possible calls' (ILO 2011).
4 Under the SEC, 'employers who have obtained the Director of Immigration's approval before 1 April 2003' are allowed to continue letting their workers reside at a different address, 'so long as they continue to employ Helpers without a break of more than 6 months' (Hong Kong Immigration Department 2022).
5 In several of the interviews, workers noted that some placement agencies would encourage employers to terminate employment contracts and change the worker, which would incur additional 'transfer fees' for workers that they then have to pay to the placement agencies.
6 This is lower than the stipulated minimum wage.

References

Akalin, A (2015), 'Motherhood as the value of labour', *Australian Feminist Studies*, 30(83): 65–81.

Anderson, B (2016), *Worker, Helper, Auntie, Maid?: Working Conditions and Attitudes Experienced by Migrant Domestic Workers in Thailand and Malaysia*, International Labour Organization, Asia Pacific, https://www.ilo.org/wcmsp5/groups/public/---asia/---ro-bangkok/---sro-bangkok/documents/publication/wcms_537808.pdf

Anderson, B & Rogaly, B (2005), 'Forced labour and migration to the UK, Trades Union Congress', London, http://www.ituc-csi.org/IMG/pdf/Forced_labour_in_UK_12-2009.pdf

Andrees, B (2008), *Forced Labour and Trafficking in Europe: How People Are Trapped in, Live Through and Come Out*, Working Paper 57, International Labour Organisation, Geneva, https://www.ilo.org/wcmsp5/groups/public/---ed_norm/---declaration/documents/publication/wcms_090548.pdf

Barker, DK (2012), 'Querying the paradox of caring labor', *Rethinking Marxism: A Journal of Economics, Culture & Society*, 24(4): 574–591.

Barua, P, Haukanes, H & Waldrop, A (2016), 'Maid in India: Negotiating and contesting the boundaries of domestic work', *Forum for Development Studies*, 43(3): 415–436.

Blackett, A (2019), *Everyday Transgressions: Domestic Workers' Transnational Challenge to International Labor Law*, Cornell University Press, Ithaca.

Chiu, MYL (2018), 'Familization of Indonesian domestic workers in Singapore', in R Ogawa, RKH Chan, AS Oishi & LR Wang (eds.), *Gender, Care and Migration in East Asia*, Palgrave Macmillan, Singapore, pp. 97–116.

Chuang, JA (2017), 'Contemporary debt bondage, "self-exploitation" and the limits of the trafficking definition', in P Kotiswaran (ed.), *Revisiting the Law and Governance of Trafficking, Forced Labour and Modern Slavery*, Cambridge University Press, UK, pp. 112–133.

Coghlan, D & Wylie, G (2011), 'Defining trafficking/denying justice? Forced labour in Ireland and the consequences of trafficking discourse', *Journal of Ethnic and Migration Studies*, 37(9): 1513–1526.

DeVault, ML (1990), 'Talking and listening from women's standpoint: Feminist strategies for interviewing and analysis', *Social Problems*, 37(1): 96–116.

Duffy, M (2005), 'Reproducing labor inequalities: Challenges for feminists, conceptualising care at the intersections of gender, race and class', *Gender & Society*, 19(1): 66–82.

Ham, J, Segrave, M & Pickering, S (2013), 'In the eyes of the beholder: Border enforcement, suspect travellers and trafficking victims', *Anti-Trafficking Review*, (2): 51–66.

HOME & Liberty Shared (2019), *Behind Closed Doors: Forced Labour in the Domestic Work Sector in Singapore*, HOME, Singapore.

Hong Kong Immigration Department (2022), *Guidebook for the Employment of Domestic Helpers from Abroad*, viewed 1 Feb, https://www.immd.gov.hk/eng/forms/forms/id-e-969.html

Hong Kong Labour Department (2022), *A Concise Guide to the Employment Ordinance*, viewed 1 Feb, https://www.labour.gov.hk/eng/public/ConciseGuide.htm

Huang, S & Yeoh, BSA (1996), 'Ties that bind: State policy and migrant female domestic helpers in Singapore', *Geoforum*, 27(4): 473–493.

Huckerby, J (2015), 'Same, but different: Assessing the interaction of the migrant workers' rights and anti-trafficking regimes under international law', *Journal of International Law and Politics*, 47(3): 593–645.

Human Rights Watch (2005), *Maid to Order: Ending Abuses against Migrant Domestic Workers in Singapore*, vol. 17, no. 10, Human Rights Watch, Singapore.

International Labour Organization (ILO) (2011), *C189 – Domestic Workers Convention*, Geneva, viewed 9 Dec, https://www.ilo.org/dyn/normlex/en/f?p=NORMLEXPUB:12100:0::NO::P12100_ILO_CODE:C189

Lan, PC (2003), 'Negotiating social boundaries and private zones: The micropolitics of employing migrant domestic workers', *Social Problems*, 50(4): 525–549.

Lan, PC (2006), *Global Cinderellas: Migrant Domestics and Newly Rich Employers in Taiwan*, Duke University Press, Durham.

Miles, M (1999), 'Working in the city: The case of migrant women in Swaziland's domestic service sector', in JH Momsen (ed.), *Gender, Migration and Domestic Service*, Routledge, London.

Moras, A (2008), 'The private home as a public workplace: Employing paid domestic labour', *Journal of Workplace Rights*, 13(4): 377–400.

O'Connell Davidson, J & Anderson, B (2006), 'The trouble with "trafficking"', in CL van den Anker & J Doomernik (eds.), *Trafficking and Women's Rights*, Palgrave Macmillan, New York, pp. 11–26.

Parreñas, RS (2015), *Servants of Globalization: Migration and Domestic Work* (2nd edition), Stanford University Press, California.

Parreñas, RS & Silvey, AR (2018), 'The precarity of migrant domestic work', *The South Atlantic Quarterly*, 117(2): 430–438.

Paul, AM (2017), *Multinational Maids: Stepwise Migration in a Global Labor Market*, Cambridge University Press, UK.

Pickering, S (2014), 'Floating carceral spaces: Border enforcement and gender on the high seas', *Punishment and Society*, 16(2): 187–205.

Poon, A (2009), 'Maid visible: Foreign domestic workers and the dilemma of development in Singapore', *Crossroads: An Interdisciplinary Journal of Southeast Asian Studies*, 17(1): 1–28.

Romero, M (1992), *Maid in the USA*, Routledge, New York.

Segrave, M & Powell, R (2015), 'Victimisation, citizenship and gender: Interrogating state responses', in D Wilson & S Ross (eds.), *Crimes, Victims and Policy: International Contexts, Local Experiences*, Palgrave Macmillan, UK, pp. 53–83.

Shahvisi, A (2018), 'Hermeneutical injustice and outsourced domestic work', *Women's Studies International Forum*, (69): 18–25.

Skrivankova, K (2010), 'Between decent work and forced labour: Examining the continuum of exploitation', *Joseph Rowntree Foundation Programme Paper: Forced Labour*, JRF Foundation, York.

Tan, EKB (2010), 'Managing female foreign domestic workers in Singapore: Economic pragmatism, coercive legal regulation or human rights', *Israel Law Journal*, (43): 99–125.

Wessels, A, Ong, M & Daniel, D (2017), 'Bonded to the system: Labour exploitation in the foreign domestic work sector in Singapore', *Research Across Borders*, https://www.researchgate.net/profile/Anja_Wessels/publication/321298753_Bonded_to_the_system_Labour_exploitation_in_the_foreign_domestic_work_sector_in_Singapore/links/5a23672a4585155dd41cc58b/Bonded-to-the-system-Labour-exploitation-in-the-foreign-domestic-work-sector-in-Singapore.pdf

Chapter 7

Conclusion

Rethinking the Parameters of 'Exploitation'

The lived realities of women migrant domestic workers challenge the definition of 'labour exploitation' predominantly used in academic policy and public discourses. As detailed in Chapter 3, discourses have tended to focus on interrogating and responding to labour exploitation as it is defined by legal and regulatory frameworks. Correspondingly, reform efforts have emphasised the identification of clear terms of employment and indicators denoting exploitation, as well as the need for changes to labour and migration laws designed to reduce legislative precariousness and to enhance access to legal protections. It is assumed that a focus on labour exploitation and in particular the objective indicators of such exploitation as stipulated in legal and regulatory frameworks that demarcate employer responsibilities will be sufficient to protect the welfare and rights of these women migrant workers. However, the clarity of the legal justice rhetoric around exploitation belies the complexity of the lived experiences of women migrant domestic workers.

In both Singapore and Hong Kong, labour law and, to a lesser extent, criminal law dominate the conversation in relation to what constitutes acceptable, substandard or unacceptable (that is, unlawful) working conditions for these workers. However, these legal and regulatory systems are not capable of capturing and accounting for women migrant domestic workers' lived realities and the messiness of life and work in the domestic workspace. The analysis of workers' experiences brings to the fore two different but interrelated findings.

First, the legal benchmarks utilised in Singapore and Hong Kong to demarcate acceptable and unacceptable employment practices and behaviours do not fully capture the range of practices that workers themselves consider to negatively impact on their day-to-day employment and quality of life. Existing legal and regulatory frameworks are focused on ensuring workers' physical safety and responding to moments of crisis, with minimal regard for the more mundane and ordinary problematic practices, some of which are normalised as a regular and expected component of women's labour in the home. Consequently, there is a clear lack of alignment between what are legally and formally recognised as

DOI: 10.4324/9781003250364-7

workplace breaches and what workers themselves identify as bad employment practices or unsustainable employment conditions. Yet the potential laws and protections that might govern the practices of workers in this study identified as harmful to their well-being and security (such as excessive working hours, restricted access to communication devices, working on rest days and verbally abusive employers) are viewed by the state as too 'difficult to enforce in the private home'. Workers and employers are instead expected to negotiate the specifics of employment conditions themselves and come to a mutual agreement on what works best for both parties.

However, workers' capacity to negotiate better conditions is constrained by significant financial and legal disincentives. As the discussion throughout this book illustrates, the way in which the legal and regulatory system is set up in Singapore and Hong Kong – rendering employers responsible for workers' welfare and presence in the jurisdiction (and in the case of Singapore, their conduct) and providing inadequate policies to support workers' employment security – means that workers' negotiation of better working and living conditions is often dependent on their making 'sacrifices' to leverage trust and build good relationships with their employers. Consequently, even though both city-states offer some legal protections for women migrant domestic workers, there are simultaneously mechanisms that undermine the accessibility and effectiveness of these protections. In addition, as discussed in Chapter 7, these limitations of the existing frameworks are partly the result of the adoption of an 'ungendered' lens to understand and define domestic labour, despite that this labour is strongly associated with and grounded in gendered norms and expectations around women's domestic work. The structural undervaluing of women's labour in the home had a significant influence on the experiences of the workers I interviewed and implications for their access to work protections, as well as their negotiation of work-related problems and management of employment relationships. This highlights the need to value women's work and foreground its significance within laws and regulations governing migrant domestic labour, rather than having a siloed focus on labour exploitation.

Second, the scholarly and state preoccupation with identifying and demarcating the threshold of labour exploitation via an objective list of indicators contrasts sharply with how women migrant domestic workers understand and evaluate their employment conditions. In this study, the workers did not often talk about their work and work conditions in relation to a checklist of indicators or formal labour standards as set out within legislative and regulatory frameworks, even though they were aware of their labour rights and legal entitlements. Instead, the workers' views of the positives, negatives, challenges and management of domestic labour were clearly shaped by a convergence of complex factors including, but not limited to, their relationship with their employers, their subjective calculation of longer-term material and immaterial benefits, their expectations of employment standards and their personal interpretation of the norms and culture surrounding domestic work. Exemplified here were the workers' descriptions of the situations in which they considered employers and work conditions to be bad. Their awareness of labour standards enabled workers to appraise whether their employer's behaviour was unlawful. But in practice, the workers' determination of good or bad and subsequent negotiation and response to these work conditions were dependent on the overall conditions of their employment, not just on any isolated employment practice.

The value and importance of establishing what constitutes labour exploitation and setting minimum labour standards cannot be understated, as it has tangible benefits for workers' rights and access to formal protections and entitlements. Nonetheless, frameworks that silo labour exploitation and harm are limited in their capacity to capture and account for women migrant domestic workers' voices and experiences, which are considerably more diverse and relational than such frameworks envision. In limiting our interrogation of migrant domestic labour and employment experiences to a binary division between exploitation and not exploitation, we risk missing the messiness of life and work that characterises the gendered domestic workplace. In particular, in this research, the workers' discussion of the intersections between the reality of providing domestic labour in an intimate space, their relationship with their employer and other household members, and their experience of negotiating safe work underscored the fact that a range of workers' experiences, needs and standpoints remain unacknowledged in dominant discourses on migrant domestic labour. The exploitation/not exploitation dichotomy that continues to dominate our understanding of domestic labour and women migrant domestic workers' employment experiences – and the conceptualisations of security and protection arising from that dichotomy – does not fully reflect workers' lived realities of domestic labour, in particular, the relational and affective factors that shape their everyday employment experience and their interpretations in different work contexts. Yet the affective relations between worker, employer and other household members play a very important role in informing workers' perceptions of their employment situations.

Alternative Understandings of the Employer–Worker Relationship in Domestic Labour

As discussed in Chapter 6, 'being part of the family' and the maintenance of a good relationship between worker and employer has important implications for how workers interpret and navigate their daily work, as well as what they decide to do when subjected to bad employment conditions. Yet these are issues and dynamics that cannot be neatly captured or addressed through the lens of legislative and regulatory frameworks on labour exploitation, as these frameworks are not set up to account for the gendered complexities of domestic and care labour in the home workplace. The social and affective dimensions of domestic labour may not be considered relevant for state mechanisms tasked with identifying objective thresholds of substandard and unlawful employment practices. However, there is still a need to be cognisant of the analytical limitations that legal categories or indicators of labour exploitation may have for researchers. The tendency to assume that the presence or absence of particular practices can explain everything about workers' experience and negotiation of risk and security in the domestic workplace risks reinforcing a contrived binary between the all-powerful employer and the powerless worker. It also limits our understanding of the complex interplay between the state, placement agents, households and workers, and how these actors interact to shape relationships of power and affect within the domestic workplace. For example, the powerful employer/powerless worker binary to some extent can inform our understanding of the limitations of the options that women migrant domestic workers have in relation to decisions made within the household (for example, the installation of surveillance cameras), where workers are generally not in a position to influence their employers' decisions despite being directly affected by them. However, the experiences of workers and employers in this study also bring to the fore a much wider diversity of work relationship configurations and power dynamics that remain under-recognised in domestic labour research.

Chapter 5 in particular illuminated the dynamic nature of the employer–worker relationship and how it is differentially navigated depending on broader state structures and frameworks, relational experiences, and employment and conditions, such as the type of work being carried out (housework or care work), the level of trust in the relationship, labour and migration laws and regulations, and past employment experiences. The numerous variants of work relationships described by the women migrant domestic workers and employers in this study suggest that there is a need for researchers to have a clearer sense of how the worker–employer relationship influences (and is influenced by) the performance of intimate and emotional labour in the domestic workplace, as well as the nexus of legislative protection and regulatory practices. During the analysis, the challenges associated with capturing the myriad of familial, emotive, contractual and regulatory elements of the employer–worker relationship became quickly apparent. The traditional employment relationship on which labour exploitation and legal frameworks are premised appeared to be clearly inadequate for reflecting the employment dynamics and experiences in the private sphere. In particular, this framing does not adequately account for the emotional work in which both workers and employers must engage to ensure their respective needs and interests are met, and to enable a sustainable employment relationship. This raises the question of how to reconcile and organise the complexities and contradictions in this particular form of employment relationship. For example, is there a way to discuss the live-in domestic work relationship beyond a reductive categorisation of all employers as exploitative and all workers as vulnerable victims?

Greater clarity around and understanding of the employer–worker relationship will not only have empirical implications for researchers, but will also have practical implications for authorities tasked with protecting and enabling safe work for women migrant domestic workers. The finding that both employers *and* women migrant domestic workers are differentially insecuritised by labour and migration laws can be used to develop alternative measures and responses to those that focus solely on policing employers' behaviours to enhance protection for workers. Moreover, the fact that many women migrant domestic workers do not perceive the lodging of a formal complaint to be an accessible or practical measure to enable their everyday security may shift the discussion from one that is focused on legal approaches as a solution to one that recognises the affective aspects of workers' employment experiences and the implications for safe work. For instance, this could include recognising that considerations of safe work for women migrant domestic workers necessitate talking about the emotional work in which both workers and employers engage, making this emotional work central to the operations of migrant domestic labour. These findings highlight the need to shift the debate away from labour exploitation to adopt a stronger gendered and sectoral focus to identify the employment norms, expectations and culture related to live-in waged domestic labour. Specifically, we need to begin by valuing women's waged and unwaged labour in the home and understanding the gendered and emotional dynamics that underpin the performance of domestic labour in the intimate home workplace. Correspondingly, this points to a need for alternative ways of understanding what is necessary to secure the safety and well-being of women migrant domestic workers.

Everyday Security: Making a Case for Sustainable Labour and Livelihoods

Theoretically, this book challenges the emphasis on 'protection from or resistance to labour exploitation' as the frame for understanding and responding to the employment-related issues encountered by women migrant domestic workers. For researchers working from a labour rights perspective, interrogating law, legal frameworks and their capacity to improve formal protections and entitlements for workers remains an important imperative, particularly as women migrant domestic workers continue to have inequitable employment rights and access to law. In this regard, this study's findings do not contradict global calls for more comprehensive labour law protections for women migrant domestic workers; however, they do highlight the limitations of law in understanding workers' experiences and ensuring their safety. The discussion of workers' management of workplace problems and relations in Chapters 4 and 6 suggests that security is fluid for women migrant domestic workers – influenced not only by institutional structures of labour and migration laws and regulation but also by these workers' day-to-day employment experiences.

Consequently, researchers should be cautious about allowing theoretical debates about exploitation and safe work to be solely framed by a legal lens. This strategy risks forcing women's experiences into a pre-existing category of employment standards borrowed from a labour market economy, which have not conventionally accounted for or even recognised women's work in the home. As Fudge and Mundlak (forthcoming, p. 8) remind us, even though laws and legal norms can be a platform from which to contest and address market failures and inadequacies, 'the substance of labour standards needs to be tailored to the wide variety of life situations of workers who invoke them, rather than tied to the life course of a male breadwinner'.

In addition, what emerged from this study as a key priority for workers, and what remains absent in dominant discourses, is how women migrant domestic workers navigate their everyday workplace to facilitate a safe and sustainable work environment for themselves. Women migrant domestic workers' experiences and expectations clearly highlight their distance from law, particularly in terms of how they define their experiences, and manage and enable their safety in the everyday. While resistance to workplace exploitation may be part of this experience, it is not the whole story. Instead, ensuring financial and livelihood security is central to shaping workers' work-related decision-making. In other words, 'making money' can matter as much as safety when making decisions about work, as evident in the workers' assessments and use of regulatory frameworks presented in Chapter 6. Providing financial support to their children and/or parents is the major reason why the majority of the women in this study migrated into domestic labour. Thus, for workers who are driven to find work to make money to cover such basic needs, having access to and the ability to remain in paid employment abroad is their main priority, and deportation or the inability to find alternative employment is something to be avoided at all costs.

However, wanting to access work and maintain one's employment status does not mean that workers will passively accept any and all employment conditions or practices. The discussion of workers' management and negotiation of work conditions in Chapters 4 and 5 suggests that workers do seek other forms of support to achieve sustainable workplace environments, particularly through the assistance of third-party intermediaries and/or the development of a fictive kin relationship with their employers. Complex, intersecting factors and interests influence their decisions around which individuals or organisations are best positioned to provide assistance and enable workers' safety and security when work-related problems arise. As detailed in Chapter 5, the women migrant domestic workers in this study consistently reported that, among the various formal and informal service providers, their first call would be to their placement agencies as they are the most well-equipped to ensure workers' employment security. Even if placement agencies were not generally perceived to be an ideal source of assistance, due to market factors and the restrictive labour migration regime in both Singapore and Hong Kong, they were seen as the 'safest' source of support for distressed workers seeking to negotiate with employers to secure better working and living conditions, or a contract transfer when the employment relationship breaks down. Thus, the following finding is critical for policy and academic discourse to consider: placement agencies occupy a complex position insofar as they are not protection-focused (nor financially incentivised to be), yet play a significant role as first responders in ensuring safe work and support for women migrant domestic workers in Singapore and Hong Kong.

The emphasis that the workers in this research placed on employers' attitudes – specifically, being respectful, able to reciprocate and treating workers with dignity – points to the ambiguous category of worker psychological well-being, which contrasts with the clear identification of (physical) harms in labour law and criminal justice frameworks. In public discourse, conceptualisations of good or decent working and living conditions for women migrant domestic workers often align with legally defined employment standards, but women's experiences demonstrate that, on a day-to-day basis, what affects their assessment of work conditions are often issues and matters that lie outside the remit of law and are therefore arguably difficult to regulate. For the workers in this study, the notion of safe work was more closely linked to working in a sustainable work environment, which did not necessarily reflect an absence of unlawful employment practices but did reflect an overall employment situation where workers felt respected, cared for and valued. For many workers, these affective sentiments are associated with employers' general compliance with labour laws and standards, as such compliance is perceived to guarantee at least a basic level of employment security. However, laws and employment standards are only able to capture a small proportion of the realities and messiness of domestic labour as performed in a highly intimate workplace, where social relations and interactions with employers and other household members determine the everyday working and living conditions for women migrant domestic workers.

These findings have direct relevance in terms of informing new approaches to and conceptualisations of safe work for women migrant domestic workers and theoretical understanding of waged domestic labour more broadly. This is all the more crucial given that some of the issues that have been dismissed by frontline NGO staff members (such as a mismatch between employers' and workers' expectations, depression and homesickness) are the very issues that workers identify as critical to their well-being and sense of security (Anjara et al. 2017). State regulations and recommendations introduced during the COVID-19 pandemic, which has reinforced workers' isolation,[1] suggest that these issues continue to be disregarded (Lui et al. 2021). If policy and research discourses and efforts are to effectively support and protect women migrant domestic workers, stakeholders will need to recognise what these workers value, and how they negotiate their work environments to protect their safety and facilitate a sustainable workplace. In this context, empirical studies of the domestic labour industry have an important role to play in challenging and deconstructing the static categories and definitions utilised to account for women migrant domestic workers' employment experiences, assessment of risk and search for safety.

Much of the analysis presented throughout this book complements what is known about domestic labour as performed by women migrant workers. It does not represent a complete departure from the dominant understandings of female migrant domestic labour. However, in examining workers' lived experiences and interrogating how these experiences are structured or constrained by the labour migration regime in Singapore and Hong Kong, this research prompts a broader reflection on the empirical and theoretical concepts that underpin the contemporary body of scholarship in this area and highlights the need for a gendered examination of these workers' employment experiences. In particular, the way that gender, labour, emotional work, affective relations, legal protection and security intersect in waged domestic labour and its regulation warrants further attention. In addition, the analysis brings to the fore the importance of applying a critical feminist lens to understanding women's lived realities: the exploration of women's experiences and the identification of the limitations of dominant understandings of domestic labour illuminate the need for us to continually interrogate the gender norms that underpin dominant structures and the implications of these norms for the translation of women's lived experiences into analysis.

Note

1 Both the Hong Kong and Singapore governments had made recommendations encouraging women migrant domestic workers to stay home even on their rest days.

References

Anjara, SG, Nellums, LB, Bonetto, C & Van Bortel, T (2017), 'Stress, health and quality of life of female migrant domestic workers in Singapore: A cross-sectional study', *BMC Women's Health*, 17(1), 98.

Fudge, J & Mundlak, G (forthcoming), 'Law and gendered labour market segmentation', *International Labour Review*, 10.1111/ilr/12339

Lui, ID, Vandan, N, Davies, SE, Harman, S, Morgan, R, Smith, J, Wenham, C & Grépin, KA (2021), '"We also deserve help during the pandemic": The effect of the COVID-19 pandemic on foreign domestic workers in Hong Kong', *Journal of Migration and Health*, 3: 100037.

Index

For Product Safety Concerns and Information please contact our EU
representative GPSR@taylorandfrancis.com
Taylor & Francis Verlag GmbH, Kaufingerstraße 24, 80331 München, Germany

www.ingramcontent.com/pod-product-compliance
Ingram Content Group UK Ltd.
Pitfield, Milton Keynes, MK11 3LW, UK
UKHW020007200926
475702UK00015B/2522

9781032168067